IBSEN

IBSEN

Harold Clurman

A DA CAPO PAPERBACK

ACKNOWLEDGMENTS:

My thanks to the John Simon Guggenheim Fund for making the writing of this book possible

and

To Yaddo (Saratoga Springs), where under ideal conditions I was able to complete the first draft of all but the final chapter.

Library of Congress Cataloging in Publication Data

Clurman, Harold, 1901–
  Ibsen.

(A Da Capo paperback)
  Reprint. Originally published: New York: Macmillan, 1977. (Masters of world literature series)
  Bibliography: p.
  Includes index.
  1. Ibsen, Henrik, 1828-1906 – Criticism and interpretation. I. Title.
PT8895.C55 1989   839.8′226   89-11732
ISBN 0-306-80365-8

Published by Da Capo Press, Inc.
A Subsidiary of Plenum Publishing Corporation
233 Spring Street, New York, New York 10013

TO *JOAN UNGARO*

"*No mind can engender till divided in two.*"
—W. B. YEATS

"*Contraries complement one another.*"
—NIELS BOHR

"*A man must live in his own times, but he can
try to make the times worth living in.*"
—IBSEN, *Love's Comedy*

Contents

A PERSONAL PROLOGUE

I FIRST HEARD the name "Ibsen" pronounced in 1912 when my parents went to see *Brand* presented by a Russian company headed by Paul Orlenoff and his leading lady Alla Nazimova. They were appearing in a small East Side theater in New York. The first four acts were given on one evening, the fifth and longest act on the following night. I myself did not see the play till forty-seven years later—its first London production—in a slightly abridged version. The earnestness with which my parents discussed the play has always haunted my memory and endowed Ibsen's name with a special resonance.

IBSEN

1

The Riddle of Fire and Ice

T HE OPENING LINES of *Catiline*, Ibsen's first play, written when he was twenty, are "I must! I must! Deep down within my soul a voice commands, and I will do its bidding."

Who was Catiline? He was the Roman against whom Cicero railed in that famous (and boring) diatribe which many of us had to construe when we set about to learn Latin. Burckhardt in his *The Civilization of the Renaissance in Italy* calls Catiline "the worst of all conspirators, a man in whose thoughts freedom has no place." But in the play, Ibsen makes Catiline a tragic hero, because he rebelled against the state.

Just as Cicero excoriated Catiline, so Ibsen's plays were flayed and hissed on many occasions, when they were not dismissed as dull by critics and audiences alike. The most flagrant instance of this was the reaction to *Ghosts* when first performed in London in 1891. "An open drain," one reviewer called it, "a loathsome sore, an abominable piece, a repulsive and degrading work."

Ibsen anticipated such a reception. In 1881, he wrote to its publisher, "*Ghosts* will probably cause alarm in certain circles, but that cannot be helped. If it did not, it would not have been necessary to write it."

Ibsen, throughout his life, was a rebel. Still, he often appeared

to doubt his own convictions. Set side by side, many of his statements made at different times create an impression of constant
vacillation. What is permanent is a compelling force ("I must!
I must!") to combat meanness, outworn modes of thought,
hypocrisy. He was in quest of a binding unity, a dominant truth.
"The only thing I care about liberty is the struggle for it," he
said. "I care nothing for the possession of it." We discover in
this both a passion of assertion and an ingredient of negation.
Ibsen's last words on his deathbed were "To the contrary."

He is all self-contradiction. Almost every play seems to be a
correction or a rebuttal of the one or several which preceded
it. Those who know only Ibsen's most frequently produced
plays—*A Doll's House, Ghosts, Hedda Gabler, The Wild Duck*
—must remain ignorant of the total impact of his work. To
comprehend Ibsen's significance as an artist and as a figure in
cultural history we must read most of his twenty-six plays and
several of his poems. To overlook any of the plays written after
The Vikings at Helgeland, when Ibsen was thirty, is to lose track
of the main line of his thought.

Ibsen's plays are deeply autobiographical. I say "deeply" because plots are rarely "documentary"—that is, recorded events
of his personal history. They are dramatizations of his emotional,
spiritual, social and intellectual life. In his own words, "Everything that I have written is most intimately connected with what
I have lived through, if not personally experienced. . . . " His
plays reveal the processes of his "self-anatomizing." The severe
discipline of his turbulent subjectivity guides his craft. It masters
the contentions of his spirit, and gives his plays a good part of
their staying power.

"Environment," Ibsen said, "has a great influence upon the
forms in which the imagination creates." A person's environment consists of his family background, the locale and period of
his education, the places he chooses or is obliged to live.

Henrik Ibsen was born March 20, 1828, in Skien, Norway, a
town of scarcely three thousand inhabitants about a hundred
miles south of the capital, Christiana (now Oslo). In 1895 Ibsen
described Skien as "a town of storming, surging, seething wa-

ters." One of the first of his English translators described Skien as "existing solely for purposes of mariners' merchandise, and depending for prosperity and life itself, on the sea."

Ibsen, his most recent biographer Michael Meyer tells us, was wont to assert that he had not a drop of Norwegian blood in his veins. He was in fact approximately two-thirds Norwegian, one-sixth Danish and a little less than one-sixth German with a slight admixture of Scottish. The possible reason for Ibsen's puzzling statement is that, like many another artist who was to bring honor to his people, he did not "like" his native land. Apart from his father, at Ibsen's birth a prosperous merchant who ran a general store selling groceries, dairy products, glass, etc., Ibsen's paternal ancestors had for over two hundred years been sea captains, and, Meyer adds, "towards the end [of] his life [he] is said to have looked and walked, more and more like a sea captain."

The sea is the dominant feature of Norwegian geography. And in one crucial aspect of his nature, Ibsen was a man of the sea. In *The Lady from the Sea*, the heroine is told by her husband, "Ellida, your mind is like the sea. It ebbs and flows." So did Ibsen's.

In 1864 at the age of thirty-six Ibsen left Norway in voluntary exile for Italy, and settled in Rome for a few years. After a year in Dresden and a move to Munich, with visits to Copenhagen and a two-month return to Norway, he went back to Rome in 1874 with an intermittent stay in Berchtesgaden and Munich and a summer in Sorrento. He left Rome for good in 1885. All told he lived in Italy for seven years. The rest of his travels took him to Denmark, Sweden, Austria and Hungary and included a month in Egypt to attend the opening in 1869 of the Suez Canal. With the exception of two brief returns to Norway, his exile lasted for twenty-seven years.

"How one longs for the sun" is an oft-repeated note in Ibsen's works. In Italy Ibsen "discovered" the sun. "Here [in Norway]," Oswald says in *Ghosts*, "they look on life as a wretched, miserable business . . . But you see, abroad people don't look at it like that . . . The mere thought of being alive seems to them joyous and marvelous . . . "

That is not all Oswald says in the speech which contrasts the gloomy atmosphere of his homeland with the radiance elsewhere. I shall revert to this further on, but it touches upon a vital vein which runs throughout the body of Ibsen's writing. Two strains of sentiment inform his being. There is the need to escape the dark constraints in the environment in which he had been bred, and the complementary impulse to enter and embrace the bright realm of freedom.

Ibsen was an atypical Norwegian, even in his looks. We remember him chiefly as the grim and grizzled old man of most of the photographs we have seen, but in his youth he was of swarthy complexion, his hair and beard black. Still, the Norwegian and what it betokens were, in more ways than he at first cared to acknowledge, in his every fiber. There was a never-ending conflict within him which, for the moment, may be metaphorically set down as a conflict between the sea and the sun or between fire and ice. "The conflict of opposites," Strindberg said, "generates power, as fire and water create the power of steam."

A self-conscious man, Ibsen was quite conscious of the tensions of opposites embodied in his art. *Emperor and Galilean*, the play on which he worked longer than on any of the others, is his most specific attempt to give philosophic as well as dramatic form to the turmoil of his spirit.

In his book on Greek tragedy, H. D. F. Kitto says, "Criticism, it seems to me, can without discredit begin with what is in the poet's head, without inquiring how it got there." This may generally be true and it is certainly a safe precept when we deal with artists of whose lives we know very little (as is the case with the Greek dramatists), but there is, to say the least, an irresistible fascination in tracing the reflection of biographical factors on modern works.

Certainly the decline in his father's fortune when Ibsen was six (and the near-bankruptcy later) must have had a most depressing effect on the boy. It may have even struck him as a betrayal, for his father, besides having been a heavy drinker, was a negligent businessman. During the six years that he (Knud

Ibsen) enjoyed prosperity, the child Ibsen, always a loner, locked himself away with books—most often the Bible—and occupied himself with dolls, puppets and drawing.

He developed proficiency in the performance of magic tricks as well as ventriloquism (aren't all playwrights ventriloquists?). He shook with unnerving laughter when he drew caricatures in which his three younger brothers were limned as animals. This was one of the practical jokes in which he was also adept. Standing on a barrel, he was given to wild harangues to the siblings. His favorite subjects of study were history, especially that of classical antiquity, and religion. He also took art lessons.

Due to his father's penury, Henrik at the age of sixteen was obliged to go to work. He became an apprentice pharmacist in Grimstad, a reputedly bleak town with a population of eight hundred. It is possible that he chose the job because he thought of studying medicine. He lived for six years in this shipping community which numbered a few wealthy merchants and bureaucrats. He was regarded as an outsider. His meals were as skimpy as his wages. The quarters in his employer's home were appallingly cold. It must have been humiliating for the youth, who liked to dress meticulously, to wear suits as "shiny as the stove." In short, he was wretchedly poor with only an occasional free Sunday.

Worst of all, he begat a son when he was eighteen. Its mother was a servant girl ten years his senior, whom he had seduced (or vice versa). For the next fourteen years he had to support the child. No one has explained how he managed this. His son lived until 1916. It has been reported that Ibsen did not see him again till he himself was an old man.

Whenever he could steal the time, he read. He borrowed novels by Dickens from the local reading society, and Scandinavian romantic poets, playwrights, historians. Voltaire was apparently one of his favorites, and so was Kierkegaard, according to most biographers, who see the Danish philosopher's influence on *Brand*. I am disposed to doubt this. Ibsen himself avowed that he did not understand Kierkegaard. Literary correspondences or parallels are frequently to be found among writers of contemporary or contiguous periods without there being any direct or immediate relation between them. These are more similarities of cultural atmosphere than results of actual contact.

Ibsen also painted. I have seen a picture-postcard reproduction of a painting, "Farm near Skien," he was supposed to have done at the age of fourteen. It is a cheerful landscape of cottages beside a stream, and it is not without promise. In Grimstad he also wrote his earliest dated poem (1847), uncharacteristically entitled "Resignation." Though Ibsen prepared himself for university study, he never completed it. He was hardly a voracious reader (except perhaps of newspapers), and for all the research he engaged in while planning *Emperor and Galilean*, he can hardly be thought of as having been highly learned.

Perhaps the deepest scar on Ibsen's psyche was the rumor of his illegitimacy. One day in his late teens in a state of great excitement, induced in part by drink, he exclaimed that he was not Knud Ibsen's son. True or not, it is a fact that for over twenty-five years after 1853 he had no contact with his father. After the age of twenty-two he never saw either of his parents. His only tie with his family which might be considered close was with his sister Hedwig. If he was his mother's favorite son, as has been said, it is strange that he should have several times repeated, "Neither my father or mother loved me."

At the time of Ibsen's emergence into manhood, Norway, a small country in area and population, was late in its industrial, economic and technical, not to mention cultural and educational, development as compared to Germany, France or even Italy. Then too we should remember that Norway had not been truly independent for 450 years. Norway had come under Danish rule in 1387, until in 1814 it was at last freed from her union (or bondage) to Denmark. But the great powers, England and Russia in the forefront, handed her over to Sweden as a reward for the latter's support in their rivalry with Napoleon. The Norwegians attempted to fight for their freedom but were defeated and forced into another union with Sweden. Politically Norway became a province of Sweden; culturally she remained a province of Denmark.

At the time of Ibsen's birth, Norway was still a primitive

country. The towns were very tiny. Even the capital, Christiana (which had been Oslo until 1624 but was not to regain its old name until 1925), had less than thirty thousand inhabitants. Ibsen was a grown man before the first railroad was seen in Norway.

It is precisely because of Norway's retarded state that its growth as a modern civilization is brought into sharp focus. The study of social phenomena is more readily observed in a small community than in a large one. Norway then may be regarded as a microcosm of the whole of bourgeois society. The parochialism of Ibsen's plays so many European critics used to complain of actually proved an advantage. Ibsen's prolonged residences in the more advanced countries gave him an added insight into his own. But in many moral and cultural respects the backward and the progressive nations were strikingly akin. As late as 1891, as we have already had occasion to note, *Ghosts* appeared scandalous to the presumably more enlightened English, and Haldvan Koht, one of Ibsen's most distinguished Norwegian biographers, speaks of the bombshell effect of *A Doll's House* on its production in 1879. "It pronounced a deathknell on accepted social ethics." To which we may add Michael Meyer's comment, "No play [in 1889] had ever contributed so momentously to social debate, been so widely and furiously received among people not normally interested in theatrical or even artistic matters." Can we even today maintain that there no longer exist among us, and in considerable numbers, our Noras and husbands very much like hers? And are there none left who do not somehow resent the play? It may be possible that our views of Ibsen's drama have been shortsighted.

Like many other artists, he was most careful in money matters. He noted down all expenditures even to the cost of every cheap cigar. He calculated each year's royalty receipts from every source, and personally scrutinized all statements of these accounts. He lived like the most scrupulously exact bourgeois. There is something of this in his dramatic method. The Norwegian, one of the country's novelists has said, is part horse-trader and part poet. But Ibsen was above all and forever a heretic.

Though in this regard as in so many others it is no easy matter

to place him within any steady or readily definable category,
he was certainly no mealy-mouthed reformer. In a poem written
at the age of forty, "To My Friend the Revolutionary Orator,"
he declared among other things:

> Your changing pawns is a false plan:
> Make a sweep of the chessboard and I'm your man.
> Was never but one revolution unfaltering
> That was not marred by half-hearted paltering.
> . . . .
> You deluge the world to its top-most mark;
> With pleasure I will torpedo the Ark.

A year later he wrote to Georg Brandes, the liberal Danish
critic, a man fourteen years his junior, and the only one he
listened to with genuine respect, "Liberty, equality, fraternity,
are no longer what they were in the days of the late lamented
guillotine. That is what the politicians will not understand; and
that is why I hate them. They only want their special revolution,
external revolution, political revolution . . . "

It would be foolish to regard Ibsen's sallies about cutting off
the heads of the bourgeoisie as anything but café talk. Though
still nebulous and farfetched, we may gather more of his social
attitudes from a statement in another letter to Brandes: "I hope
for nothing from isolated reform. The whole human race is on
the wrong track." As we shall see, he seemed to veer from one
party to another; actually he abjured all parties. The labor
forces, the liberals, the conservatives all claimed him in turn, but
he disappointed and angered them all.

One reason for this may be found in an answer to Brandes'
complaint that Ibsen isolated himself and did not actively participate in work as a progressive. "You are right," Ibsen replied,
"when you say that we must all try to spread our opinions. But
I firmly believe that an intellectual pioneer can never gather a
majority around him. . . . The majority, the masses, the mob,
will never catch him up; he can never rally them behind him.
A crowd now stands where I stood when I wrote my earlier
books. But I myself am there no longer, I am somewhere else—
far ahead of them—or so I hope."

"I have no gift for politics," he said. "I have not even a gift for citizenship." The call to action only elicited the observation, "We poets have other tasks." Writing was his action. He was incensed that Norway had not come to the aid of Denmark when in 1864 Prussia wrested the province of Schleswig-Holstein from the Danes. And though he disclaimed the duty to enlist as a war volunteer, there is evidence that he suffered pangs of conscience on that account. He could only thunder in verse:

> Those generous words that seemed to rush
> From bold hearts swelling high
> Was but a flood of empty gush
> And now their stream is dry.
> . . . .
> 'Twas but a lie in festal song
> A kiss that Judas gave.
> When Norway's sons sang loud and long
> Beside the Danish wave.

Under the royalist regime in Italy, Ibsen is an ardent republican, and later in 1880 he asks a friend, "Haven't I always maintained your republicans are the worst tyrants of all? You don't respect the freedom of the individual." In 1885 during one of his return visits to Norway he said, "The reshaping of social conditions now underway in Europe is concerned chiefly with the future of working men and women. That is what I hope for and what I wait for. It is what I intend to work for and what I shall work for all my life so far as I am able."

Could he have been a socialist? He told a journalist in 1887 that he believed so firmly in the splendid future of socialism that he could very well call himself a socialist. His psychological investigations, he added, had led him to the same conclusions as the social-democratic philosophers had arrived at in their scientific research. But he could not join a party because "it has become a necessity for me to work entirely on my own."

There are positively weird aspects to Ibsen's tergiversations. In 1874 Brandes found Ibsen "loud in his praise of the Russians. 'A splendid country,' he said with a smile. 'Think of all the grand oppression they have.' 'How do you mean?' 'Only think

of the glorious love of liberty it engenders. Russia is one of the
few countries in the world where men still love liberty and
make sacrifices for it.'" Making supreme sacrifices for one's
beliefs was for Ibsen the acid test of sincerity.

Funnier still than his undoubtedly tongue-in-cheek quip about
Russia is his reaction to the 1870 Italian revolution. "They have
finally taken Rome away from us human beings and given it to
the politicians. Where shall we take refuge now? Rome was the
one sanctuary in Europe, the only place that enjoyed true freedom—freedom from the tyranny of political freedom . . . All
that was delightful—the unsophisticatedness, the dirt—all that
will disappear." Ibsen needn't have worried: "law and order"
never, even under Mussolini, has obtained in Italy; the spon-
taniety and dirt never disappeared.

Was Ibsen then anti-democratic? Set down in an album Ibsen
in 1895 delivered himself of the following opinion: "The absolute imperative task of democracy is to make itself aristocratic."
For *aristocracy* read *nobility*, "not the nobility of birth or talent
but a nobility of will and spirit." Brandes was often disturbed
by this aspect of Ibsen's character, and spoke of him as the
most aristocratic personality he ever met. Ibsen had little faith
in "the emancipatory power of political measures."

Ibsen's constant clamor is for freedom. The closest he ever
came to a definition of the word was in a letter: "The important
thing is to remain true and faithful to yourself. It is not a question of willing this or that, but of willing what you must do
because you are yourself and cannot do otherwise." Even this
is not conclusive. We must seek our answer in the whole body
of his work, in its perpetual dialectic. He refused the encapsula-
tion of his thought in any single designation. One is therefore
hardly astonished to read in an 1892 letter to his publisher Jacob
Hegel that he is in "the happy position of knowing and daily
experiencing that I have both the right and the left behind me."

Ibsen's disposition has sometimes been set down as anarchist.
He expressed suspicion and contempt for all governments, all
constituted states. That is why his eagerness to acquire and his
direct solicitation of official orders of merit, medals, decorations,
doctorates, so often dismayed his friends. But if he went out

of his way in his approach to heads of state to confer such tributes, it was not only the practical bourgeois which impelled him—he wanted the homage of the authorities back home—but the artist in him as well. Most artists, despite haughty expressions of disdain for such honors, thirst for recognition and acclaim, especially if they have long suffered neglect.

Another recurrent word in the Ibsen lexicon is "liberty." For him this meant the spiritual regeneration of humankind. "Liberty is the first and highest condition for us. Liberty is not the same as 'liberties,' just as freedoms are not the same as Freedom." In a most remarkable 1877 letter to Brandes he writes: "I shall never agree to making liberty synonymous with political liberty . . . He who possesses liberty as something already achieved possesses it dead and soulless . . . Anyone who stops in the middle of the struggle, and says, 'Now I have it,' shows that he has lost it. It is exactly this tendency to stop dead when a certain given amount of liberty has been acquired that is characteristic of the political state—and it is that which I said was not good—the state is the curse of the individual—by absorbing the spirit of the individual into a political and geographical conception. Now turn to the Jewish nation, the nobility of the human race. [Is it possible that Ibsen used this example because Brandes was a Jew?] How has it preserved itself—in its isolation—despite all the barbarity of the outside world? Because it had no state to burden it. Had the Jewish people remained in Palestine, it would have long since been ruined in the process of construction like all other nations. The state must be abolished! . . . making intelligence and spiritual kinship the only essentials for union—and you have the beginning of liberty of some value."

All the extravagances of assertion, the heated rhetoric characteristic of the romantic personality, which Ibsen inexpugnably was, might be summarized in his one fundamental conviction: the individual's inner self is the wellspring or true warrant for all just action. The interposition or rule of official authority or dogma by state, church, party, traps the person in one manner or another, cripples the self, destroys authenticity and spells spiritual ruin. External authority can be valid only if it wins the assent of the individual soul. This is perhaps what Spinoza had in mind when he said, "Happiness consists in a man's being able to maintain his own being."

But the nature of the self which Ibsen posited as a first principle was not something he was entirely sure about. There was much more of the Old Faith in Ibsen than is generally recognized. In this regard a German writer tells a rather significant story. "Although Ibsen enjoyed jokes, he disapproved of any joke concerning religion, surprisingly for so ostentatious a freethinker. When the writer made such a joke, Ibsen became very tight-lipped and snapped, 'There are some things one doesn't make fun of,' and left the table." Ibsen was never entirely sure of anything. His lifework was the dramatization of this dilemma.

The Italian critic Nicola Chiaramonte defined Ibsen's contribution by saying: "[He] questioned on the stage the *morality* of the part the individual plays in order to adapt himself to the society in which he lives." This limits Ibsen to what he is commonly held to be: a social playwright. But that is less than half the story. To confine him within the bonds of social measure is to see him narrowly. He reaches beyond any of his "positions." He looked forward to further search and perhaps new revelations, when he suffered a stroke and could write no more.

Was it because he was possessed and tormented by the many questions which he had raised and left unanswered that the staid and stolid man more than once was found in the gutter overcome by drink? In 1891 a humorous magazine published a series of epitaphs for various notables. Ibsen's read:

> Here I lie struck by
> the shaft of death.
> Is the riddle solved now?
> I have my doubts.

None of Ibsen's generalizations or, if one chooses to designate them so, his thought, would be of great moment if he had not been a consummate dramatist. "You are like two people who cannot agree," Svanhild tells the poet Falk in *Love's Comedy*. The same is true of Ibsen. The dialogue of his spirit would find its natural expression in drama, the art *par excellence* of conflict.

The crosscurrents of his soul became eloquent in his stage characters. The inner fire which racked and might have destroyed him was checked by the icy discipline of his craft. Driven by inner necessity, he was a "born dramatist."

Ibsen wrote several volumes of poetry; six of his plays are in verse, a few combine prose with verse. But he always referred to himself as a poet and to his plays as books. This may be explained by the fact that for him and other writers of his day most creative writing was called poetry (*Dichtung* in German). His plays were published before they were produced; they were therefore books. But everything he wrote is marked by his dramatic gift. This in itself would not have sufficed to make him what he became. He studied and thoroughly trained himself for the theater.

His boyhood theatrical bent manifested itself in making puppets and in his eagerness to display them. His mother was a theater buff. In the 1830s and 1840s a touring company presented some eighteen plays in Skien. By the time he was twelve he had occasion to see, among others, six plays by Scribe, whose tricky pieces dominated the commercial theater of Paris as well as being popular elsewhere. It is believed he read Schiller's *Wilhelm Tell*, and he is known to have admired the work of the Danish dramatist Ludvig Holberg, sometimes referred to as "the Molière of the North," and the Danish poet-dramatist Adam Oehlenschläger. His lessons and practice in painting, which for a while he thought of pursuing as a career, stood him in good stead in the theater.

When he abandoned his plan to become a doctor—he was not a particularly good student—he turned toward literature. He became an avid reader of Corneille, Racine, Shakespeare, Byron, Hugo. Still a "pharmacist" at twenty, he wrote *Catiline*, which through the kind office of a friend was published under a pseudonym in an edition of 250 copies of which no more than fifty were sold.

No new play by a Norwegian had been published since 1843. And though the capital had had a regular theater since 1827, Norway had not yet produced a living dramatic literature. The theater produced almost nothing but translated plays. It was thus practically inevitable that an attempt to produce *Catiline* in Christiana should fail.

Another play, the one-act *The Warrior's Barrow*, written during Ibsen's pre-med student years, was staged at the Christiana in 1850 for three performances. It was the first Ibsen piece ever produced. He was twenty-two.

Shortly after this debut he engaged in semi-political journalism and wrote theater criticism. Through his verse and other miscellaneous writings he began to attract a little attention as a nationalist poet. In the meanwhile the renowned violinist Ole Bull had unsuccessfully pleaded with the Storting (the Norwegian parliament) to support a *Norwegian* theater he had established in Bergen on Norway's west coast. I italicize "Norwegian" because for all the nationalist puffing, the stage language of the official theater in Christiana was still Danish.

This needs clarification. The translator of Haldvan Koht's *Life of Ibsen* supplies it: "Although Denmark and Norway had a common literary language, pronunciation of this language differed widely in the two countries. Danish, with its extensive changes from the old Scandinavian, could at times be difficult for the Norwegians to understand. Danish actors using Danish pronunciation were traditionally preferred on the stage until well after the middle of the nineteenth century. In Ibsen's generation a change occurred; thanks to the agitation of Bjørnson and others, cultivated Norwegian pronunciation was introduced on the stage to replace the characteristically Danish sounds. The difference was comparable in degree to that between an extreme Oxford pronunciation and a general American pronunciation."

When Ole Bull encountered Ibsen, who shared his views, both knew they could create a theater together. They began a heated campaign to this end. In 1851 they arranged a musical evening to raise money. Ibsen contributed a prologue in verse, read by an actress, and Ole Bull composed a song with music sung by a choral ensemble. Ibsen's poem was a "triumph," reported by the newspapers. In Skien, Ibsen's birthplace, a local journal ran a proud squib: "Mr. Ibsen is a son of the merchant Knud Ibsen of Skien."

Shortly after, Ibsen signed a contract to assist the theater as an author. The theater's directorate decided to grant him two hundred dollars to go to Copenhagen to study stage technique. He could then qualify as a stage manager and director, under a five-year agreement at three hundred dollars a year.

He was not, however, to become the theater's "artistic director." Ibsen's assignment was to be a "scene instructor": he had to "block" (stage) the scenes and supervise the dialogues. Interpretation was left to the "role instructor" (or "artistic director") —a very odd arrangement. Small wonder the two were not always on friendly terms.

We should bear in mind that stagecraft at this theater was fifty years behind the times: The sets had no side-walls, but a painted backcloth and a sequence of painted wings, with hanging strips of cloth overhead. The backcloth had to be rolled up like a home cinema screen before being hoisted into the flies to make way for another. The lighting consisted of chandeliers above the stage and auditorium. Gas was not introduced at the Bergen Theater until 1856, the year Ibsen left; until then chandeliers, footlights and wing lamps provided with candles or petroleum, etc., were used. Rehearsal periods were ridiculously brief.

As stage manager, besides having to make budgetary estimates, Ibsen was also required to supervise the settings, costumes and properties. I have seen and liked some of his Bergen designs for settings and costumes. But because of his lack of previous experience and an absence of confirmed directorial authority, he was extremely shy about venturing to do more than his technical duties called for.

As the house author, he was commissioned to dramatize "the life of the nation" (the assignment was very much in the vein of our federal project of the 1930s when artists were instructed to "paint the national scene"). He was expected to have a play ready in 1853—when he would be twenty-five—and to supply one a year every year after that. The first of the plays written to order was *St. John's Night*. It was a resounding flop. The house was empty the second night and it was never put on again. The second of the "series," also a flop, was a version of *The*

Warrior's Barrow, which had been well received in Christiana, but instead of three performances as it had there, it had only one in Bergen.

A year later he wrote *Lady Inger of Østråt*, a play supposedly inspired by a "quickly formed and quickly ended love affair." *Lady Inger* was performed for the theater's anniversary celebration on January 2, 1855. (According to Ibsen's contract his Bergen premières were always due to open at the beginning of each year.) But though Ibsen himself thought well of *Lady Inger* it too failed after two performances.

In September of the same year, for the first and last time in his career Ibsen directed a play by Shakespeare: *As You Like It*. It was no more successful than his own plays had been. "The play," it was reported, "was too difficult for the company's talents."

With his next play, *The Feast at Solhaug*, Ibsen enjoyed his first taste of "success." Presented on January 2, 1856, under his own direction, it was given six times in the first few months— a good run for a city as small as Bergen. It was also accepted by the Christiana Theater when it opened the same year and achieved another six performnces that spring.

Olaf Liljekrans was a revised and completed version of an early unfinished play. It too was a disaster at its opening in 1857, and was withdrawn after two performances. Ibsen never wished to have it published.

Ibsen's contract now having expired, he signed a new one for another year at the same salary and still in a relatively subordinate position. He was then offered the post of "artistic director" at the Christiana Norwegian Theater at a salary of six hundred dollars a year. The Bergen Theater granted him a release. He occupied his new position at the Christiana for five years. Among his other duties he was expected to salvage the reorganized theater, which had run into financial difficulties.

He announced an ambitious program, as do most directors of new theatrical enterprises. He began by condemning the entire French dramatic school *à la* Scribe, because of its basic frivolity. "Now," to quote Haldvan Koht, who paraphrases all Ibsen's pronouncements, "he insisted that the inner life of drama, not

just its outward action, should reflect the spirit of the nation—
an idea in keeping with the constantly reiterated plea that a
work of art should do more than simply strive to imitate nature
or life. Art must search out spiritual truths (in Ibsen's words),
'that higher symbolic representation of life that would clarify
the questioning thoughts of people.' He looked for actors [who]
would share these ideals. One of his critiques deals with stage
directing: the director must try to express the author's real
intention, so that even lines that seem on the surface insignificant
can be made to assume dramatic and psychological meaning."
All this several years before Stanislavsky's birth.

Ibsen's next play, *The Vikings at Helgeland*, was written for
the Christiana Theater in 1858, but the trustees postponed its
production because, so he was informed, they could not afford
to pay royalties for a new work that season. He published a sharp
attack on the theater's management in a national liberal newspaper. The postponement meant, he claimed, that the theater
"was unable to support, encourage or in general bother itself
about Norwegian dramatic literature." A representative of the
theater defended its action on the ground that Ibsen was "a
small time poet," and went on to attack his other output. He
was put down as "a major nonentity."

The controversy made Ibsen even more determined to become
the national Norwegian dramatist. He would bend all his efforts
toward realizing "the great ideal of Scandinavian beauty," Scandinavia which had to achieve equality with other nations: independent, in all things independent. Norway was not to achieve
complete national independence till 1905, a year before Ibsen's
death.

This brief sketch of Ibsen's early theater experience must be
interrupted for a moment to note that during the period of
his controversy over *The Vikings*, just before the opening of
the next season, Ibsen returned to Bergen to marry Suzannah
Thoreson on June 18, 1858. This occurred after a brief romance
with another girl, but of Ibsen's love life and marriage more
will be said in a later chapter. Ibsen's and Suzannah's child,
Sigurd, was born December 23 of the next year.

After the publication of *The Vikings at Helgeland* in a magazine, the dispute between Ibsen and the theater management was
terminated by the production of the play despite the theater's
inadequate company and poor technical resources. A revival
of *Lady Inger of Østråt* followed in 1859. *The Vikings* drew
well, ran for eight performances, but was not a financial success. The production of *Lady Inger* was a pronounced failure.

A year's experience as a theater director taught Ibsen, as it
has many others, that "one learns to be practical in the theater
. . . learns to put one's higher ideals aside for a while when one
can't do otherwise." He had to replace *Lady Inger* with two
"petite English dancing girls," who filled the house all through
the spring.

During Ibsen's tenure at the Christiana Theater from 1857 to
1863, bad adaptations of plays by Shakespeare, Molière, de Mus-
set, Calderón, Holberg, Scribe, Sardou and other French and
Danish writers were presented.

When Ibsen applied for a government grant to study the
theater in London, Paris, Stockholm and major cities in Germany he was not thought worthy of it. He wrote many poems,
venting his bitterness and confusion over the course of his career
and the blocks in the way of fulfilling his aims in the theater.
He was unable to complete a new play and began to lose hope
in his future. His work as a director grew lax, for which he
was dressed down by the theater's trustees and others.

He recovered from this interval of depression, and encouraged by Bjørnstjerne Bjørnson, poet, novelist and dramatist four
years younger than Ibsen, he mounted a series of interesting
plays. Bjørnson was then already a leading literary figure and
was soon to become a political force as well. He had taken over
the directorship of the Bergen Theater after Ibsen's resignation
and later of the Christiana Theater. He directed some of Ibsen's
plays and was godfather to Ibsen's son, who in 1882 was to
marry Bjørnson's daughter. Ibsen's relation to Bjørnson was to
be intimate all through their lives, though their friendship blew
hot and cold—sometimes to the danger point of enmity.

When because of heavy financial losses the Christiana Theater
was forced to close, Ibsen was left without an income. He now

applied for a grant to collect country legends, ballads, folk tales; above all to make contact with people along the way. The trip proved of inestimable value.

In 1862, while brooding over a new play, he took a job as a theater critic. No doubt because of his intimate knowledge of conditions in the theater, he now evinced greater lenience of judgment than he had previously done. He hoped to stimulate interest in a living Norwegian theater and attacked all those who like himself had previously been inclined to a sentimentally nationalistic ancestor worship which masked neglect of the present.

Now thirty-four, he wrote *Love's Comedy*, his first play with a contemporary subject or setting. On publication it so angered the public and the critics—for reasons which will be apparent when we arrive at a discussion of the play—that it could not then be produced.

On assuming the position of literary consultant for the Christiana Theater, Ibsen dropped his assignment as a reviewer. The new job was poorly paid and he was heavily in debt. To help keep himself financially afloat he wrote festive and other occasional poems for the Student Society and similar groups.

Again and again he applied for a foreign travel stipend. He asked for six hundred dollars "to study art, art history and literature," preferably in Rome or Paris so that he might gain "an all round education," for his work as an author. The requests were met either by rejection or delay.

While waiting anxiously for an affirmative response, he wrote and published his most important historical play, *The Pretenders*, which was produced at the Christiana Theater. Though the performance under his own direction lasted nearly five hours, on the opening night it was greeted with thunderous applause and cries for the author.

The Pretenders was the first Ibsen play to be produced outside Scandinavia: in Copenhagen in 1871 and in 1875 by the famous Meiningen Players, a pioneer company in the modern approach to staging. First given as a court production at the Duchy of Meiningen, Germany, and later brought to Berlin, new productions of *The Pretenders* followed. In 1904 Max

Reinhardt scored a great hit with the play in Berlin. But by that time Ibsen had become world-famous, though in some cities merely notorious.

The government in 1863 finally granted Ibsen four hundred dollars for travel, two hundred less than he had requested. Bjørnson managed to collect another seven hundred dollars from a number of his influential acquaintances. On April 5, 1864, Ibsen set sail for Rome, with a stopover in Copenhagen. It was just then that Denmark's defeat in the war with Prussia over Schleswig-Holstein was announced. Ibsen's indignation over Norway's betrayal (already mentioned) knew no bounds:

> With forgotten promises, treacherous words
> With solemn treaties torn,
> With this year's lie given to last year's oath
> You have manured history's soil.

After two weeks in Copenhagen and a brief stay in Berlin, where, to his mortification, he saw the Prussians gloat over their victory, he went on to Vienna. On the railroad from the suburb of Semmering, he took a train which led over the Alps toward Rome. He reached Rome on June 19, 1864, where the Italian sun dispelled the Northern gloom. After a short stay in a mountain town to avoid the summer heat, he settled with his wife and son in the Eternal City. There he reveled in its monuments, art treasures, churches, castles and palaces.

It was in Rome, after being salvaged from further financial duress by Bjørnson's intervention on his behalf and a grant from a Norwegian scientific society, that Ibsen, at the age of thirty-seven, wrote and in 1866 published *Brand*, the play that was to bring him international renown. As a book it achieved an unprecedented sale and ran into numerous editions during the next few years. Though twice the length of the average play and probably never intended for the stage, it was given its first performance in 1885 in Stockholm, where, with cuts, it ran for six and a half hours. It was nonetheless a success.

After *The Pretenders* Ibsen never again directed any of his plays or actually participated in their production except as an adviser on casting and in certain matters of interpretation. The writing of *Brand* confirmed him in his conviction that he was above all a dramatist. Whatever verse he wrote would henceforth serve as dialogue in his plays.

It is not altogether a metaphor to say that Ibsen's conception of drama and art in general was a priestly one. "The gift of writing," he wrote in a letter to Bjørnson from Rome, "is not a privilege, it is a responsibility." If he ever entertained an aesthetic rather than an ethical attitude toward his work, he abandoned it with his first steps into manhood. "Aestheticism of this kind [art in isolation]," he wrote in an 1865 letter, "seems to me as great a curse to poetry as theology is to religion." In 1869 he tells Brandes, "Of course I bow before the laws of beauty, but I have no regard for its conventions. You mention Michelangelo: no one has ever sinned more against the established conventions of beauty than he. Nevertheless everything which he has created is beautiful because it is full of character. Raphael's art has never really moved me. His people belong to a period before the fall of man. Besides, the Latin's aesthetic principles are quite different from ours: he wants absolute formal beauty, while to us conventional ugliness may be more beautiful by virtue of its inherent truth."

At the very moment he was engaged in shaping *Brand* he writes to his publisher: "I find it my godgiven talent to arouse my countrymen from their lethargy and make them understand what direction the great issues of life are taking." He is a man with a mission: " . . . to awaken the nation and to lead it to think great thoughts." Though no crass "pulpit-thumper," he was able to say, "Every one of us must strive to improve the state of the world."

For all his self-questioning he could honestly affirm, "I have an impression that my new work [*Brand*] will not dispose [the Norwegian parliament] more charitably toward me. But hang me if I can or will, on that account, suppress a single line, no matter what these 'pocket edition' souls think of it. Let me rather be a beggar all my life! If I cannot be myself or what I

want, then everything is nothing but lies and humbug . . . " At
a later period—1885–86—Ibsen admitted that his polemic interests were decreasing.

His attitude toward the theater was very much as Schiller's
had been when in 1783 he said of Germany, "Had we a national
theater, we could become a nation." Ibsen worked long and
arduously in the preparation of his plays. More than a year
elapsed between one play and another—in some instances much
longer. There were rough drafts and numerous revisions in
which many changes of motivation and characterization were
effected. The tone and vocabulary of the dialogues were often
altered in conformity with each personage. It is said that even
the season and time of day were factors in the modes of speech
employed. Ibsen's account of his schedule of composition is
more explicit:

"As a rule I make three drafts of my plays, which differ
greatly from each other—in characterization, not in plot. When
I approach the first working out of my material, it is as though
I knew my characters from a railway journey; one has made a
preliminary acquaintance, one has chatted about this and that.
At the next draft I already see everything much more clearly,
and I know the people roughly as one would after a month
spent with them at a spa; I have discovered the fundamentals
of their characters and their little peculiarities; but I may still
be wrong about certain essentials. Finally, in the last draft I
have reached the limit of my knowledge; I know my characters
from close and long acquaintances—they are my intimate
friends, who will no longer disappoint me; as I see them now,
I shall always see them."

A friend made note of Ibsen's work day: "He liked to rise at
four a.m., and take a stroll in the woods or the park before the
day grew hot. As the sun rose higher in the heavens he sat down
at his desk where he would work more or less uninterruptedly
till the day ended." He brooded over his plays in the winter;
wrote them in the summer.

His suggestions as a stage director were, to quote one of his
actors, "brief, clean, precise and helpful." He had a sense, rare
in his day, of theatrical *ensemble*. To actors who thanked him

for writing great roles for them he replied with some asperity, "I have not written roles for actors and actresses. I have written to portray human beings, not to create roles." Plays were entities of which each character was part of the total structure and idea of the play.

In answering an actress from Munich who inquired for interpretative instruction in playing the role of Rebecca in *Rosmersholm*, he wrote, "The only piece of advice I can give you is to read the whole play closely over and over again and carefully observe what other persons say about Rebecca. In earlier times our actors often committed the great mistake of studying parts in isolation without paying sufficient regard to the character's position in connection with the whole work—Furthermore, you should bring to your assistance your studies and observations of life.

"No declamation! No theatrical emphasis! No pomposity at all!" Ibsen went on, "Give each mood credible, true-to-life expression. Do not think of this or that actress you have seen. But stick to the life that is going on around you, and give us a true, living character."

Still another actress reported from the Christiana Theater that one of her colleagues in the cast, a Mrs. Wolf, wished to be released from playing Berte in *Hedda Gabler*, because she felt that the part could be given to any other actress—implicitly an inferior or less important actress—in the company. "She is mistaken," Ibsen replied. "There is no one else there who could play Berte in the way I want . . . But apparently she has not taken the trouble to read the play through attentively . . . Tesman, his old aunts and the faithful servant Berte together form a picture of complete unity . . . In a performance of the play the harmony that exists between them must be conveyed. And that could happen if Mrs. Wolf takes the part. But only if she does."

Ibsen continued shrewdly with a proper sense of how to conduct a permanent repertory company: "Out of regard for Mrs. Wolf's good judgment I cannot seriously believe that she considers it beneath her dignity as an artist to portray a maid.— Here in Munich this unassuming individual is represented by one of the foremost actresses of the Court Theater. And she now embraces her task with love and interest. For besides being an actress, she is also an artist. I mean she does not pride herself on 'acting parts' but in creating real people from their fictitious roles . . . *An Enemy of the People* is now being played at the Burgtheater in Vienna. Among the many subordinate characters of the fourth act, there is a drunkard with only a few lines to say. This character, who disappears in the play, is portrayed by the great Gabrillon, well known throughout Europe . . . "

The summation of Ibsen's lifelong attitude toward writing—a fit motto for all artists—is to be found in the dedication in a copy of one of his books: "Writing means summoning oneself to court and playing the judge's part."

Despite the hardships of his early years, Ibsen always enjoyed good health. As a youth he was described as thin, and "pale as gypsum." When Brandes visited Ibsen, then forty-three, Brandes observed he was "not very tall, but handsome, athletically built, with a mighty head, a big neck, powerful shoulders—looked as if a club would be needed to overpower him. In general, he spoke little, though he was communicative to me; but the curious thing about his speech was its calm and slowness and the fact that he never smiled except when the person to whom he was talking smiled first. This sometimes had an effect that was almost one of timidity. Yet if one had to choose a single adjective to describe him, it would be 'menacing.' He looked terrifying, as he sat with his watchful eyes. Then he resembled a judge. He looked a man who was accustomed, in intercourse with other men, to occupy the standpoint of a schoolmaster, confronting his pupils, and to instill fear. For all his hostility toward the Norwegians, he was in essence very Norwegian . . . He was an aristocrat to his fingertips."

Due to his youthful troubles in Bergen and Christiana, "he felt most painfully that he was not accepted in the best society . . . he longed not to be excluded from what was best in high society . . . " "Through the rest of his life," Michael Meyer writes in this connection, "he maintained a special sensitivity in matters of protocol."

"The black clothes and white cravat which he always wears,"

another observer relates, "and the searching, penetrating glance, which issues from behind his spectacles, gave him the appearance of a French notary rather than that of an artist." A woman of his acquaintance remarked in 1864, "So dual a character it is difficult to imagine. To meet day by day he is the most socially cheerful man you could conceive. But sometimes his eyes glow cruelly, and then all he wants is to play the devil . . . He likes to take a glass of wine, because it heightens his spirits, and since they are not always lively, it is easy to get a false impression. But when he is writing, he drinks less."

He liked to "dress up"; he often wore his many medals. Princess Louise, Queen Victoria's granddaughter, noticed that "he carried a small mirror in the crown of his hat and used it like a woman when combing his hair." He often stopped in the street to look at himself in the glass of a store window to see if he looked as he thought he should.

One of the most vivid impressions of Ibsen after his return from exile is that of Richard Le Gallienne (Eva Le Gallienne's father), who describes a "forbidding, disgruntled, tight-lipped person, starchily dignified, straight as a ramrod, there he was . . . with a touch of grim dandyism about him, but with no touch of human kindness about his parchment skin or fierce badger eyes . . .

"As he entered and proceeded with precision to the table reserved in perpetuity for him, which no one would have dreamed of occupying, a thing new and delightful—to me a mere Anglo-Saxon—suddenly happened. As one man, the whole café was on its feet in an attitude of salute, and a stranger standing near me who evidently spoke English, and who recognized my nationality, said to me in a loud and reverent aside, 'That is our great national poet, Henrik Ibsen!' And remained standing till he had taken his seat, as in the presence of a king . . . "

The café he entered must have been the one which was pointed out to me on my visit to Oslo. It is an enormous place on Karl Johan Street, Oslo's main thoroughfare. On the café wall there is a painting, a reproduction of which has been made into a picture postcard on sale for tourists. We see the café interior crowded with famous artists, intellectuals, "bohemians." In the far distance from the viewers' eye, the figure of Ibsen in great-coat, cane, "stovepipe" hat enters with the steady tread of a self-contained, relentless potentate. As he himself said in 1889, he had brought "more credit to the Norwegian nation than any other Norwegian had ever done in the field of literature—or in any other field, for that matter."

Soon he would be able "to look back on forty years of uninterrupted work as a writer." Today an imposing statue of Ibsen stands, along with that of his staunch champion, Bjørnson, outside the National Theater in Oslo.

2
Stumbling

IN IBSEN'S EARLIEST PLAYS we find the seeds of the later ones. There is in *Catiline* the direct and immoderate expression of his passionate self-assertiveness. But there is also still a note of contrary disposition. In the very first speech, "No, they can never still my inner urge," after a moment's hesitation he curbs the impulse with the exclamation, "Mad ravings!"

At the time of its writing, Ibsen, as previously mentioned, was still the apprentice pharmacist in Grimstad, which on the whole was a sorry time for him. Apart from the burden of his ill-paid job and the discomfort of his lodgings, he was studying Latin in preparation for university examinations. He could devote only the night hours to his literary efforts. He had written the poem "Resignation" a year before he set to work on *Catiline*. Though he must have felt despondent he was surely not resigned. He quells his doubts as to his gift for poetry with:

> Glimpses from my spirit's depths
> Break through the dead of night,
> Flash like a stroke of lightning.

Note: All the citations from the plays in this chapter are from the translations in the Oxford University Press edition.

Beside the subjective stimulus there was the excitement of historical events. The revolution of 1848 with its repercussions in Hungary, Germany and elsewhere in Europe roused the insurrectionary and polemic sentiments which were to be characteristic of him for many years. He indited resounding poems of encouragement to the Magyars, urging them in the name of honesty and freedom to fight on in their rightful war against the "tyrants."

Studying, he came upon Sallust on the subject of Catiline and, inevitably, on Cicero's speeches against that much vilified conspirator. What attracted him to the personage was not only his rebelliousness but the fact that Cicero was so vehement against him. Ibsen saw in Cicero "that indefatigable spokesman of the majority." And we know what the arch-individualist Ibsen thought of the majority. Then too, of course, it is always the victors who write history.

Ibsen realized from the first that his play would have only a tenuous relation to historical data. He used what little he knew or anyone else then knew for the purpose of an idea, his idea. More latent than explicit in the play is the portrait of a flawed person who, in revolt against an empire he deems complacent and decadent, is still to be regarded as a hero.

It was not Rome Ibsen scorned—he had a limited knowledge of ancient history—but Norway. It was Norway in its peaceful slumber of reclusion from the "big world" that Ibsen wished to arouse. Surely it is Norway rather than Rome he has in mind when he has the aptly named Furia say:

> here soaring pride is repressed—
> here business stifles every spark of brilliance
> before it bursts forth in leaping flames . . .

Furia also speaks of "proud and lofty plans within [her] breast":

> How it is crushed between the narrow walls,
> where all life ossifies and hope is quenched,
> where drowsily the weary day drags on,
> where thoughts can never find a concrete goal!

To which Catiline replies:

> Ah, Furia, how uncanny are your words,
> like sounds which seem to come from my own breast!

and goes on to say that they [his countrymen] do not know how fast

> this heart is beating,
> for right and freedom, for each noble cause
> which has strained in any human breast!

Furia asks him to flee with her. "We will set up our home in distant lands . . . " For a moment Catiline is tempted by the prospect but then challenges it:

> . . . But why, pray should we flee?
> . . . here too the flame of freedom can be fed . . .
> here also there is ample scope for deeds,
> as great as any even your soul asks . . .

She rejects the challenge:

> Ah! Are you also one of those
> who must shamefacedly recall Rome's past?
> What was she once? What has she now become?
> A land of heroes then, now a crowd
> of wretched slaves . . .

The reference here to sentimentally pompous oratory and past glory amid inertia and lethargy is the situation in Norway as Ibsen viewed it. It was a form of romantic historicism which he despised if it was merely to serve as a prop to sloth and complacency. He espoused it if it could be evoked as a spur to positive action; to a renewal of proud ("progressive") deeds.

The play was read by only a handful of students and a few like-minded reviewers who were on the whole sympathetic to it, but it would surely have fallen on deaf ears if it had been staged at the time of its publication. The audience would hardly have been capable of seeing any connection between the Rome of the play and the conditions in Norway. In fact the play was not produced till 1881 in Stockholm and not till 1935 in Oslo. In the latter production it was given a contemporary interpre-

tation: drunken Romans entered the stage to jazz music, dressed
in top hats, and Catiline and his fellow conspirators wore German steel helmets! But neither that production nor the one in
1976 was a success: the play after all was the first flight of a
fledgling dramatist.

In retrospect, however, it presents another feature of greater
interest. It reflects something of Ibsen's ever-abiding feeling for
two contrasting types of women. When we first meet Catiline
he declares himself a "man who always answers to freedom's
cause, an enemy of arbitrary power . . . a friend of the defense-
less and oppressed, with pluck and strength to bring the mighty
down!" He is also described as being endowed "with nobility of
soul and unflinching courage." With all this, on the very day
Cicero is denouncing him in the Senate, Catiline surreptitiously
enters the temple of Vesta to introduce his friend Curius to one
of its virgin priestesses whom he had first beheld in a festive
procession along the streets of Rome. Catiline has become violently attracted to her, and means to seduce her.

He is married to Aurelia, a gentle, compassionate, forever-
constant wife. She is the very opposite of Furia, in whom we
immediately recognize a smolderingly passionate and vindic-
tively fiery woman. How, Catiline wonders, can he love them
both? But it soon becomes evident that much of Furia's fascination for him is that she burns with a rage which is the
counterpart of his own.

The spark that has ignited the flame of hate in Furia is the
seduction of her sister by an unknown Roman, followed by her
suicide. Catiline feels compelled to confess himself that "unknown Roman." "I'm cursed, and soon forever more to hate
myself." (We recall—and it is a factor which was to weigh
heavily on his conscience and sexual behavior for the rest of
his life—that two years before the writing of this play Ibsen
had seduced a servant girl.) Furia vows to revenge herself on
him. Later, because through neglect she has allowed the flame of
Vesta to become extinguished, she is punished and dies in consequence of it. But she returns as a "ghost"—Catiline's evil
genius—to prod him to conspiratorial battle in which she fore-

sees his defeat: she has incited his friend Curius to betray him to the governing powers.

The absurdity in all this is that Furia's "ghost" continues to torment Catiline and is both audible and visible to Curius as well as to Aurelia. We are, therefore, never entirely sure whether she is a ghost or whether she has actually survived.

When Aurelia presses Catiline to tell her what so disturbs him he can only reply:

> —on my head
> a horrible and oppressive fate
> the curse is inherent in that combination
> of noble spiritual energies,
> of ardent fervour for a life of deeds,
> with sordid bonds which cramp the striving soul . . .

This symptom of a discomfiture many of Ibsen's near heroes and heroines were to suffer, a suffering which in Ibsen himself could only be assuaged by its expression in art. Throughout the play Catiline vacillates between his nobler instincts, patriotic zeal, fidelity to Aurelia and the malefic hold Furia exerts on him, impelling him at times to acts of courage and at others to crime. He is, by turn, magnanimous and vile, a liberator and a traitor, a libertine and a man capable of renunciation and self-sacrifice. Though Furia may be regarded as his nemesis, she also inspires exalted action.

Furia promises that if he will follow her urgings, which are really his own, his life "would shine with a brilliant clarity

> across the ages, if with strength and vigor
> you found a passage through the madding crowd,
> and through your radiant spirit clouds of thralldom
> had given way to new-born skies of freedom.

"You seem to me a spirit of revenge," he tells her; "Indeed, I am an image of your soul," she says.

The play is not so much a dramatization of an objectively conceived situation as the hectic ruminations of a man wrangling with his conscience. Catiline is defeated, as he must be, after he has been betrayed by his followers and even more by his own uncertainties. Should we consider it "symbolic" that he is also driven to the murder of his wife?

In Furia we recognize by hindsight the prototype of the "dangerous women" who were to become the most arresting of Ibsen's creatures, and in Aurelia the first model of the tender and supportive women who, while they may at times strike us as pallid, at others rise to angelic heights. The destructive women, some of them unconsciously or unwillingly so, possess faculties which lead to valuable ends, but more often to their own and other people's downfall. "Victory" generally attends the unassailably good women, though we rarely find them as dramatically absorbing as the others. Ibsen's "devilish" women in the later plays are as remarkable, significant and real as Emma Bovary or Anna Karenina. Even those Ibsen women who might be designated "anti-heroines" are usually more aggressive, stronger and more intelligent than the males around them. They are victims of their strength as much as of their weaknesses.

Furia and Aurelia are conceptual rather than fleshed characters. Even as such there is a staginess about them which smacks of flagrantly romantic theater. Still, some of the lineaments of the more mature Ibsen are to be discerned here. Except for its initial impetus, the play as a whole with its many hastily contrived scenes lacks sound substance. None of the main personages are much more than stock characters. The writing strains for but rarely achieves either strength or striking eloquence. In the climactic scene after Furia has plunged the dagger given her into his chest, Aurelia staggers in, her bosom bloody, and after some words of contrition Catiline sinks his head on her breast, while day dawns in the background!

Ignorant of the original Norwegian, one cannot expatiate on the merits or faults of the play's versification. (In speaking disparagingly in his first review of *Peer Gynt*, Georg Brandes nevertheless spoke of Ibsen's "incredible gift for versification" and "wonderful command of language.") In translation, Ibsen's verse tends toward the sense and sound of prose, while at its best the dialogue of his prose plays takes on the ring and afflatus of poetry.

The critics of Ibsen's day found the influence of Greek trag-

edy on *Catiline*. But there is much more of Schiller-like melodramatics and in spots a filching from Shakespeare. A Phantom
appears in the course of the play very much on the manner of
the witches in *Macbeth*:

> Though thou shalt fall by thine own hand
> Yet shall another strike thee down.

The play nevertheless interests by what it portends:

> Is life then not an unabating struggle
> between hostile forces in the soul?
> And in this struggle lies the soul's true life . . .

There is little to be said about and not much to be recommended in *The Burial Mound*, a one-act dramatic poem written
during the winter of 1850. Originally composed in Grimstad
shortly after the completion of *Catiline* and revised on Ibsen's
arrival in Christiana where he was to prepare himself for the
university entrance examination, the play was submitted, again
under a pseudonym, to the theater in that city—and accepted
by it.

It tells of a Viking incursion into Sicily (in the second version, into Normandy), where the warrior king has come to
avenge his father's death, which he had met in battle eleven
years before. Ready to kill anyone who may have been responsible for it, he forgoes his savage purpose when he becomes
enamored of Blanka, a Norse girl who has been reared in the
mildness of the Southern clime and protected by the grace of
Christian kindness.

In every respect inferior to *Catiline*, the only explanation for
the play's acceptance, apart from the fact that it calls for only
a single setting and therefore is much less costly to produce,
is that it resounds with nationalistic sentiment, the revival of
which swept through Norway, particularly among the students
in Christiana. The play failed after three performances. A new
and rather better version was presented in 1854 in accord with
Ibsen's contract with the Bergen Theater. The failure there was
even more shattering than it had been in the capital.

Though the play echoes the author's enthusiasm for the poetic

evocation of Norway's past there is very little of the subjective
fervor that informs *Catiline*. Still there are certain traits which
foreshadow Ibsen's later physiognomy. The 1854 version contrasts Northern virility with Mediterranean softness. Implied in
this is the notion that softness bespeaks decadence.

> *Here* [in Sicily] the god-like lives no more;
>   stone alone its features bear.
> *There* [in Norway] it breathes a vigorous air
>   like a warrior strong and bold!
> . . . .
> *Here* it's all a crumbling ruin,
>   drowsy, slothful, heavy dull
> *There* a plunging avalanche,
>   a life of spring, a winter's death!

Yet one of the Vikings complains:

> Oh, what a stagnant time is this we live in!
> Our faith and customs from the older days
> are everywhere unhappily in decline.

Further on, the king himself confirms this:

> A blight has fallen on this present age,
> that's sapping all the goodness of the North,
> just like a poison feeding on its blooms,
> I shall go home! And save what still there is
> to save, before it falls down in ruins.
> (*Pauses, during which time he looks about him*)
> How pleasant within this Southern grove!
> My pine woods cannot boast so strong a scent.

Several contrasting, very nearly opposing elements are discernible. On the one hand, Ibsen, while eschewing chauvinism,
celebrates the stern vigor of Norse paganism; on the other, with
more personal animus, he denounces the decline of his country's
sturdy nature. The play however concludes on a rallying upbeat:

> The North shall rise from out the tomb
> truer deeds of spirit on seas of thought.

As in other areas, Norway was late in its religious development. It hadn't become Christian till the latter part of the tenth
century. The play suggests that the Norse strain of martial stal-
wartness required the mollifying influence of Christian idealism.
When the Viking king enters into marriage with Blanka, the
maid of Norse extraction and Southern breeding, the ceremony
begins with:

> Eternal blessings be upon this pact
> Combining Nordic strength with Southern mercy.

Another significant note, to be given full expression in *Love's
Comedy* and in other plays where the *skald* (the court noble-
man's bard) recites, sings and speaks as a prophet, is first struck
here:

> The monument the poet's tongue creates,
> outlines the memorial stone upon the mound.

More personal is the reiteration of Ibsen's keynote when
Blanka responds to the Viking's speech about the glory of war,
which he calls "strife":

> Ah yes! The *inner strife*, the *spirit's battle*,
> And light's resounding victory over dark.
> Such struggle gives life its purpose, heathen!

While still at the university, editing a student newspaper, contributing articles to the Workers Union paper, doing a stint as
theater critic, writing poems and serving on the staff of a short-
lived satirical journal, Ibsen dashed off a political spoof called
Norma or *A Politician's Love: A Tragic Opera in Three Acts*.

Published in *The Man*, the aforementioned journal, the three
acts come to little more in Ibsen's collected works than eight
pages and never, of course, were meant to be performed.
Norma's only importance now is that it is the first example of
Ibsen's comic verse. *Peer Gynt* and other of his plays attest to
his humor—an attribute which often escapes notice in the consideration of his writing. Theater folk who understand Norwegian—Eva Le Gallienne and the actor Earle Hyman, to name

only two—assure us that much of Ibsen's dialogue is actually *funny*, "with laugh lines galore" as certain American reviewers used to say. The humor is for the most part shrewd, truculent, Mephistophelean. This is not the case in *Norma*, which is one long joke.

In the prologue, Ibsen explains how he came to write it. "The other day I found myself in the gallery of the Storting, the nature of the matter under discussion was like most of these things, so I no longer remember what it was about . . . I gave free play to my imagination and yielded myself up to that agreeable state of suspended animation . . . when either the soul feels weary or the surrounding world produces the appropriate soporific impression . . .

"In the evening I saw [Bellini's opera] *Norma*, and suddenly I realized, 'The Storting is a dramatically talented company.' The Opposition in general is the coquette, which every young fellow wants to pay court to, but of whom finally he usually has doubts about taking to wife (especially when her rival tends to bring a more substantial dowry) . . .

"It was these considerations which moved me to arrange the opera 'Norma or the Politician's Love' . . . which I heartily invite Parliament to perform on some festive occasion or other. They will have to see to the music themselves, and as they have virtuosi in all possible instruments from trumpet to drums and trombone, one hopes that this will not prove difficult."

As in Bellini's opera, the characters are all Druids. The Druids, we are reminded, "were heathen dogs who, like owls and bats, preferred to carry on their activities in dark forests, where enlightenment—from sun and moon—found difficulty in penetrating." Listing the characters according to the nomenclature of the original opera, the author Ibsen says *his* Norma is to be played by the Opposition; her good friend Adalgisia is the Government; Severus, lover of both ladies, is a Liberal. Norma and Severus' two consumptive sons represent the Address 71848, the Chorus of Druids are Sensible Members of the Opposition, etc.

The piece opens with Ariovist, Norma's father and the head of the Male and Female Druids:

> Here we stand on freedom's forest land.

Chorus of Male and Female Druids in unison:

> Yes, yes, yes, yes:
> Yes, yes, yes, yes:

All:

> In the good old ancient North!

Ariovist continues:

> But we must watch, and we must pray . . .
> . . . .
> (*Aside*) It has always been my practice, from my
>   earliest days
> To keep myself in any case a horse's length behind
>   the times.

The characters are all caricatures of well-known parliamentarians, projected in the manner of lightfingered journalism and political cabaret. In the final scene of the first act, when Adalgisia (the Government) finds Severus (the Liberal) pretty much *in flagrante delicto* with Norma (the Opposition), a fracas breaks out between the two. Severus begs forgiveness for his transgression and is taken to Adalgisia's breast. The stage direction then reads: "touching embrace; the curtain then falls for the sake of the proprieties."

At the end of the second act when the tables have turned and Norma finds Severus back at the same antics with Adalgisia, still another hullabaloo erupts. Severus tries to make them both shut up and whispers to the stagehand in the wings "Oh let the curtain down, this is a scandalous scene." To which the curtain man offstage shouts, "You're right there," and the curtain descends rapidly.

Ibsen himself referred to his next play, *St. John's Night* (Midsummer Night), as "a miserable thing," and refused to have it published during his lifetime. He was not mistaken. Written while he was abroad on his three-month study tour in Copenhagen and Dresden, it was the second of his plays to be produced and like his first, *Catiline*, a flop. The Bergen public looked forward to it—the first night was sold out—but was bitterly and justifiably disappointed.

The play is clumsy in execution, confusing in style and plot, and though it contains a few entertaining scenes, most of its humors are heavy-handed. It is in prose, except for the verse of an interwoven fantasy. A goblin, like Puck in *A Midsummer Night's Dream*, pokes his head into the contemporary scene and at one point—its only major action—squeezes the juice of a flower into a bowl with the same discombobulating effect on a brace of lovers as in Shakespeare's comedy.

If one is to read the play at all, there are two passages which merit notice. In the prologue written for the Bergen performance in 1853, one finds lines which reveal the author's state of mind at the time and anticipate his future. Thus: "If on foreign strand you voyage, your yearnings fly across the sea to the dear old country buried in the distance behind the waves, to the place where your cradle stood you wander in waking dreams, and would gladly exchange the blood of the grape for a draught of the mountain stream." Further on he asks, "Why should art build its pavilions only in Southern lands?"

He then concludes with monetary instruction, and acknowledgement of his past failures and a forecast of the faltering steps on the bumpy path ahead: "Remember that an artistic career can only be opened up foot by foot."

The happiest chord in the play is in a jocular portrait of a student poetaster, Julian Paulsen. He is pretentiously affected in his self-regard as a deep thinker and aesthete. He admits that his natural self does not conform with his aestheticism. He is a committed and "passionate nationalist" in the mode of the day. He advocates the use of the old Norse language to stress Norway's difference from Denmark. A sensible girl suggests that if he were to employ the archaic tongue, no one would understand him. He makes a fetish of local folk tales and mythology, though it puzzles him that they contain distinctly "unaesthetic" features. The following exchange exemplifies the kind of kidding to which Ibsen subjects the character:

PAULSEN: O nature's bosom is so delightful to rest in . . .
JULIANA: Yes, if it weren't so dirty.
PAULSEN: Yes, but one has to rise above that . . .

There were many such types among the young literary youths of the time. There is the prick of self-caricature and self-correction here. After the joke just cited, we read this:

PAULSEN: . . . You see, to put it bluntly, I'm still not absolutely clear about myself . . . I vacillate.
JULIANA: But you only just said you had a firm basis in—
PAULSEN: Exactly! In theory I really have . . . but it's one of the peculiarities of my theories that they don't always work out in practice.
JULIANA: Really?
PAULSEN: Yes, because the world is out of joint. That's an axiom I always cling to.

Lady Inger, Ibsen's first play entirely in prose, marks an advance over his three previous ones. That is what Ibsen meant when he called it his "best." But since the earlier plays hardly deserve to be considered "good," the compliment in which Michael Meyer and Haldvan Koht join, the praise is surely overzealous. *Lady Inger* is, at any rate, broader in scope and more intricate in plot than anything Ibsen had thus far undertaken.

It deals with Norway's struggle for independence from Danish rule in the late middle ages. Ibsen called it an "historical drama," but more reliable scholars challenged its historicity. This could not have troubled him because what he chiefly intended was to draw a parallel between Norway's past and its present. It was an appeal to public patriotism, an effort characteristic of the Norwegian intelligentsia in the 1850s to renew their pride in their national identity and to arouse the people's former vitality. That at least was what the Bergen theater audiences looked forward to. But the play itself with its long soliloquies and the asides by which the plot is made to progress and through which the psychology of the characters is revealed are dramatically awkward, at times ludicrously inept. Worse still, the play's tangle of mistaken identities, its melodramatic ploys, its crude means of inducing suspense, make its plot difficult to follow.

It begins provocatively enough with a dialogue between two retainers in the service of the suzerain Lady Inger, a woman who plays the perilous game of appeasing the Danes while conspiring as a Norwegian to overthrow them. The great hall of her palace is bedecked with relics of several knights from before Norway's subjection to Danish hegemony. The retainers are polishing the helmets and armor which once belonged to the defeated noblemen. One of the retainers, who later proves to be a traitor, mocks, "So Knut Alfson was our last knight, was he? And now he is dead and gone! (*Holding up the helmet*) Then you might as well resign yourself to hanging all bright and polished in the Great Hall because you are nothing but an empty nutshell now; yes, the kernel was eaten up by the worms many winters ago . . . couldn't we also speak of Norway as a hollow shell, like this helmet—bright on the outside and worm-eaten inside?" When told to shut up and to scrape the rust off the sword, he asks, "Is it worth it? The edge has gone . . . and the strap's missing."

This is Ibsen at his perpetual game of needling his countrymen's complacency. A moment later the same character adds, striking a note which would resound in full blast in Ibsen's later plays, "You know the old saying: only a knight is a real man. And now we've no more knights left in the country, we haven't any real men either, and when there are no men the women have to be in charge."

There are too few such sharp shafts in the play, and though its two strong women, Lady Inger and her daughter Eline, may be said to foreshadow Ibsen's later feminine portraits, the drawing in this instance lacks special insight or variety, depending too heavily on theatrical convention.

Apropos of his next play, *The Feast at Solhaug*, presented at Bergen in 1856 and a little "triumph" there, Ibsen much later said, "The present play is the inevitable result of my life at a given time." He was perhaps alluding to a love affair when he was twenty-five with Rikke Holst, a girl ten years his junior to whom he had written several ardent poems. Ibsen had asked her to marry him. But her father was violently opposed to his daughter's marriage to an impecunious poet of radical views. When the old man found that Rikke was still seeing Ibsen, after his having forbidden any further meetings between them, he threatened Ibsen physically.

Many years later when Ibsen met Rikke again—she was a married woman by then—he asked, "I wonder why nothing ever came of our relationship?" "But my dear Ibsen!" she answered with a laugh. "Don't you remember? You ran away!" "Yes, yes," he replied, "I never was a brave man face to face."

In *Lady Inger* Ibsen has a woman say, ". . . a woman is the greatest power in this world, and only through her can a man fully realize his potentialities." Ibsen must have agreed, for after his failed love with Rikke Holst, he met the intelligent, well-read, resolutely radical Suzannah Thoresen six days after the première of *The Feast at Solhaug* in 1856, and in 1858 married her. Ibsen needed, admired and depended on his wife, but later evidence makes one suspect that something of his disappointment at his behavior on the occasion of the earlier love may have been involved in his union with Suzannah.

The *Feast at Solhaug* is, except for *Olaf Liljekrans*, which followed it on the boards of the Bergen Theater, the most uncloudedly romantic of his plays. In prose and verse this comedy is composed in folk-ballad style, of very light texture. At moments one expects the characters to burst into song. In subsequent years seven composers wrote incidental music for the play, among them Hugo Wolf, when it was produced in Vienna's Burg Theater in 1891. In 1893 he made an opera of it.

The play, which takes place at the beginning of the fourteenth century, contains elements of lively drama but nothing comes of them. They all dissolve into traditionally comic complications. Margit, the young wife of Bergt Gauteson, married him because he was the wealthy master of the great estate of Solhony. She had been in love with Gudmund Alfson, in exile on being falsely accused of siding with the enemy while Norway was at war with Denmark.

When the play begins, Gudmund has stolen back to the homeland and takes refuge with Margit and her younger sister Signe. Gudmund's return stirs Margit, bored to death in her marriage, with renewed ardor for him. She is tempted and very nearly succeeds in poisoning her husband. But Gudmund has fallen in love with Signe. She in turn is about to be married to the King's Sheriff, whom she does not love. There follows a criss-cross of misunderstandings in a pattern similar to that woven in the later *Olaf Liljekrans* and the earlier *St. John's Night*, but all ends happily. Bengt escapes death, Gudmund gets Signe, the King's Sheriff does not arrest his rival, no blood is shed.

Though Ibsen later denigrated *The Feast*, it was the first of his plays to be produced outside Norway. In a rebuttal of certain critics who accused him of having borrowed certain of its features from someone else's play which had also employed the meter of the old ballads, Ibsen in the 1853 edition wrote, "What makes a work of art its creator's spiritual property is the fact that he has imposed upon it the stamp of his own personality."

Though it is another trifle, *Olaf Liljekrans*, unpublished until 1902, is a much more accomplished play, though it proved less pleasing to audiences than the preceding one. It was first written under the title *The Grouse in the Judestall*, a "national play in four acts" of which only two were completed. Something of the early version's quality may be gathered from one of its speeches.

> —I've noticed for some time [it is said of its hero]
> that all your thoughts of late [are] inclined to
> fairy tales and stories.

In verse and prose, *Olaf* resembles a fairy tale. Ibsen later thought of turning the early versions into a "romantic opera," to be named *The Mountain Bird*. A fragment, also called *Olaf Liljekrans*, is still extant. If it had been written by an American it would have been turned into a musical. "Woe, woe, to the house," one of the characters in *The Grouse* exclaims, "where songs are not heard." Despite its melodramatics and other devices of the early-nineteenth-century stage, *Olaf*'s total effect has, for all its padding, something gay and lighthearted about it.

Critics have remarked that the play contains more than a hint of one of Ibsen's major themes: the opposition of dream and reality. Olaf roaming about in an uninhabited mountain valley becomes enchanted with its sole female survivor, Alfhild, an old minstrel's daughter. But he has plighted his troth to Ingeborg, the daughter of a rich landowner, Arne of Guldvik (again a contrast between two types of women). Olaf's mother, the widowed Lady Kirstin, no longer as well off as in former days, is anxious to have Olaf's marriage to Ingeborg take place, though in her view it will be a misalliance because of her high feudal station in respect to Arne. On the eve of the wedding feast Olaf is nowhere to be found.

Olaf, Lady Kirstin fears, is "troll-struck." And so, one might add, through most of his life was Ibsen. A troll in Norwegian lore is a supernatural being, sometimes conceived as a dwarf, sometimes as a giant, dwelling in caves, hills or other strange abodes, usually of evil influence and endlessly bewitching.

Though Olaf has declared his love for Alfhild, which she reciprocates, he is duty-bound to marry Ingeborg, and is rather frightened by the spell Alfhild has cast upon him. All ends well, however, because to prevent Olaf's marriage to Ingeborg, Alfhild burns down Lady Kirstin's mansion. Ingeborg has all along been attracted to Hemming, her father's page, who is in love with her. They do not at first feel free to declare their feelings, he because he is a servant and she for that very reason. But after the fire, the quartet meet in the mountainous region of Alfhild's birth; Olaf has gone to seek her where Ingeborg and Hemming have eloped.

At last the couples pair off, but not before Ibsen has had his fun with the situation and introduced some sly animadversions on the subject of romance and reality. Olaf warns Alfhild against her headlong devotion to him, for he is aware of the peculiarity of their relationship:

> Don't come too close—it's easily done
> You may find you may have burned your fingers
> In truth it [their love] may shine like the stars
> in heaven
> But only when seen from a distance.

In like fashion after Ingeborg and Hemming have run off together, she soon realizes that now neither of them has any means of subsistence, and that they cannot live at the height of the mountain so far from the "world." She very sensibly suggests that it may be the best for her to go back to her father. "But then," he asks, "what will become of me?"

SHE: You shall ride to the wars!
HE: To the wars! And be killed!
SHE: Certainly not. You shall perform some famous deed, and then you'll be knighted, and then my father will not stand against you.
HE: Yes, but what if they do kill me?
SHE: Well, we can always think about that.

The play opens with a chorus which sets the tone for what follows:

> Oh, Christian men, pay heed to our song,
> And wake from your dreamy enchantment.

There is much talk about the "valley below," that is, the valley where the "realists" reside in contrast to the mountains where Alfhild and her minstrel father live. "Let life down below go its own sweet way," Olaf tells her, "my home is up here, my dearest, is up here with you . . . " and again, "I bid farewell to the distant world . . . "

The contrast of the "village down below" with the high mountains is no momentary fancy on Ibsen's part; it will recur more somberly and significantly in his later plays. The call of the chorus that he hears in the mountains, "Olaf Liljekrans! Olaf Liljekrans! Why sleep you so long and so heavy," comes to him as a half-forgotten memory on which he muses: "It bodes me ill, for it summons me below!" All this while Alfhild protests to her father that she wants to follow Olaf back to where he lives down in the village. "I want to take part in the great game of life!" Nor will she heed her father's warning, "It will shatter your peace of mind. Do stay!"

The airiness of the play's atmosphere brings to mind not only the metaphoric opposition between mountain and valley but of open space and the stuffiness of middle-class interiors from which many of Ibsen's characters seek escape. Mountains and other such natural environments in Ibsen's plays are always magical places where minstrels, trolls and other unfettered spirits dangerously but freely rove. The connotations are personal, aesthetic, metaphysical. They offer a clue to Ibsen's *loftiness*.

The closing lines of *The Vikings at Helgeland* (produced by the Christiana Theater and directed by Ibsen himself in 1858) proclaim Ibsen's overall intention in writing the play:

> Sing of these heroic battles,
> mighty deeds on Norwegian strand,
> down through Iceland's generations
> thrilling every Northern land.

Set in the tenth century, based on old Icelandic Family Sagas, it is a blood-and-thunder melodrama, full of killing, oaths of vengeance, duels and fierce heroics to sustain codes of honor. This in part explains its success in Norway, Denmark, Germany. It was less successful in its first English production in 1903, possibly because Ellen Terry was miscast as the play's most memorable character, Hjördis. It is also interesting to record that for that production Gordon Craig designed the settings, costumes and lighting in a manner wholly novel at the time: no foot or border lights, no flies, cloth borders or backdrops.

Certain critics have praised the play's construction. I find it jumbled and stiff, hardly the work of a skilled dramatist. The essential exposition is initiated in the following lines, spoken by Ornulf, an Icelandic chief: "I want you all to hear now what this matter is about: five winters ago, Sigurd and Gunnar came as Vikings to Iceland! All that winter they took shelter on my land close by my house. Then Gunnar carried off Hjördis, my foster daughter, by force and cunning! But you, Sigurd, took my own child, Dagny, and sailed away with her. For this I demand that you pay three hundred pieces of silver, and with that atone for your crimes."

This contretemps is soon peacefully resolved, but many others follow thick and fast in an incessant stream of violent action.

Years later Edvard Grieg contemplated making an opera of the play.

The real focus of interest is Hjördis. Her scenes exert the greatest impact. Beside her stands Dagny. She is gentle, virtuous, graciously loving; Hjördis has a fiery temperament: daring and vindictive. What further inflames the heat of her nature is that she is obsessed by a passion for the stalwart Sigurd, who, through circumstances too intricate to narrate here, married Dagny, while Hjördis was obliged to wed Gunnar, who is a softer man than Sigurd and whom she does not love. All four are ill-matched.

Though Ibsen's intention may have been to write an epic drama of national-historic interest, it is unmistakable that his creative impulse led him to a depiction of the first of "problematic" women of which Furia in *Catiline* is the abstract prototype. Hjördis is the epitome of "all the bold women who refused to live a tame life." We are to meet them later in more individualized guise in specifically modern environments. As usual they are placed beside those of opposite complexion.

Such turbulent women as Hjördis often attract powerful men —or men presumed to possess power. Hjördis' husband, Gunnar, tells her, "The very day we sailed away from Iceland, I saw that things would not go well with us. You are proud and strong. There are times I am almost frightened by you. But strangely, it is this that makes me love you most. There is a fearful fascination about you. I feel as if you could get me to do anything you wanted, commit any crime and—no matter what—I would think it well done. Sigurd should have been your husband."

Hjördis is unwilling to yield to the fate which has deprived her of the man she desires, who, under her pressure, confesses his own desire. "The cruel Fates make the world," she says, "but their power is small unless they find helpers in our own hearts. Happiness is his who is strong enough to do battle with the Fates." In this Ibsen asserts his central conviction: nothing, apart from natural forces, is valid which does not have the assent of the self. It is what he called "the revolution of the spirit."

This leads to a strange love scene:

SIGURD: . . . There is only one woman Sigurd has ever loved. And that was the woman who treated him coldly from the very first day they met . . . Now let us part. To you, Gunnar's wife, I say good-bye. We shall never meet again.

HJÖRDIS: No stay! Alas for us both! Sigurd, what have you done!

SIGURD: Done? What is this?

HJÖRDIS: All this you tell me now! Yet, no . . . it cannot be true?

SIGURD: This is the last time we shall talk together. Every word is true. I wanted you to think more kindly of me, and that is why I had to speak.

HJÖRDIS: Loved . . . loved me . . . you! I don't believe you. (*Looks fixedly at him and bursts out in wild anguish*) Yes, it is true and a sad thing for us both. (*She buries her face in her hands*) . . . Sigurd, you have not finished your story. That proud woman you were talking about . . . She loved you too!

SIGURD: You!

HJÖRDIS: Yes, Sigurd! I loved you . . . I was silent and cold with you. What else is there for a woman to do? If I had made a show of my love, I would scarcely have been worthy of you. You always seemed to me the finest of all men. And then to see you as the husband of someone else, that caused me a kind of bitter pain I never properly understood.

SIGURD: This is a wretched web the Fates have spun around us.

HJÖRDIS: You have yourself to blame. Men should act with strength and courage.

In the midst of many other violent deaths, Sigurd and Hjördis perish. Just before this moment, Ibsen strikes a note which will be developed and become full-bodied in a future play:

HJÖRDIS: Sigurd! My brother! . . . Now we belong together!

SIGURD: Less now than ever—For I am a Christian . . .

HJÖRDIS: (*in despair*) And I . . . [a pagan!]

Another recurrent chord is sounded here by way of a healing or "catharsis." In the tradition of his Icelandic countrymen, Ornulf, all of whose sons have been killed in the cross-currents of the play's feuds and battles, is asked to chant a dirge. Ornulf speaks of Hjördis, who was responsible for the murder of his youngest and most beloved son:

One thing I would strive for:
her abrupt destruction . . .
she who robbed and plundered
All I hold most precious
Has she taken all things!
No! I keep one asset!
still in my possession . . .
the gift of poetry.
(*with rising enthusiasm*)
Of my sons she stripped me,
yet the arts of language
still are mine, by which to
voice my grief in singing.
To my speech she granted
gifts of lyric power—
so my song shall echo
though my sons lie lifeless.
Hail, my sons courageous!
Hail, returning warriors!
thus the gift god-given
heals our grief and anguish!
So! Ornulf is sound and strong again!

Through his art, the poet dispels and transcends sorrow and pain. It was one of the hopes of the nineteenth century.

3

On the Threshold

A T THIRTY-FOUR Ibsen announces himself in his feisty play
Love's Comedy. Falk (the falcon), Ibsen's spokesman
here, proclaims, "The joy of battle surges through my veins."
He is youthfully bumptious and rude in speech. The play
trumpets a "program"—on wings of song. It is an epithalamium
in reverse.

For at least four years before 1868, when Love's Comedy was
published, Ibsen was no doubt an angry young man. He had
cause: he was a poor and, despite some eminent defenders, suffered misgivings as to his talent. He had not been successful
either as director or dramatist. At this juncture he might have
been considered a failure. Had he been an American most of us,
especially reviewers, would have pronounced him "finished."
In Love's Comedy, Ibsen bared his teeth, but reading it today
one is delighted by the muscle and liveliness of its writing. The
effect is tonic.

It is Ibsen's first play in a contemporary setting. One is somewhat puzzled by its having been couched in verse. An earlier
incomplete version was in prose. Perhaps the exultation and

Note: All the citations from the plays in this chapter are from the translations in the Oxford University Press edition.

annunciatory, almost prophetic, urge which incited it explains the change. The play abounds in epigrams and pithy phrases; it is comedy of sarcastic bent, though its humor can hardly be called "black."

There was much more anger in its public reception than in the play. A critic who had liked *Catiline* called *Love's Comedy* "an offense against decency," an example of "the loose thinking and debilitating nihilism that is now fashionable." The play appears to be based on the axiom that marriage is the murderer of love. But even in this there are ambiguities; the play's spirit breathes something more refreshing than its "thesis."

Ibsen's momentary bias is expressed here with self-conscious swagger. Not only do we find an amalgam of contempt for the smugness of middle-class existence and mockery of the money-marriage syndrome but also extreme individualism and idealistic or "bohemian" romanticism, which among other things suggests an espousal of free love. Still there are inner contradictions and reversals. All Ibsen's flags wave bravely over the play while he remains self-admittedly immature.

One may detect an uneasy, quizzical autobiographical element in it. At the time of its publication Ibsen had been married for less than four years after a two-year period of engagement. In the play's first scene there is this jocose exchange:

FALK: Romance, like varnish, wears away in time, but were you
         once . . .
STYVER: (*a copy clerk in a government office*): Well, you know, that
         was when I was in love.
FALK: What, when you *were* in love? I didn't know that you were
         cured already!
STYVER: Ah, now I am officially engaged, that's more than merely
         being in love!

. . . .

    Strange, do you know I find it hard to credit
    Old things I remember from that time.
    Would you believe it, seven years ago
    I secretly wrote poetry at the office.

Had Ibsen become disillusioned with his own marriage? Some people inferred as much. Ibsen resented this and said, "Only after I married did my life acquire a weight or content . . . The only person who approved of my book [*Love's Comedy*] was my wife. She is just the sort of character I need—illogical, but with a strong poetic instinct, generous and thoughtful and with an almost violent hatred of anything petty."

It has been said that Svanhild, the play's understanding and noble heroine, was modeled on his wife, Suzannah; but paradoxically she was also thought to be the model for the murderously enraged Hjördis of *The Vikings*, who was married to the wrong man.

The play also contains a not-so-vague echo of his courtship to Rikke Holst, the early love he renounced because her father threatened him with a beating. But then Ibsen might say as Falk does, " . . . I hate to wear my soul indecently exposed, like courting couples who parade their love in every street—to show my naked heart like a young lady with uncovered arms!"

Let us turn back to the play's text, in which Ibsen does expose himself more directly than in any other play of the period. He begins with a generalization which in another man's mouth might appear a banality but which in him, as we shall discover, is most revealing. "I'm paralyzed between two alternatives, flesh on the one hand, on the other, spirit." Giving vent in a torrent of quips and eloquent set pieces, he sums them all up with, "Marriage has no more to do with love than mathematics has." He derides all the company of married couples and their aunts, who seem to be their inevitable appendages. In Ibsen they (the aunts) become bulwarks of the petty bourgeoisie. Through Falk he spouts his credo as man and poet: "Each man alive must aim to stand alone, in truth and freedom."

He finds a kindred soul in Svanhild. "We shall not shirk that duty, you and I," he says. "A living spirit pulses through your veins." Her answer, fine person that she is, throws light on the situation of middle-class girls in those days: "And don't you think I've been hurt for it too . . . I wanted to break free, and stand alone." "Yes, in your silent thoughts?" "No," she says, "in my life. But then the aunts came around with their advice . . . they all discussed, and worried, and considered . . . "

She wanted to paint, but she was persuaded to take a govern-

ment post. Falk encourages her: " . . . My proud Svanhild; I've
shown the goal beyond the abyss; now leap it . . . show that
you have the courage to be free . . . for freedom lies in fully
answering your inmost call . . . "

He suggests that they join together without the bonds of
marriage. Again, as we have remarked, women in Ibsen are
more resolute and levelheaded than men. She apostrophizes him:

> I'm going to speak seriously now
> as a return for what you offered me.
> You used an image that helped me to see
> just what your "flight to freedom" really means.
> You likened yourself to a falcon, who
> must beat against the wind to reach the heights;
> I was the breeze that was to bear you up,
> And without me you couldn't rise at all.
> How pitiable! How utterly puny . . . yes laughable
> And yet your simile bore fruit, for I soon
> saw in my mind another, different emblem,
> not like yours, impatiently lame and false.
> I saw you as a kite, not as a falcon,
> a paper kite, fashioned of poetry,
> which in itself is and remains a trifle
> while the important thing is the string.
> The body was of paper obligations
> payable, some day, in poetic gold . . .
> And in this guise you lay before me, crying
> "Send me aloft wherever the wind takes me!
> "Let me soar upwards with my little rhymes;
> "Though your mamma should scold you, don't forsake me!"

Falk is aroused by this. "No more words, now, but deeds . . .
Action now, I've slept too long!" On Svanhild's injunction, "Go
with God, then, from poetry to performance," he decides to
take action: he will *marry* her! And the first act concludes with
an offstage chorus:

> Perhaps you will sail your poor vessel aground;
> Yet putting to sea is delightful.

His proposal of marriage begins ringingly with " . . . we will
show the world that love has not lost its power, that love can

face the dull and grimy weekday round and still remain stain-
less and dismayed." The stage direction reads, "With gay confidence she throws herself into his arms as the curtain falls."

This, however, is by no means the end. "We stand united; no
one can strike me down," Falk says. But there is Gulstad, a
businessman and a widower, on the premises; he talks common
sense. He too offers Svanhild marriage and calmly and sym-
pathetically asks her to chose between Falk and himself. The
canny fellow turns Falk's initial condemnation of marriage
against him:

> —love is blind; love chooses not a wife
> but a woman . . .
> For a happy engagement is a matter
> of getting on with the family,
> of sharing the same attitudes and tasks.
> And marriage? That's a veritable ocean
> of obligations and demands and claims
> that haven't very much to do with love . . .

"Use your experience," Gulstad advises, "look around in life,

> where every pair of lovers talks as though
> they had been handed out a million pounds.
> You see them rushing headlong to the altar,
> setting up house, and walking round on air;
> at first they're carried on a flood of courage,
> but then a day of settlement comes . . .
> And then they find the whole concern is bankrupt,
> gone is the bloom on the wife's cheek,
> gone is the bloom that flowered within her mind;
> Gone is the man's all-conquering courage, and
> gone every spark that once shone in his soul.

Falk cries out, "No! It's a lie!" To which Gulstad replies:

> And yet it was the truth
> but a few hours ago. Those were your words
> when you stood hero and battled single-handed,
> alone against the entire tea-table . . .

The fatal blow falls when Gulstad, addressing Falk, craftily
and generously adds, "You spoke just now of money; believe

me it's rather more than a mere decoration. I'm quite alone in life—I've no relations; everything that is mine I'll share with you; you shall be my son, and she my daughter . . . "

Falks cries out to his beloved, "What he said is true for other people, not for us!" To which Svanhild quietly tells him, "No, once a hailstorm has laid down the corn it cannot stand proud and erect again." In a last effort to convince her that she is mistaken, Falk continues, "The others

> set themselves too many goals;
> I only want your love, and nothing else . . .

SVANHILD: And can you swear, solemnly, before God that it will never lose its fragrance and hang like a withered flower? That it will last a lifetime?
FALK: (*after a short pause*): It will last a long time.
SVANHILD: Oh, "a long time," poverty-stricken words! What can "a long time" mean for love, except its death warrant, the mildew on the seed? "I believe in a love that lasts forever" —that song is silenced now, and we're to have instead: I was in love with you last year!

She gives him up and accepts Gulstad's proposal. There is nonetheless beauty in the gesture. She wants to preserve his love forever bright: "Now, Falk, I have renounced you for this life . . . but I have won you for eternity!" and further adds, "And you'll go upward in your goal to poetry . . . "

FALK: Yes, I go upwards; the winged steed is saddled; I know you have ennobled my whole life. And now farewell!
SVANHILD: Farewell!
FALK (*embarrassed*): A kiss!
SVANHILD: The last! (*She tears herself away from him*) Now I can leave you gladly for this life!
FALK: Though every light on earth should be extinguished, the thought of light will live, for it is God.

This odd mixture of romantic idealism and down-to-earth pragmatism, this separation of unalloyed love (to prevent its withering) from practical considerations, is especially poignant when we speculate in foresight or hindsight of the bitter regret on this score Ibsen expressed in his last two plays, written when he was sixty-eight and seventy-one.

Regarded in its day as irate and offensive, *Love's Comedy* can now be enjoyed as a flash of young bravado and hope. It is buoyed up by a swell of vigorous optimism in something more than personal confidence. "Young Norway," Falk declares, "is awake in a new dawn, a thousand warriors troop to the gay banner that streams so bravely in the morning breeze."

The contradictions here are also self-criticism. Svanhild chides Falk about his having written a pamphlet to aid the Christians in Syria but not fighting on their behalf. Falk is about to answer but doesn't—for hadn't Ibsen behaved in the same way in respect to the Danish-Prussian conflict raging at the time? Falk is shown to be something of a fool, somewhat as Gregers Werle in *The Wild Duck* will prove to be, with a touch of Don Quixote in him and a bit of Brand's highmindedness.

The derisive tone in the depiction of the civil servants and of the other "ordinary" citizens present becomes rather more indulgent than ironic at the end. "As for me," Falk smiles his goodbye, "the future lies ahead." He takes leave of Svanhild in tender quiet. "God's blessing be with you, my sweet young bride; farewell; my fame shall reach you, believe me!" As the final curtain descends we hear most of the company shout "Hurrah" after the chorus of students have repeated their refrain in a slight variation:

> And what if I've run my poor vessel aground?
> Still, putting out to sea was delightful!"

Love's Comedy is certainly no diatribe; it is a gallant song to celebrate the ambition of a dedicated artist.

With the prose play *The Pretenders*, Ibsen is on the threshold of great achievement.

It is a historical-chronicle play. To anyone ignorant of Ibsen's earlier work and life story the reason for its writing might not be evident, but its intrinsic power would be manifest. It contains three epic figures and several dazzling scenes of extraordinary psychological penetration. Brilliant in texture, a few passages waver in style, yet even these show the hand of a writer of vast gifts.

The plot is overcomplicated, the play overlong, and the battle scenes verge on film spectacle. On the surface it is the story of Norway's greatest king, Haakon, and the challenge to his throne by Earl Skule. Haakon, still young, is called upon by Skule and his followers to prove the legitimacy of his birth, hence his right to rule. In a thirteenth-century trial, the Queen Mother is forced to grasp a burning iron in her hand and swear that Haakon is her son.

Having successfully sustained this ordeal, Haakon's legitimacy as the royal heir is unquestioned. Still the Earl is tempted to further doubt by Bishop Nicholas, who, viciously envious of kingship, harbors an irrepressible passion to govern. He devises a series of intrigues so that neither Haakon nor Skule shall command absolute sway over the land. After a constant switching of fortune from one man to the other—at one point Skule is pronounced king in the north so that the country is racked by civil war—Haakon triumphs, and Skule is slain.

By itself the plot—except for the multiple machinations and battles which arise in the cause of the contest—would have little interest for those not specifically concerned with the intricacies of Norway's past history. What Ibsen has done is to make a personal document of the material, a dramatization of a struggle with broad-based moral connotations.

Haakon is the hero, radiant in his conviction of having chosen the right course in leadership. To end the strife among his people, he conceives his kingly task to be the conversion of Norway from a kingdom to a *nation*. Skule is deeply impressed by the grandeur of Haakon's far-reaching vision and would make Haakon's goal his own. But he lacks confidence in himself; he is only capable of recreating "the old saga." And to a large degree the play is his tragedy. For his is a divided self, uncertain in everything except in his desire to reign. Between the two—Haakon and Skule—stands Bishop Nicholas, one of the most fascinating and closely studied of Ibsen's personages, a genius of negative capacity who would ruin so that he may rule.

Acting as counsel to Skule, the Bishop utters the "Balzacian" credo of most dictators (whether in government or in business) from time immemorial: "There is no such thing as good or evil. No such thing as up and down, high and low. You must forget such words or you will not take the last step, you will never leap the ditch. You must never hate the Party, or the cause for which it fights, because the Party, or the cause, stand for *this* and not for *that*. But you must hate every man in the Party because he is against you, and you must hate every man who rallied to a cause because the cause will not forward your desire —everything that obstructs your path is bad."

When Skule asks, "Bishop Nicholas, are you more or less than human?" the Bishop replies, smiling shrewdly, "I am in a state of innocence, because I do not know the difference between good or bad."

Skule bemoans his lack of what Haakon possesses: a firm belief in himself. The Bishop tells him, "Hide the fact that you have no such confidence. Talk as if you had it. Swear loud and long that you have it—and everyone will believe you!"

The Bishop finally divulges a plan to both Haakon and Skule which will assuage his own mortification at not having attained supremacy. Moribund, he calls out to Haakon, "Divide the kingdom with him [Skule]. I shall have no peace in my coffin . . . unless you two share alike! Neither of you shall add the other's height to his own stature, for if so, there would be a giant in the land and there shall be no giants here, for I was never one!"

In a truly magnificent speech after he has declared himself a "corpse in the bud" (what a phrase!) the Bishop reveals the root and secret of his character: " . . . Yes, I have hated much, hated every man in this country who raised himself above the crowd. But I hated because I could not love. Lovely women— oh, I could devour them still with glistening eyes. Eighty years old I am, and still this desire to kill men and embrace women . . . But it was the same with me with women as in battle; only longing and desire, impotent from birth—the gift of passion, and yet crippled. So I became a priest; for the man who wishes to wield power must be either a king or a priest . . . "

A medieval religious atmosphere permeates the play. At times the effect is awesome even in its repetitiousness; at others almost comic. "Oh, if one had more than *one* soul—or else *none* at all!" cries the Bishop while planning the final blow against Skule's party. He must only live a little longer. "Get more priests to help" (with a Mass to be said for him). "Eight is not enough! . . . " But reflecting on the Bishop's terrible fear, his chaplain, shaking his head as the servants carry out the body, says, "I think it will be safer to say fourteen."

As with so many hateful characters in the theater, one is sorry to see the Bishop die as he does in the third act. But Ibsen brings him back in Act Five in the unearthly guise of a monk. He is a vision which appears before Skule in support of his final effort to win the crown of the entire kingdom before he too at long last surrenders to Haakon and prepares to let himself be killed. The "monk" scenes here are grotesquely funny: they shatter the tragic mood of Skule's ultimate conversion. But there is a special purpose in bringing the Bishop back which requires further citation.

Speaking to the "monk," Skule says, "I hear you have been studying the arts of poetry, you old warhorse!" "Yes," the "monk" explains:

> Versification! And masses of Latin!
> It was never my strong point, Latin, somehow;
> Yet I doubt if you'd find any keener one now
> Down there, if you want to keep up with the pace,
> in fact, even just to get into the place,
> there is nothing else for it—you must know your Latin.
> But progress is rapid, I hasten to say,
> with such learned companions at table each day:
> more than four dozen Popes, as they'd once been before,
> and hundreds of clerics, and poets galore.

I have mentioned the play's subjective aspect. It relates to a dilemma in the course of Ibsen's life and progress as an artist. There can be little doubt that Haakon, his country's great standardbearer, is in some measure modeled on Bjørnson, four years Ibsen's junior, the liberal leader in Norway's reawakening literary nationalism. Despite their close ties and Ibsen's reasons for being more than grateful to Bjørnson, a coolness not without an absurd element of competitive envy (more on Ibsen's part than on the younger man's) had for a time developed between them.

Ibsen had planned to dedicate *The Pretenders* to Bjørnson but then thought better of it, probably because the analogy between living persons and the play's characters might prove unmistakable. For while Bjørnson, like Haakon, enormously admired his older rival, Ibsen, like Earl Skule, was as troubled as much as he was in awe of the shining self-confidence, the unvarying good luck of the younger man. Ibsen, at thirty-five, for all his brash trumpeting in *Love's Comedy*, was sorely shaken by the acrimony it had provoked. He had garnered very few trophies from his other ventures in the theater and had suffered poverty and official neglect to boot.

Ibsen has still another "face" in *The Pretenders*; it is the Icelandic poet, Jatgeir, of Earl Skule's retinue. Through this alter ego, Ibsen not only engages in self-examination but once again voices reverence for the artist's role in society. On both accounts the scene in which Skule and Jatgeir confront each other warrants extensive citation.

SKULE: There are two men in you, Jatgeir. When you sit drinking with the men, you cloak your real thoughts, but when a man's alone with you, he sees in you the sort of man he wishes for a friend. How is that?

JATGEIR: When you go to bathe in the river, Sire, you will not undress where all the Churchgoers will pass you. You would pick a private spot instead.

SKULE: Of course.

JATGEIR: My soul is also shy, therefore I do not undress it when the hall is full of people.

SKULE: Hm! Tell me, Jatgeir, how did you become a poet? Who taught you the art of ballad making?

JATGEIR: One cannot be taught to be a bard, my liege.

SKULE: Cannot be taught? How did you learn then?

JATGEIR: I received the gift of sorrow, that made me a bard.

SKULE: So the gift of sorrow makes a poet?

JATGEIR: I needed sorrow; there may be others who need faith, or joy or doubt.

SKULE: Doubt also?

JATGEIR: Yes, but then the doubter must be strong and sound.

SKULE: And who do you call an unsound doubter?

JATGEIR: He who doubts his own doubt.

SKULE: That seems to me like death.

JATGEIR: It's worse—it's twilight . . .

SKULE: Have you any . . . unspoken ballads in your head, Jatgeir?

JATGEIR: No; but many unborn; they are conceived one after the other; they are given life and are born.

SKULE: And if I who am king and have the power to do it, if I had you killed, would every unborn thought within you die with you?

JATGEIR: My lord, it is a great sin to kill a fine thought.

SKULE: I do not ask whether it is a *sin*, but whether it is *possible*.

JATGEIR: I do not know.

SKULE: Have you never had another poet as a friend and has he never told you of a great and noble ballad he wished to compose?

JATGEIR: Yes, my lord.

SKULE: Did you then not wish you could kill him and take his idea and make his ballad yours?

JATGEIR: My lord, I am not barren; my brain has children of its own. I do not need to covet those of others. (*Goes*)

SKULE (*alone*): The Icelander is certainly a poet. He speaks God's deepest truths unknowingly. I am the barren woman— therefore I covet Haakon's royal brain child, love it with all the passion of my soul. Oh, if only I could take it to myself. But it would die in my hands. Which is most to be desired—that it should die in my hands or that it should grow to full strength in his? Shall my soul have peace if that occurs? Can I renounce it? How dead and empty is everything within me—and around me! No friends . . .

He calls Jatgeir back. He resumes: "I cannot sleep, Jatgeir; my thoughts, all my great and majestic thoughts keep me awake."

JATGEIR: No doubt the thoughts of a king are like a poet's. They soar higher and prosper best when surrounded by silence and the night . . . no song is born in daylight. It may be

written in sunshine, but it is composed in the still hours of
the night.

SKULE: Who gave you the gift of sorrow, Jatgeir?

JATGEIR: She whom I loved.

The scene ends with Jatgeir telling Skule, "Believe in yourself, and you will be saved."

Haakon and Skule share a common fault. Both are unthought-
ful of women. Skule says that his former mistress deceived him,
but it is much more likely that he abandoned her, for she re-
appears and brings him a son who was born to them. And though
Haakon speaks Ibsen's sentiments when he asserts, "Every man
needs a woman's advice," he sends his mother away so that he
may be free to carry out his mission, while he uses his touchingly
loyal wife (Skule's daughter) more to bear him a son than for
her good counsel.

It is also the Haakon in Ibsen who proclaims, "I am only just
beginning! I have done so little up to now, but I hear the unmistakable voice of Heaven within me, 'Thou shalt carry out a
kingly task in Norway.'"

For all Ibsen's dissatisfaction with and frequent denunciations
of Norway, he was a patriot at heart. He was a patriot like many
others in literary history who have proved themselves national
heroes through the very scorn and wrath they aimed against
their homelands' shortcomings, impurities and crimes. There are
moments when, as Brand is soon to say, "the best love is hate."
As *The Pretenders* approaches its resolution, a further castiga-
tion is cunningly expressed through the "monk's" (or devil's)
words:

> Whenever the men of Norway go
> drifting aimlessly to and fro . . .
> Whenever hearts shrivel, whenever minds change
> and bend like willows before the wind
> In one thing alone they are united:
> that greatness is merely to be dreaded . . .
> When they run up the flag of shameful abuse,
> when they take pride in defeat and fall . . .
> Then it's old Bishop Nicholas out on the loose.

When Haakon is told that he may now rejoice that his enemy
Earl Skule is dead, he says, "All men judged him wrongly; there
was a mystery about him . . . [he] was God's stepchild on earth,
that was the mystery."

This perhaps was then Ibsen's verdict on himself.

4

Of Greatness

A T THIS POINT I cannot forbear from repeating a perhaps apocryphal anecdote which the distinguished Italian critic Paolo Milano insists is a fact. On his arrival in Italy, Ibsen was ignorant of its language. He spoke Latin instead and was rather astounded that he (or it) was not understood.

In an 1866 letter to a friend in Norway, Ibsen wrote, "Rome is beautiful, wonderful, magical." In the Eternal City Ibsen came into his own, achieved spiritual and aesthetic maturity. And it was during a casual visit to St. Peter's, he wrote Bjørnson, that everything he wanted to say in the "dramatic poem" he was struggling with "appeared in a strong and clear light." The dramatic poem was *Brand*. Sentimentally, no doubt, one imagines or would like to believe that the place and the moment of the poem's formal crystallization contributed to its monumentality. The play itself is a cathedral.

Brand brought Ibsen unqualified fame throughout most European countries (especially in Norway and Russia), though unfortunately it is little known in America—at any rate among theatergoers. Published in 1866 when its author was thirty-seven,

Note: All the citations from the plays in this chapter, except as noted, are from Michael Meyer's translations.

it achieved an unprecedented sale and ran into numerous editions in the next four years. Though over twice the length of the average play and probably never intended as a stage piece, it was given in Stockholm in 1885 at a performance which ran for six and a half hours and where nevertheless it was a distinct success. It was not produced in Norway till 1904, though to this day it is one of the most admired and most frequently quoted plays there. The Moscow Art Theater produced it in 1907 where its political and social resonance—though it is neither social nor political— stirred revolutionary ardor. England never saw a full-length production till 1959 in Michael Meyer's slightly abridged version.

"*Brand*," Ibsen said, "is myself in my best moments." As a youth of seventeen Strindberg heard in it "the voice of Savonarola." Though to some degree apt, both statements are misleading. While *Brand* is majestic, it is not monolithic. Brand's command "All or nothing" is challenged as much as espoused by the play. Brand is a hero who, to use Emerson's phrase, is *immovably centered*, but by that very trait, tragically flawed. He is doomed as an individual, if not altogether condemned.

The play embodies "the quintessence of Ibsen" but not as Shaw defined it. Within Brand's literal and noble reassertion of Christian purity we recognize the split in Ibsen's soul. There is inspiration in the ideal to which it summons us, but it is also questioned. The play reacts against its own premise—which is one of the earmarks of its immense pathos and power. If it reaches a moral conclusion, it is very nearly the opposite of what has so long been taken to be its "message." It bursts through the dogma in which it has so long been confined. Set in the mid-nineteenth century, it is a play for all times.

It flays petty compromise. In F. A. Garrett's rhymed translation we read: "The times for greatness call/Just because they are so small." Ibsen, "Europe's angriest man," as Strindberg once called him, could not abide his countrymen's mediocrity, spiritual sloth, cowardice and hypocrisy. He calls down thunder and lightning on them. The name "Brand" means "fire." His defiance is Promethean.

Bjørnson considered the play "nihilistic," which most emphatically, it is not. It is a religious parable. Like Brand, Ibsen was in quest of a way to salvation, a true path in life. Brand, "a mission preacher" or "a diocesan pastor," travels about from one place to another to minister to the afflicted. Every man or woman, he insists, must assume the burden prescribed by the Gospel, which enjoins us to give our all to those most in need. We must enact the faith implied in the words "He that loses his life shall find it." It calls not for the commonplace human but for sanctity. Brand is determined not only to preach this very nearly unattainable ideal but to live by it and to make others do likewise. That is what he means by "All or Nothing."

The first scene is literally realistic and nonetheless symbolic—which, be it said in passing, is the soundest sort of symbolism. Brand is in the rain and the dark high up in "the wilds of the mountains" on the way to someone who requires his office. A guide and the guide's son are leading him through the snow. "We have lost all trace of the path," Brand says. The guide warns him against advancing any farther. "There is an abyss here too deep to fathom," the guide warns. "It will swallow us up." But Brand persists:

> I must go on . . .
> GUIDE: It's beyond mortal power. Feel!
> The ground here is hollow and brittle.
> Stop! It's life or death.
> BRAND: I must. I serve a great master.
> GUIDE: What's his name?
> BRAND: His name is God.
> . . . .
> GUIDE: Listen, priest. We have only one life.
> Once that's lost, we don't get another.
> There's a frozen mountain lake ahead,
> And mountain lakes are treacherous.
> BRAND: We will walk across it.
> GUIDE: Walk on water?
> BRAND: It has been done.
> . . . .
> GUIDE: You'll die.
> BRAND: If my master needs my death,
> Then welcome flood and cataract and storm.
> GUIDE: He's mad.

The Guide and his son are about to turn back:

BRAND: Didn't you say your daughter has sent you word that she is dying and cannot go in peace unless she sees you first?
GUIDE: It's true, God help me.
BRAND: And she cannot live beyond today.
GUIDE: Yes.
BRAND: Then, come!
GUIDE: It's impossible. Turn back.
BRAND: What would you give for your daughter to die in peace?
GUIDE: I'd give everything I have, my house and farm, gladly.
BRAND: But not your life? . . .
GUIDE: There's a limit. I've a wife and children at home.
BRAND: Go home. Your life is the way of death. You do not know God, and God does not know you.

To give one's life for one's ideal was something of a fixation in Ibsen's mind. Had he not written in a letter to Bjørnson that he admired the Russians because they were the only ones ready to sacrifice their lives on behalf of their beliefs?

"You're hard," the Guide tells Brand, a reproach repeated time and again in the course of the play. Ibsen, very much but not quite like Brand, was an extremist. And *Brand* may be said to exemplify the tragedy of extremism. For in *Peer Gynt* it is said, "Truth pushed to an excess reads like a wise text written backwards . . . " The passage just quoted contains the kernel of the whole. Let us now observe its growth.

The sun rises as Brand climbs upward. Two figures come into view: Ejnar, a painter, and Agnes, a girl he is courting. Ejnar and Brand were friends at school. "Yes," Ejnar says in recognition, "you are the same old Brand who always kept to yourself and never played with us." Ejnar is a hedonistic aesthete and (in F. E. Garrett's translation) says, "Don't stand there like an icicle! Thaw man!" To which Brand replies:

> Enjoy life if you will,
> But be consistent, do it all the time.
> Not one thing one day and another the next.
> Be wholly what you are, not half and half.
> Everyone now is a little of everything . . .

> A little sin, a little virtue;
> A little good, a little evil; the one
> Destroys the other, and every man is nothing.

Ejnar, somewhat shaken, asks, "And now we are to be created anew?"

BRAND: Yes. As surely as I know that I
> Was born into this world to heal its sickness
> And its weakness.

Ejnar admonishes:

> Do not destroy the old language
> Until you have created the new.

Brand is bent on laying the "old God," the God of the Philistines, in his grave. Agnes, who has listened to their discussion, asks Ejnar in awe, "Did you see? How as he spoke, he grew?"

A soliloquy follows in which Brand remembers his lonesome childhood and apostrophizes the people going to church and as much in sorrow as in contempt sums up:

> "Give us this day our daily bread!" That
> Is now the watchword of this country, the remnant
> Of its faith. Away from this stifling pit;
> The air down there is poisoned, as in a mine . . .

He encounters a fifteen-year-old girl who is throwing stones at a hawk, a large loathsome bird with red-and-gold-circled eyes. He asks the girl to accompany him to the church down in the valley. She thinks it ugly because it is too small. She's going to a church built of ice and snow that stands at the mountain's summit. That church, Brand warns, is unsafe. The black hawk, we are later to learn, symbolizes *compromise*, and she aims to kill it.

So many churchgoers! Some, Brand says, are like Ejnar, light of heart, playing along the edge of the crevices; others, like the peasant guide, are "dull of heart," plodding and slow because his neighbors are so. And there is the girl (whose name is Gerd), "the wild of heart, in whose broken mind evil seems beautiful." The triple enemy must be fought. They all stray from *home*— that is, his truth.

The first act ends with Brand's vow:

> I see my calling. It shines forth like the sun.
> I know my mission. If these three can be slain,
> Man's sickness will be cured.
> Arm, arm my soul. Unsheath your sword.
> To battle for the heirs of Heaven!

Down in the valley, Brand finds a hungry crowd of villagers fighting among themselves over who is to be first to get his order ration of bread. The Mayor and the Sexton, who distribute the food, are careful not to give too much: "A saving is a saving," says the Mayor.

Ejnar who stands by, has emptied his purse in charity. Brand watches the proceedings coldly because the starving people are so meek in begging for the dole; he would have them more demanding:

> . . . where extremity breeds no courage, the flock
> Is not worthy of salvation.

A woman appears screaming for a priest. Her husband, in mad despair at seeing their three children starve, has killed his youngest and attempted to kill himself. "Cross the fjord and save his soul," she pleads. "He cannot live, and dare not die [unshriven]." The Mayor grumbles, "He doesn't belong to my district."

Brand quietly tells the woman, "Your need is great," but he requires a boat to get to her dwelling place. A storm threatens. Brand orders a boat to be unmoored. "The soul of a dying sinner does not wait for wind and weather," Brand ordains as he takes command of a boat which has been offered by a man in the crowd. Someone is needed to bail and work the sail. This means the risk of one's life. The bereaved woman herself is afraid to undertake the crossing. So is Ejnar, but not Agnes. "I will come," she cries. "That's the sort of priest we need," the villagers shout.

Brand does not wish simply to serve as village priest: he must speak to the world. The man who thought him the needed priest now rails, "May you be cursed for quenching the flame you lit, as we are cursed who, for a moment, saw."

Brand's mother appears. After a few words he dismisses her gruffly with "Good day. My time is short."

MOTHER: Yes, you were always restless; ran away and left me—
BRAND: You wanted me to leave ...
MOTHER: It was best. You had to be a priest.

This in a nutshell is evidently how Ibsen construed the abandonment of the parental hearth. Did not Falk in *Love's Comedy* categorically say, "I never had a home"? Brand tells his mother:

> Let's be clear about one thing.
> I have always defied you, even when I was a child.
> I have been no son to you, and you have been
> No mother to me.

Brand goes on to say that when she lies dying he will come to shrive her—on one condition; that she leave all her savings, as he sees fit, to the service of God. She must repay her debt: as a child he saw her at his father's deathbed rummaging under his pillow to find the money hidden there. "More, more!" she had whispered. Now she makes only a single request of her son, that on her death his inheritance never be spent outside the family, but be left to his son or grandson. Her greed, he insists, has dragged God's image in the mire. Her only defense is that she had loved a village boy but had followed her father's advice to forget the boy and take the other. "Never mind that he's old and withered. He's clever. He'll double his money," but he never did. She has worked and slaved since then; she is no longer poor.

It is possible that this passage is a shadow of Ibsen's suspicion that he was illegitimate, and shame over his father's bankruptcy. Brand's last word to his mother at this point is: "I shall come in the hour of your repentance. But . . . everything that binds you to this world, you must renounce, and go naked to your grave."

Ejnar comes to reclaim his bride, Agnes. Choose, he implores, "between the sunny plains and this dark corner of sorrow." But Agnes has made her choice. She says of Brand, "He is my teacher, my brother and my friend. I shall not leave him." Brand warns her that he is stern in his demands. "I require All or Nothing. No half measures . . . It may not be enough to offer your life. Your death may be needed also."

Agnes marries Brand. Three years later he hears that his mother is dying. He awaits her message. Agnes, the soul of kindness and fidelity, tells him he ought to go to his mother even though she has not called him. "If she does not repent," he says, "I have no words to say to her, no comfort to offer her."

AGNES: She is your mother.
BRAND: I have no right to worship gods in my family.
AGNES: You are hard, Brand.
BRAND: Towards you?
AGNES: Oh no!

They have a son who is threatened with illness in the sunless valley in which they live. They have survived the harsh condition of their lives and he has been successful.

AGNES: Yes, Brand, but you deserve success.
You have fought and suffered, have toiled and drudged.
I know you have wept blood silently.
BRAND: Yes, but it all seemed easy to me. With you
Love came like a sunny spring day to warm my heart.
I had never known it before. My father and mother
Never loved me. They quenched any little flame
That faltered from the ashes. It was as though
All the gentleness I carried suppressed within me
Had been saved so I could give it all to you
And him [his son].
AGNES: Not only to us. To others too.
BRAND: Through you and him. You taught me
Gentleness of spirit. That was the bridge to their hearts.
No one can love all until he has first loved one.
AGNES: And yet your love is hard. Where you would caress, you
bruise.
Many have shrunk from us, at your demand
Of All or Nothing.
. . . .
BRAND: Listen, Agnes. There is but one law
For all men. No cowardly compromise!

> If a man does his work by halves
> He stands condemned.

Brand does nothing by halves. He will not visit his mother as her doctor bids him do. The doctor reproves him: "—in your ledger your credit account for strength of will is full, but, priest, your love account is a white virgin page." Brand scoffs at this: "Love! Has any word been so abused and debased? It is used as a veil to cover weakness." To which Agnes responds, "Yes, love is a snare. And yet—I sometimes wonder—is it?" But with Brand *will* comes first.

Waiting for his mother's call, Brand rushes to his son's sickbed to seek solace there. In this, Agnes sees "a deep well of love [which] exists in his soul." He loves his child because "the snake of human weakness has not yet bitten that small heart." His mother's appeal finally arrives: she agrees to give half her goods for the sacrament. His answer is that "the least fragment of the golden calf is as much an idol as the whole." The messenger leaves, saying, "God is not as hard as you." Brand's only comment at this: "—They know their old God; they know He is always ready to be bargained with." His mother dies without consolation or blessing. Her last words are: "God is not so cruel as my son." At that moment doubt begins to assail him.

The town officials, the Mayor in chief, want to rid themselves of Brand's presence. Surely, they insinuate, he doesn't wish to bury himself in their little backwater, as he now has the means to live elsewhere. His gifts are better suited to a more sophisticated community. Brand refuses to tear himself from his roots, abandon his post. He declares war on officialdom. The Mayor, according to Brand, "a typical man of the people," does more damage in a year than hurricane, frost or plague. "How much spiritual aspiration has he not stifled at birth?"

The doctor on returning to Brand after the death of his mother tells him. "Every generation must make its own pact with God . . . Its first commandment, Brand, is: Be humane." Brand asks if God was humane toward Jesus. Still he hides his head in silent grief. The doctor insinuates "If only you could find tears." "Henceforth," Brand resumes with still greater resolve, "I shall fight unflinchingly for the victory of the spirit over the weakness of the flesh . . . Now . . . I can crush mountains." It was a battle Ibsen was to engage in all his life.

The doctor, who has been called on to examine Brand's son, orders Brand to put his affairs in order and leave the cold climate where they live. Failure to do so will imperil the child's life. Brand prepares to depart at once. The doctor observes, "So merciless towards your flock, so lenient towards yourself." Brand, distraught, cries out, "Am I blind now? Or was I blind before?" We are now close to the play's turning point.

His flock wishes him to stay; they need him. Agnes is ready to leave. Gerd, who aimed to destroy the Black Hawk, appears, screams as though from within his conscience, "The parson's flown away! The trolls and demons are swarming out of the hillsides." Brand turns on her in reply: "Child, you talk crazily. Look at me, I'm still here." "Yes, you," she taunts, "but not the priest." Struck by this, Brand calls out, "Agnes! Agnes! I fear a Greater One has sent her to us." He must remain with his flock at the risk of his son's life. Agnes must make her own choice. She tells him to do as God bids him—which means they will both stay. Agnes, lifting the child in her arms, cries out, "Oh God! This sacrifice You dare demand, I dare to raise towards Your Heaven. Lead me through the fire of life," at which Brand bursts into tears, throwing himself down on the steps of the hut praying, "Jesus! Jesus! Give me light!"

Their son has died. It is Christmas eve. Agnes cannot bear mention of the graveyard. But it must be said, Brand tells her, shouted if she's afraid of it, nor must she shed tears on the Lord's holiday. She notices that his own brow is wet and the reminder of his child's death frightens him more than he will admit. He confesses his inner torment and struggle. "Listen. I want to tell you something that has come to me in our sorrow. It is as though there lay a kind of joy in being able to weep . . . then I see God closer than I ever saw Him before . . . And I thirst to cast myself into His bosom, to be sheltered by His strong, loving, fatherly arms." "Oh Brand," Agnes pleads, "always see Him so, as a God you can approach, more like a father, less like a master" (or in the Garrett translation, "more the father, less the Lord!").

He is now ready to undertake another task: to construct a new church. He will build it for Agnes, for the townspeople and even for Gerd, who thought the old one ugly because too small. "Again you guide me," he tells Agnes. "You see how much I need you. It is I who say to you: 'Do not leave me, Agnes.' " She murmurs, "I shall shake off my sorrow, I will dry my tears. I will bury my memories. I will be wholly your wife." He prays to God to be merciful to her.

The Mayor plans to build a poorhouse. Brand queries, "You want to abolish poverty?" "Certainly not," is the answer. "Poverty's a necessity in every society"; the Mayor adds, "We've got to accept that. But with a little skill it can be kept within limits, and moulded into decent forms. I thought, for example, we might build a poorhouse. And while we're at it, we might combine it with other amenities under the same roof: a jail, a hall for meetings and banquets . . . and guest rooms for distinguished visitors—" But Brand rejects all this. He wants to rebuild the church, make it great. He proposes to use the money left in his inheritance—an offer which by its "munificence" excites the Mayor, who immediately foregoes his own project and is now entirely in favor of Brand's.

In their colloquy the Mayor alludes to a gypsy ragamuffin: Gerd. She is the daughter, the Mayor tells Brand, of a penniless lad who wanted to marry Brand's mother and whom she had given up. He married a gypsy girl who bore Gerd. "So in a sense," the Mayor explains, "the woman who brought you into the world brought her here too, for the girl was conceived as a result of his love for your mother." Thus she and Brand share a peculiar kinship.

While Brand has left the room to pray, Agnes, still mourning her son, takes from a chest of drawers the shawl in which he was carried to his christening, his shirt and other such belongings. Just then a gypsy woman with a child in her arm rushes in and reaches for the baby clothes in Agnes' hands. "Share with me, rich mother," the woman begs. Agnes invites her to the

warmth of the fire and food. But all the woman wants is a rag
to protect her half-naked child, blue with cold. Brand tells
Agnes it is her duty to give the gypsy their son's clothes. This
follows:

AGNES: Come, woman, take them. I will share them with you.
BRAND: Share, Agnes? Share?
AGNES: Half is enough. She needs no more.
BRAND: Would half have been enough for your child?
AGNES: Come, woman, take them. Take the dress
          He wore to his baptism. Here is his shirt, his scarf,
          His coat. It will keep the night air from your child.
. . . .
BRAND: Agnes, have you given her all?
AGNES: Here is his christening robe. Take that, too.

With the woman's departure Agnes asks: "Tell me, Brand.
Haven't I given enough now?"

BRAND: Did you give them willingly?
AGNES: No.
BRAND: Then your gift is nothing . . . (*He turns to go*)
AGNES: Brand!
BRAND: What is it?
AGNES: I lied. Look. I kept one thing.
BRAND: The cap?
AGNES: Yes.
BRAND: Stay with your idols. (*Turns*)
AGNES: Wait!
BRAND: What do you want?
AGNES   (*holds out the cap to him*): Oh, you know.
BRAND: Willingly?
AGNES: Willingly.

She is exultant now. "Giving my child has saved my soul from
death. Thank you for guiding my hand . . . Now the weight has
fallen on you—of All or Nothing. Now you stand in the valley
of choice."

Perplexed, Brand says:

          You speak in riddles. Our struggle is over.
AGNES: Have you forgotten, Brand?
          [*Quoting him*] He dies who sees Jehovah face to face.

BRAND: No! Agnes, no! You shall not leave me.
Let me lose everything else, everything.
But not you! Don't leave me, Agnes!

Agnes dies. The new church is ready to be consecrated. The townspeople have gathered, the crowd gabbles in wonderment. But before Brand assumes his duties the Church Provost has a little request, if not exactly a complaint, to make: "Your church is of benefit to the state, and therefore you have a responsibility to the state." "By God, I never meant that," Brand exclaims. The Provost continues: "I'm not asking you to do anything wicked . . . You can minister just as well to the souls in your care by serving the state at the same time. Your job isn't to save every Jack and Jill from damnation, but to see that the parish as a whole finds grace. We want all men to be equal. But you are creating inequality where it never existed before. Until now each man was simply a member of the Church. You have taught him to look upon himself as an individual, requiring special treatment. This will result in the most frightful confusion. The surest way to destroy a man is to turn him into an individual. Very few men can fight the world alone." (These are all double-edged truths!)

Ejnar passes by. Presumably repentant, his cheerful aesthetism has turned sour; he has taken to drink and to gambling, which have left him a sick man. He now preaches total abstinence as a missionary. He is a caricature of pietism; a distortion of the Brand persona.

Suddenly Brand turns on the crowd to whom the imposing church is simply a new fetish. Most of the throng have come only to gape at the steeple, to listen to the organ and the bells. Brand had envisioned an all-embracing, a cleansing and all-redeeming religion, but the church, he now asserts, is a monstrous swindle. To the Provost's accusations that he is not a true Christian, Brand responds:

No, you are right. I am not a true Christian.
Neither are you, nor is anyone here.
A true Christian must have a soul,
And show me one who has kept his soul!

He speaks of the true church, a church beyond all Churches, a church without walls, the Church of Life. "Make the earth your temple." The people are momentarily exalted by Brand's fervor. They follow him to the high point of the village. But they are hungry, thirsty, tired. They hope for salvation, but sense danger in Brand's invocation. They demand a warrant that their devotion will be rewarded. Brand answers:

> How long will you have to fight? Until you die!
> What will it cost? Everything you hold dear.
> . . . .
> A crown of thorns. That will be your reward.

The crowd turns savage: they feel they have been tricked. They hurl stones at him, bloodying his forehead. The Mayor promises the crowd prosperity: millions of fish have entered the fjord. This, the Mayor admits after he has swayed the crowd, is a lie. Brand climbs further up the mountain. The Mayor is most concerned over the people's perhaps inhumane treatment of the man. "The voice of the people is the voice of God" is the Provost's pious reassurance. The crowd descends into the valley.

The last scene is the crowning beam of the play's towering structure. The "Mosaic man," as Brand has been called, throws himself down into the snow. He understands the people's plight: their will is weak, their fear strong. Long ago someone died to save their souls, so nothing is required of them. From this moment, as Brand sinks or rises in ecstatic agony, visions appear before him. The play now transcends the bounds of "realism" and becomes an apocalyptic poem of great beauty and wisdom.

Agnes, as wraith, speaks to Brand and summons him to her. He needs tenderness and care. Brand declares himself strong. "Not yet," the wraith answers. "Your dreams will lure you back again . . . Your mind will grow confused again unless you try the remedy." What is the remedy? "Three words," she tells him, "You must blot them out, wipe them from your memory. Forget them." The three words are: All or Nothing!

He will not relent. He would tread the same road again; let his child die; kill her. "Brand," she remonstrates, and once again he utters the signal words "I must! I must! I must!" A beautifully tragic exchange follows:

FIGURE [*who is Agnes*]: Remember, an angel with a flaming rod
Drew Man from Paradise.
He set a gulf before that gate.
Over that gulf you cannot leap.
BRAND: The way of longing remains.
FIGURE: Die! The world has no use for you.

Gerd, the half-mad gypsy "within" Brand, appears again with a rifle to kill the black hawk, the "deceitful spirit," the spirit of compromise. Gerd identifies Brand as "the Big Man, the Biggest of all" (Christ?), but he says, "I am the meanest thing that crawls on earth." He is now close to the Ice Church, the pinnacle in the climb to the Ideal.

Had he reached it he would have been isolated in the pure perfection and frozen immobility of his aspiration. Brand breaks down and weeps:

I wish I were far away. Oh, how I long for light
And sun, and the still tenderness of peace.
I long to be where life's summer kingdoms are.
O Jesus, I have called upon Your name,
Why did You never receive me into Your Bosom?
You passed close by me, but You never touched me.

Gerd, seeing Brand in tears, asks: "Man, why did you never weep before?" She then fires at the hawk. But instead of being black, he is white. Does this mean that compromise may not be all evil or that evil frequently takes on a fair color?

The rifle shot precipitates an avalanche in which Brand, along with Gerd, will perish. Brand asks the greatest question of all:

Answer me, God, in the moment of death!
If not by Will, how can Man be redeemed?
A VOICE (*cries through the thunder*): He is the God of Love.

Georg Brandes found *Brand* confusing. There are so many "inconsistencies" in it. In this instance, Brandes said, the mastermind Ibsen was not "quite clear and transparent," but this, he added, rendered the play "all the more fascinating." This may have been an acceptable judgment on the part of a critic who in 1866 was only twenty-four, but it cannot satisfy us today. Yet misunderstandings of the play still persist. They spring from an overemphasis on one or another of its aspects. It is seen as a relentless jeremiad against a morally blemished world or as a mighty warning that the absolute severity which Brand personifies must be tempered by the forgiveness of love. *Brand* says both things. It is a dramatization of moral grandeur within which we hear a distinct knell of uncertainty. There is nobility in what Brand seeks: heroic individuals free of egotistic stain. But his greatness is marred by a tragic flaw: a refusal to forbear, an hyperaesthesia of will. To confront God face to face is to die; to demand extreme righteousness is a kind of nihilism. Yet it is part of Brand's pathos and lofty stature that even in failure and defeat he breathes the inalterability of his character, "the way of longing remains." Such men, crushed though they must inevitably be, are still indispensable to humankind: they raise its sights, they impel it to noble action.

Brand's "sin" is that he rejects his own tenderness, yet it shines through the armor of his inflexibility. It is precisely because he is softer than he conceives it owing to his mission to be that he steels himself to superhuman self-discipline. If it were not so, would he hear Agnes' lovingly admonishing voice within him or the unidentified voice which calls out that God is love?

All of Ibsen is in this double consciousness. Each of his plays sets forth one or the other impulses of his nature. In Brand more potently than anywhere else in his work they coexist and find their expression in counterpoint. Neither side will yield entirely to the other, as we shall see in the pages which follow; only in the very last play do we find, at least for Ibsen, a resolution and concordance.

Though *Brand* has served as a battle cry for the radicals of its day—and may still retain such value—it is not a tribute to fanaticism. Ibsen knew that fanaticism claims too many victims.

Whatever our interpretation of the play, there can be little doubt that it is a work of grand design, mighty line and immense scope. If Ibsen had written no more than this generally overlooked and little-studied play one would still have to assign him a high place among the giants of world drama. For its stage realization, *Brand* requires inspired actors, directors, and above all a great theater with ample resources. That is one reason why it is so seldom produced.

Peer Gynt, written in Rome and in a town nearby, was published a year and some months after *Brand*. The verse of the later play is more varied, but Ibsen's most captious critic refused to concede that it was poetry. Ibsen's proud and sagacious response to this was the memorably prophetic assertion: "My book *is* poetry. And if not, then it shall be."

It can only be staged when drastically cut, which was not done till nine years after its publication. Edvard Grieg provided the music for that occasion, which has unfortunately accompanied most of the later productions. I say "unfortunately" because the score's romantic sweetness belies the play's content. It is perhaps on account of that misunderstanding that it became the most popular of Ibsen's early plays.

It is *Brand* in reverse. Both plays end in their protagonists' "failure," but while *Brand* is severe in structure and tragic in tone, *Peer Gynt* is comic, ribald and playfully "loose." In a much less murky vein, it anticipates Strindberg's "experimental" plays by some fifteen years. Ibsen must have experienced a kind of fierce exaltation as he wrote *Brand* and euphoria in writing *Peer Gynt*.

The differences go deeper. *Brand* possesses a classic universality in its theme and treatment; the appeal of *Peer Gynt*, with all its picaresque extravagance, fantasy, local color, resides, at least for a reader today, in a special contemporaneity. Though it might be described as a folk tale, it is in one sense the more "realistic" work. Its essential modernity points to the social plays which were soon to follow. Indeed only one more drama, *Emperor and Galilean*, was to revert to the older canon, and that one was in Ibsen's mind (and "workshop") before and during the writing of *Brand*. The would-be prophet Brand is a figure of heroic proportions, while Peer, under his old-time motley, is something of a lout, very much the "ordinary citizen," your neighbor or yourself. Ibsen undoubtedly saw something

of himself in Peer, though he preferred himself as Brand. There
are even more autobiographical elements in the inglorious comedy than in the stern drama.

Brand and Peer are obsessed by a single question: how is one
to be true to oneself? Brand's answer is that one finds (and re-
deems) oneself by sacrificing oneself for others. It is the way
to divinity. Peer wants to be himself *for himself alone*. Brand
is an absolute Christian; Peer an almost complete heathen. Brand
pursues his goal relentlessly; Peer shirks every crisis, is never
truly himself and ends without having any self.

By tracing the play's plot line we follow the process by which
Ibsen makes his point—though he is too complex, ambiguous
and ironic an artist for any of his plays to be reduced to a
"point." His plays are not tracts; *A Doll's House*, as we shall
see, is not an argument for femininism, *Hedda Gabler* is more
than a study of a neurotic woman. Ibsen's best plays are en-
veloped in mystery; it is a warrant for their endurance.

We first see Peer simply as a lusty farm boy of twenty who
lives alone with his widowed mother. His father, once prosperous we learn, died bankrupt and a drunk. Peer is a romantic liar,
a braggart of bounding imagination. His mother, Aase, stick in
hand, is always ready to beat the devil out of him for his way-
wardness and at the same time to protect him from all calumny
or harm.

Though crude and thoughtless, Peer is by no means ill-natured;
he is unendingly fond of Aase, whom he lovingly addresses as
"ugly little mother." To her reproach that he is a good-for-
nothing, he cries out in hot earnest, "I'll be King! Emperor!"
The future man reveals himself in the boast. Aase calls it "twad-
dle" but admits that Ingrid, a prosperous farmer's daughter,
favors him. If he were to marry her the condition of both Peer
and Aase's life would improve. But a no-account rival has proposed and is about to marry her. Peer dashes off to the wedding
party in hopes of preventing the marriage.

Among the guests at the feast in a Brueghel-like scene, Peer
encounters a shy young girl, Solveig, carrying a psalm book.
He is touched by her beauty and innocence. She is frightened
and transfixed by his alluring brashness. The other guests either

mock him for his boozing, braggadocio and mendacity or shun him in fear of his muscular aggressiveness.

While the party goes on we learn that Ingrid, the bride-to-be, has hidden herself from the ninny bridegroom. He asks Peer to pry his bride out of her hiding place. Peer complies, but instead of turning her over to the groom, he abducts and then seduces her. She begs him to marry her. They are bound, she says, by their double crime. "Go back where you came from," he tells her. Only the girl with the psalm book and the golden hair occupies his thoughts. The wedding guests, led by the bride's parents, are out to lynch him. He flees. Alone high in the mountains his fantasy wanders. "Peer Gynt," he muses, "thou wast born to greatness, and to greatness thou shalt come."

A sort of drunken dream begins. A female character, identified at this point as the Greenclad One, appears. Peer, wooing her, presents himself as a king's son. The Greenclad One is herself the daughter of another king, known as the Old Man of the Mountains. "When my father's angry, the mountains crack." She always wears gold and silk, she boasts. But he finds her rags look more like tow and straw. "That is the way of the mountain people," she explains. "Everything there has another meaning. Black seems white and ugly seems fair." The same is true, Peer warns, where he lives; greatness seems little and foul seems clean. "Oh Peer! I see it!" she gushes as she falls on his neck. "We were made for each other." She calls for a bridal steed; a huge pig canters on with an old sack as a saddle. Peer swings himself astride its back and sets the Greenclad One in front of him. And off they go to the palace of the Old Man of the Mountains.

The next scene is as weird as a painting by Hieronymous Bosch, if that artist were as funny as he is scary. Peer finds himself among Troll Courtiers, Elves and Goblins who surround their king seated on his throne. His attendants, children and nearest relations want to kill the Christian dog (Peer). But the Old Man is forbearing; the troll kingdom is not what it used to be, so he is willing to consider his daughter's marriage to Peer. Peer demands the kingdom as dowry. This agreed upon, Peer consents to go through with the marriage; it suits his temperament. But further conditions to the contract are set. First there is an oral test: "What is the difference between troll and man?" There is no difference: "Big trolls want to roast you, small trolls want to claw you. It is the same with us." There is a difference nonetheless. "Out there—men tell each other, 'Man, be thyself.' But here among the trolls, we say, 'Troll, be thy-self—*and thyself alone.*' " Peer finds the creed compatible with his own views.

Though he shudders at some of the stipulations in sealing his alliance—for example, he must eat cake which flows from the cow and mead from the bull—he figures that in time he'll get used to the taste. He must allow a tail to be attached to him. Peer agrees to this as well; "one must toe the line of fashion." He is a cooperative boy. A horrendous ballet ensues; when he speaks of it as such he is very nearly torn apart. So he concedes that "Both the dance and the music were really splendid." Peer finally rebels against forfeiting the last vestige of his human nature; to have a little cut made in his left eye so that he will see everything askew. The same operation must be performed on his right eye so that everything will seem bright and fair, his bride beautiful and the dancing sows and cows playing harps right and natural.

When Peer balks at accepting these conditions, the Old Man rages: "You human beings are always the same. You are always ready to admit an impulse, but won't accept the guilt for any-thing." Peer has lusted after his daughter; before the end of the year he'll be a father and the offspring will be sent to him. The hall crashes in ruins—a nightmare!

The significance of the scene is clear enough, but since "sym-bols" abound, one is free to choose one's own! The Mountain Kingdom and its ruler bring to my mind nothing so much as the moguls of Hollywood and their cohorts in our larger enter-tainment industries.

After Peer has seemingly bashed his way out of his hallucina-tion (and as such entirely "real") there is an intervening scene: he hears a voice which commands, "Go round, Peer." It is the voice of the Great Boyg, an apparently meaningless or untrans-latable name, whose message signifies bend, circumvent every contingency and duty, cut corners, lie, steal, but get ahead. Peer uses his fists to fight off this invisible but articulate and persuasive monster. The voice jeers, "Yes, trust to your fists. That's the way to the top . . . The Great Boyg wins by doing nothing." Peer sinks to the ground exhausted by the futile struggle. We hear the Boyg gasp, "He was too strong. There were women behind him."

After this we find Peer suffering a "hangover" outside his mother's hut. Helga, Solveig's sister, appears with a hamper of food, a gift from Solveig. She is hiding behind a wall; when she hears Peer say that the Old Man of the Mountain's daughter is pursuing him, she runs away. He gives Helga a silver button as a token for a promise: "Ask Solveig not to forget me!"

Peer is now an outlaw. The villagers are up in arms to punish him for seducing Ingrid. Unable to find him, they have ransacked his dwelling place and left his mother stripped of all her possessions. Peer builds himself a cabin hideout in the forest. For love of him Solveig has left her home. He has lost his inheritance but she has chosen her path and will never turn back. She enters his cabin. "My princess," he joyously exclaims. "Now at last I've found and won her."

Outside the cabin he is accosted by an Old-Looking Woman who has a horrible brat clutching at her skirt. The ugly child, she tells him, is the one engendered by him in the mountains. She is the troll king's daughter come to plague him, a memory which will forever haunt him. It is a mysterious course—and all this for nothing, but for *thinking*!

This hell-born phantasmagoria is associated by Ibsen's biographers with Ibsen's seduction of a servant girl when he was eighteen and his subsequent horror at the thought of illegitimate birth. The mishap is also supposed to have given rise to a "squeamishness" in regard to the consummation of desire. Ibsen, it should be remembered, was not the cold person he is often thought to have been but a man of volcanic passion, forever attracted by the opposite sex.

Peer remembers the Boyg's motto, "Go round!" He can no longer bear the thought of staying with Solveig; he would besmirch her with his shame. She is prepared to share his burden:

"I must bear it alone!" he says. As he takes leave of her he pleads, "I may be long, but wait for me. Wait for me." Solveig will wait.

A wonderfully touching scene follows. Peer comes to bid his mother farewell. She is in bed dying. She points to the now destitute hut. It's all his fault, he confesses, but she forgives him everything: "My darling boy, you were drunk." Seeing she has only minutes more to live, Peer hopes to distract and ease the final agony by simulating a ride on a fabled steed to the gate of Heaven and bidding St. Peter grant her entry. On her death, he murmurs;

> You can rest now, Grane.
> We've come to the end of our ride.
> Thank you for all your days,
> For your beatings and kisses, my dear.

After he has pressed his cheek to her mouth, he whispers

> So; the driver has had his fare.

Ibsen's mother died two years after the publication of *Peer Gynt*. Biographers would have it that Aase is based on her. If so he must have been in a particularly sentimental mood. He was supposed to have been her favorite son, the one whom she took to the theater when he was still a boy, but he showed very little disposition in later years to see or write to her. After a brief visit to his parents on the way from Christiana he never had any contact with his immediate family for nineteen and a half years. It was three and a half months after he was notified of his mother's death by his sister Hedwig—the only one in his family he felt close to—that he wrote to explain that his delay in answering was not due to indifference: "I cannot write letters; I must be near someone to give myself completely."

The first three acts of *Peer Gynt* provide a base for the rest of the work, which is much longer. The at times Rabelaisian humor is no longer good-natured but bitingly satiric. For now we find the middle-aged Peer a wealthy entrepreneur, a capitalist on a world scale, the epitome of the self-made man. He has been everywhere, traded all over, spreading largesse to earn widespread admiration and self-assurance. The international fat cats who surround him at dinner in a palm grove off the coast of Morocco flatter and despise him.

The secret of his success, he boasts, is that he has never married: *he has lived for himself and for himself alone.* How can one live, he asks, if one spends one's life burdened by other people's woes? His philosophy was "elastic." He trafficked in Negro slaves in Carolina and in heathen images in China. Every spring he sent the Chinese idols and each autumn exported missionaries, equipped with woolen stockings, Bibles, rice and rum —all, to be sure, at a profit. In sum:

> The art of success is to stand free
> And uncommitted amid the snares of life.

His goal is to become emperor, emperor of the whole world. To achieve this he needs gold. But he has gold. Still—not enough. He sees his opportunity now. In the Greco-Turkish war, he finances the Turks—though they are not Christians. He urges the others to support the Greeks. "The more you fan the flame of [their] patriotism, the more I have to gain." Furious at such undisguised cynicism, the others secretly steal away to the yacht on which they have all been sailing and leave him stranded on the shore. But the gods, it would appear, are on his side: out at sea the yacht explodes and sinks. "I was fated to live and they to die," he muses philosophically.

His conclusion is characteristic of the big businessman! I am reminded of a story told me by Stella Adler. She had accompanied a millionaire to a seaside beach where he wore nothing but his bathing shorts. He was fat and ugly. "You are rich," she taunted him, "but were you abandoned here alone, naked as you are, what would you do without outside help?" "I would make myself a millionaire all over again out of the sand on which I stand" was the prompt rejoinder.

Deserted amid the palm groves, Peer takes refuge on a treetop from a swarm of climbing monkeys. He tries to beat them off. Failing in this, he "adapts" himself: eats the filthy stuff they do, and dreams of turning this wasteland into an oasis where towns would rise and become the center of a vital culture. "I'll found my capital, Peeropolis . . . My kingdom—well, half of my kingdom for a horse," he cries. And, as luck would have it, a horse emerges from a cave.

He ranges over the earth. We meet him in oriental costume reclining on a cushion, drinking coffee and smoking a large pipe in the tent of an Arabian chieftain. He is treated as a prophet by a bevy of dancers and singing girls. He now regrets that he has spent many years grubbing around in the "garbage cans of commerce." Though the girl who leads the dance is exceedingly plump with legs like drumsticks, he makes amorous advances. He can always revise his interpretations. "If one has a soul one wastes so much time on introspection."

The girl steals his horse. He doffs his Turkish costume and once again dresses in his European clothes. He comes to Egypt. There he recognizes the Boyg in the Sphinx; a German emerges from behind it and hails him as Emperor of Interpreters, the Prophet of Self. He will be hailed as such in Cairo.

The welcome accorded him there is in a madhouse, where it is announced: "Absolute learning passed away at eleven o'clock last night." And here, as in a fable, the play openly reveals its author's mind: to be oneself, and nothing whatever but oneself, is to be shut in the cask of the self, is to be "beside oneself," that is, to be insane.

There are different kinds of individualism. Brand's consisted of giving oneself to those most in need; Peer's individualism is only selfishness. He constantly forfeits himself to avoid confrontation with any difficulty; he is the emperor of compromise, a spiritual cipher.

The fifth act is more abstractly symbolic than most of what has preceded it, and thus more subject to a variety of interpretations—a boon to exegetes. Peer is now a grizzled, bent but still vigorous man aboard a ship sailing the North Sea; he is on his way home from Panama. Dressed in sailor clothes, his face is weatherbeaten and hard. "There's no one awaiting this rich old bastard." He envies those who live a normal life, with wives and children. He is still tough, uncharitable—and yet bitter at the world's lack of Christian faith. A premonition of death appears to him in the guise of a Strange Passenger.

The ship founders on the rocks. Peer saves himself by preventing the ship's cook from climbing onto a small rescue boat
which has come to the surface. The cook drowns. In a second
encounter with the Strange Passenger on the keel of the over-
turned boat, Ibsen resorts to an "alienating" witticism very much
like the one in Ionesco's *Exit the King*. "Get away! Leave me!"
Peer screams. "I must get ashore! I will not die!" "Oh, don't
worry," the Strange Passenger reassures him. "You won't die in
the middle of the last act."

Peer comes upon the figure of the Button Moulder who has
to "collect" him. Peer must go into the Button Moulder's casting
ladle, the same sort of ladle Peer used to play with as a boy.
He is to be melted down to a button! He pretends that he
doesn't deserve such a fate, he hasn't been so wicked. He has
merely splashed around between good and bad. He has never
been himself, the Button Moulder specifies; he is a waste matter.
He begs for time to prove that he has been himself. The Button
Moulder concedes him a chance to find a witness to testify that
he has been thoroughly sinful or wholly good. (We remember
Brand's contempt for those of petty virtue or petty vice.) Peer
happens on the Old Man of the Mountains, who declares that
Peer is not a person with a true self, only a troll. For the hall-
mark of the troll is one who wholeheartedly believes in the
adage "To hell with the rest of the world."

"To be oneself is to kill oneself," says the Button Moulder.
This is a rephrasing of what Jesus said to his disciples: "Who-
ever cares for his safety is lost, but if a man will let himself die
for my sake, he will find his true self." It was also Brand's creed.
But Peer in his constant effort to save himself for himself alone
deteriorated into something less than a mediocrity. He is not
worthy of hell's torment. (In an 1865 letter to his mother-in-law
Ibsen wrote: " . . . there is something more worth having than
a clever head and that is a whole soul.") In his quest for salvation Peer meets a Thin Man who tells him that at the moment
"There just aren't any souls about. Just the odd stray now and
then." Peer, now in total despair, cries out, "I was a dead man
before I died."

He dashes toward a cabin, and there he finds Solveig, erect

and gentle, still waiting for him. He is doomed if no one can tell him where his self, his whole self, his true self, is to be found, "the self that bore God's stamp upon its brow." She tells him, "In my faith, in my hope and in my love." Peer, bathed in tears, cries out, "My mother! My wife! Oh thou pure woman! Oh hide me in your love!" But the Button Moulder still lingers in the background. Peer's fate remains undetermined.

The coda is beautiful, but hardly a "happy ending." As he approaches the last judgment, Peer realizes that he has been like the peeled onion which when stripped layer by layer reveals nothing at its core. The Strange Passenger had asked him, "Have you once in life won the victory that only defeat can bring?" But it's now too late to ask such questions of Peer. When he saw the scapegrace lad who hacked off his own finger to avoid going to war, he was overcome with incredulity. Yes, it is possible to think of such a thing, but to *do* it, *that* Peer could not understand. The lad, still publicly shunned as a traitor years later, was not, in the words of the priest officiating at his funeral, "a cripple in the eyes of God."

Brand was crushed, but with head held high, a death not without glory. Peer's end is slightly shabby and pathetic. In Ibsen there is no "out" or total redemption for mortal man, but of the two personages the less heroic is more "sympathetic." There is an Asiatic proverb which tells us, "The tree that bends bears the fruit," which might have been a maxim of possible benefit to Brand, but in his self-absorption Peer was a tree which hewed itself down. In his central conviction Brand contains something of Ibsen's best self, as he himself put it, but "happy-go-lucky" Peer somewhat resembles the Ibsen who schemed and plotted to acquire honors at every hand. Ibsen harbors something like veneration for Brand; he regards Peer with a wry affection.

I have called *Peer Gynt* a more "realistic" play. Obviously I was not alluding to its style. If such designations are at all useful one would have to categorize Peer Gynt as distinctly "anti-realistic." But there is in the play the adumbration of a rather new social type. In 1867 Ibsen extrapolated from the tardy capitalism of his country such figures as the international speculators and tycoons of the more advanced societies. It is always something of a betrayal with such plays to speak of their general importance without reference to their immediate relevancy.

No less striking in *Peer Gynt* and most crucial to an enjoyment of it is the ring and robustness, the sweep, pithiness and savor of its imagery. There is an abundance of humor in individual lines as well as in entire scenes. When the smoke lifts on the explosion of the yacht which has rid Peer of his competition, he looks back at the sea where the yacht has sunk, thanks God for having been spared and murmurs, " . . . but He certainly isn't economical." Peer calls the Strange Gentleman, death's surrogate, "a damned freethinker" and a "boring moralist!" He also thinks that "nature," in its incalculability, "is witty."

Peer Gynt looks toward the future in its theatrical form. Though written as a dramatic poem, it is eminently playable. Even more than *Brand*, it calls for a highly endowed and most versatile actor, a genuinely "total theater" production. When the play was produced in Paris in 1895 (with Alfred Jarry, author of *Ubu Roi* and patron devil of "the theater of the absurd," in the cast, and with sets and costumes by Bonnard, Vuillard and Toulouse-Lautrec) the time was not yet ripe for the creation of a style befitting the play. Still the play's quality did not escape the notice of the London dramatic critic who reviewed it on that occasion: Bernard Shaw.

I have myself never yet seen a satisfactory production of the play, though I have heard of several in Europe: Pitoeff in Paris, one in Yugoslavia and possibly the late Tyrone Guthrie's production with Ralph Richardson at the Old Vic. It is perhaps something for Peter Brook to essay when he is finished with his experiments. Or for Andrei Serban.

If *Brand* is not Ibsen's masterpiece, then surely *Peer Gynt* is.

5

Forward and Backward:
Backward and Forward

After *Peer Gynt* Ibsen never wrote another play in verse. Prose is clearly the proper medium for *The League of Youth* (1868–69), a comedy about small-town politics in Norway, but why did he employ prose for *Emperor and Galilean*, a "world-historical drama," the action of which extends in its first part from A.D. 351 to A.D. 361 and in its second from A.D. 361 to A.D. 363? His explanation was that he "wanted to produce [the illusion] of reality. I wished to produce the impression on the reader that he was reading something that had really happened . . . We are no longer living in the age of Shakespeare. Speaking generally, the style must conform to the degree of ideality which pervades the representation. My new drama is no tragedy in the ancient acceptation; what I desired to depict were human beings, and therefore I would not let them talk in the language of the gods."

This is plausible enough, though one might object that the satiric businessmen's dinner on the yacht in *Peer Gynt* is more "real" than anything in *Emperor and Galilean*, and that there are several scenes in the latter play which might be set down

Note: All the citations from the plays in this chapter are from the translations in the Oxford University Press edition.

[90]

as "mystic." Yet *Peer Gynt* is entirely in verse. The truer reason for the stylistic change in Ibsen's plays after 1867 is that the social milieu had changed, and he was eminently an author who lived in his times.

The plays of old dealt with the gods of heaven and the gods on earth (royalty): exalted heroes who were at odds with transcendental forces. Their speech could not be that of ordinary citizens. But by the middle of the nineteenth century the audience was largely composed of the increasingly dominant middle class and its immediate dependents. They wanted to see themselves on the stage; they wanted to hear people speak more or less as they did about matters that concerned them more intimately than the recondite issues with which the older dramatists had dealt. They were no longer deeply moved by the towering edifices reaching to the occult; they wanted dramas built around their hearths and homes where everyday talk was to be heard. That was what Ibsen was to give them, to build his worldwide reputation on, and ultimately, to give signs of regretting.

Though *The League of Youth*, written in Germany in 1869, was to become his most popular play in Norway during the nineteenth century, its present interest is clearly academic. It marks Ibsen's transition from the broad canvases of his poetic drama (whether in verse or prose) to modern realism. The student seeking clues or origins of the dramatist's later work will find many here. *The League of Youth* is a first step on the road to the typical "Ibsenite" play, those by which he is best known to the general public: the most influential ones but certainly not his profoundest.

It is called a comedy but reads like and certainly should be played as farce. Its plot, once its premise has been set, moves at rapid-fire pace with twists and turns so complicated that it would take an inordinate amount of time and space to make a lucid summary—and it would hardly be worth the trouble. But its success in its day is understandable. A topical play, it attacks phony liberalism and thus pleased conservatives, unaware that its target is politics and politicians in general.

Practically the entire political community as represented in the play consists of blackguards. Toward the very end, as the last of the blackest among them is disposed of, someone predicts that the rascal will return. Had not Napoleon said the more double-dealing a man, the more likely he is to make a politician.

Except for a number of incisive thrusts, scattered at random through the text, the play is all surface—a fact which Ibsen surely knew. Artistically it is a step backward compared to his three previous plays; technically, however, it marks a change, if not an advance. We can only speak of a technical advance if progress toward box-set realism is considered to be inherent in the purpose of modern drama. The play avoids soliloquies and asides; in other words, it conforms to the stage requirements of the new day. To master the appropriate method for its dramatic composition, Ibsen worked on this play for a whole year.

Its central character, Stensgaard, is a pipsqueak Peer—that is, Peer Gynt without any of Peer's panache, charm or depth. Young Stensgaard, an obviously deceitful opportunist, has come to forge his way in the "stagnant backwater" of a southern Norwegian township. His fraudulence is so apparent that one finds it incredible that it is not immediately unmasked. He is referred to as a "split personality," but one does not discern any "split" at all: he is an unmitigated swindler. He first presents himself as a "liberal," not to say an anti-capitalist. But it is clear from the outset that he has no convictions at all; he only wants to get ahead and will do anything within the shortest possible lapse of time to further his deceits. If Stensgaard has any attractiveness at all, it is due to the fact that in addition to being a scoundrel he is a fool! Today our political personages are at least a little more complex than that. In the end the crisscross of intrigues makes it inescapably evident that all parties are tarred with the same brush. But, to repeat, the play is a farce.

One readily understands why Ibsen thought of Brand as himself in his best moments and why he acknowledged kinship with Peer, but was he not libeling himself when he confessed to having something of Stensgaard in himself as well? Was he alluding to his envy and literary politicking and in his occasional slander of Bjørnson? In a speech to working men after he had returned for a brief visit to Norway in 1888, he said, "During these eight days at home I have experienced more of the joy of life than in all the eleven years abroad," after which he resumed his exile—though it is true he did end it two years later. Or did he suspect that he had entered upon a marriage of convenience just as Stensgaard repeatedly attempts to do? Speaking to a friend in a moment of self-revealing exasperation, Stensgaard exclaims, "You are not trying to tell me that I should be so blindly obstinate as to risk my entire future, miss my chance of reaching my objective for the miserable satisfaction of being consistent?"

One might certainly ask who among us has not now and then recognized a contradiction between word and deed or behaved with reprehensible selfishness. But with Stensgaard such action is constant and therefore dramatically of meager interest except as caricature.

The success of the play in its day—no doubt enhanced by the very anger and controversy it aroused—may be explained by the fact that all over Europe the mid-nineteenth century was a period of intense political agitation. Radicalism put heavy pressure on governments and their societies in general, while the reactionary powers fought hard to stem the tide.

The play contains jibes at war profiteers, electoral treachery, newspapers. The wily printer-journalist Aslaksen says, "A newspaper needs a large public to support it, but a large public is a bad public—and a bad public demands a bad paper. I can't make a living out of a good paper."

As to the new capitalist class, we read, "No one asks any more how a fortune was acquired . . . All they ask is how much is so and so worth?" And this about politicians: ["Stensgaard's] got the gift of carrying the crowd with him. And because he's lucky enough not to be hampered by either character or social status, he can very easily be liberal-minded."

In *The League of Youth* we also note the first expression of another of Ibsen's preoccupations. A young woman who has been treated with solicitude by her husband, her sister and her father-in-law but told nothing of the family's money troubles bursts out at last with: "Oh, what I've had to suffer from you! The shame of it—from all of you! Always I had to be the one to take—never was I the one to give. I've been a pauper among

you all. You never came to ask me to make any sacrifices—I've
never been good enough to bear anything. I hate you! I loathe
you! ... How I've longed for even a little share in your worries.
But when I asked, all you did was laugh it off as a joke. You
dressed me up like a doll. You played with me as you might with
a child. Oh, how joyfully I could have helped bear the burdens!
How earnestly I longed for some part in the storms and thrills
and excitements of life! Now I'm good enough. Now when Eric
[her husband] has nothing else. But I don't want to be the one
people turn to last. Now I don't want any of your troubles. I'm
leaving you!"

Here we have something of the Nora in *A Doll's House*, who
was to be brought on stage ten years later. But everything we
associate with the later Ibsen was in gestation in the younger.
In *Brand*, Agnes tells of her child's asking ecstatically about a
candle: "Mother, is it the sun?"—a line made memorable in its
transformation in *Ghosts*. There are parallels between Ejnar in
Brand with Molvik in *The Wild Duck* and Ulrik Brendel, whom
we are to meet in *Rosmersholm*. Hjördis in *The Vikings* resembles Rebecca West in *Rosmersholm* and the glamorous dream
of "with vine leaves in his hair" many think peculiar in *Hedda
Gabler* is to be found in *The Pretenders*. The legendary white
horses which haunt the minds of men and women in *Rosmersholm* are part of the "racial memory" gleaned by Ibsen from
his readings in Norse mythology. Aslaksen in *The League of
Youth* may be the pusillanimous printer of the same name in
An Enemy of the People. Knowing only one or even a few
plays of Ibsen's middle period is not sufficient for an evaluation
of his work as a whole.

"To be a poet means essentially to see," Ibsen declared in his
1874 speech to Norwegian students, " . . . to see in such a way
that whatever is seen is perceived by the audience just as the
poet saw it. But only what has been lived through can be seen
in that way and accepted in that way . . . All I have written these
last ten years I have lived through spiritually."

This is true even of *Emperor and Galilean*, the most impersonal of Ibsen's plays. What has Julian the Apostate, Emperor

of Rome, to do with Ibsen? Yet however removed the subject is from Ibsen as an individual, however arcane the play's probings, it is central to a dilemma in his thinking and feeling in regard to world history and his position within it. Even before he prepared and wrote *Brand* he was wrestling with the thematic material of *Emperor and Galilean*. Its composition occupied him from 1864 to 1873.

It is divided into two parts, each of them in five acts. Though it has been staged, it is the least playable of Ibsen's plays. Without being entirely clear, it is the closest to being a "preachment" as well the most "symbolic" of all his plays. Ibsen considered it his masterpiece, probably because it attempted a statement of a "world view," an effort to enunciate a credo, however abstruse its terms.

Part One is called "Caesar's Apostasy," though Julian's official proclamation of paganism as the state religion does not occur till Part Two, which is called "The Emperor Julian." Though in preparing it Ibsen engaged in strenuous research, its historicity is doubtful. On the one hand it suffers from too much "homework," on the other there is more of Henrik in it than of Julian.

As a youth of nineteen, Julian, like his emperor cousin Constantine, is a devout Christian. But from the very beginning we observe Julian's inclination toward "philosophy," which in those days was chiefly Greek, that is to say, pagan. He wants to study Plato and Aristotle, the better to defend Christian doctrine.

The play opens ironically. An anthem is being sung in a church, "The Lamb hath won the day; all earth of peace doth tell!" while outside Christians are not only at loggerheads with pagans but squabbling among themselves with regard to mutually antagonistic factions within the Faith.

Julian is attracted by that "whole world of splendor, which you Galileans [i.e., Christians] are blind to . . . Life there [among the pagans] is an endless festival, among the statues and temple songs, with foaming goblets full, and roses in our hair." (Though the terms are different this speech reminds one of Oswald's already-quoted paeans to the "free life" in the great European centers—outside of Norway.) As Julian begins to be ever more seduced by the intellectual and physical charms of his student

days in Athens, he finds himself riven by an uncertainty which
both Christianity and paganism arouse in him. "Was sin beautiful in Sodom and Gomorrah? Didn't Jehovah's fire avenge what
Socrates did not shrink from? Oh when I live this gay and
reckless life, I often wonder whether truth *is* the enemy of
beauty."

The writings of the holy men fail to satisfy Julian. His appetite for a fullness of being cannot be appeased by "books . . .
always books." "Don't you have that horrible feeling of nausea,"
he asks, "tossing backwards and forwards between life, scripture,
pagan wisdom and beauty? There must be a new revelation. Or
a revelation of something new. There *must*, I say." What he
has come to feel is that the old (pagan) beauty is no longer beautiful and the new (Christian) truth is no longer true.

In this the sore spot in Ibsen's spirit become palpable. Apart
from his resistance to socially received dogma and other ephem-
eral dissatisfactions he could not achieve that wholeness of being
he considered the essential human goal. He believed that we
must act according to the dictates of our innermost selves, but
what hope is there for us if we find division in ourselves? All
appearance to the contrary, Ibsen was never wholly sure of
anything; everything basic remained an open question.

As master of mysteries, Maximus brings Julian as near as he
(or Ibsen) was ever able to come to the "new revelation." He
must, Maximus instructs him, become the founder of a "new
empire."

JULIAN: What is the empire?
MAXIMUS: There are three empires.
JULIAN: Three?
MAXIMUS: First, the empire which was founded on the tree of
            knowledge; then the empire which was founded on the
            tree of the cross.
JULIAN: And the third?
MAXIMUS: The third is the empire of the great mystery; the empire
            which shall be founded on the tree of knowledge and
            the tree of the cross together, because it hates and loves
            them both, and because it has its living springs under
            Adam's grave and Golgotha.

The "tree of knowledge" is science and the spirit of paganism; the tree of the cross is the Christian religion. By what means can the new empire be established? By *willing*. What must Julian will? The answer: what you *must*.

We come no nearer to clarity than this. "The signs conflict." All, except the travail of the quest, is muddle. Julian is warned against becoming emperor, but the temptation is too great. He now believes the new empire will be established through him. Was this Ibsen's secret intellectual dream and temptation?

One could go on much longer to trace allusions to Ibsen's ambitions, his cares, friendships, fears—indeed his whole life story. The play is rich with the ore of Ibsen's speculations and memories. For example, he has no dependable friends, Julian says, to aid him in his battles: not even Sallust (Brandes), who offered to share in all his dangers. But he couldn't be of use to him at the imperial court: "He is one of those they call pagans there." There are hints of Ibsen's enemies at home, all tagged with Roman titles and names. They do not want him to return to his native land. There is talk of dying of homesickness, "it consumes a man," and we think of Ibsen in exile. There are cosmological and theological musings, a constant groping to capture the ineffable.

Julian as emperor adopts paganism as the state religion: their gods are not burdensome, "they leave a man plenty of scope for action . . . Oh happy Greeks with their sense of freedom!" His assumption of paganism is a rebellion against the faith of his youth. He justifies his conversion by pontificating: "All human emotions have been forbidden since that day the seer of Galilee began to rule the world. With him to live is to die. To love and to hate are to sin. But has he changed man's flesh and blood? Is man still not earthbound as before? With every healthy fiber of our being we revolt against it . . . and yet we are told to *will* against our will! . . . " Still he continues to live in awe and fear of the finally triumphant Christ.

The play's second part, which is much too long and generally inferior to the first, dramatizes the history of Julian's rule and defeat. To establish his empire in every sense he sets out to conquer Persia and most of Asia. He fails in every respect.

The reason for his failure, his master Maximus tells him, is that "You want to unite what cannot be united . . . to reconcile two things which are not to be reconciled." This is a blatant self-contradiction unless Maximus means what we suppose Ibsen to mean: that the establishment of a religion through the power of the state must entail falsity and havoc.

Much more interesting than the battles in which Julian is constantly baffled is the picture of the social life of his regime: the contradictions between creed and practice. We find Julian, now the declared and resolved pagan, enjoining simplicity and modesty in dress, and the Christians taking to sybaritic fashion. Though Julian at the outset of his reign proclaims that neither Christians nor Jews shall be persecuted, his head of state and his appointed officers become coercive and tyrannically cruel. The ruler of men soon develops the craving to rule as god: "I shall possess the world." It is this ambition which spells his ruin.

Now Maximus tells Julian, "You know that I have never approved of what you have done as Emperor . . . drawing your sword against what shall be, against the third empire, where he who is two in one shall rule!" And who may that be? "The Jews have a name for him. They call him the Messiah; and they are waiting for him . . . He shall swallow up both Emperor and Galilean. Both shall lose . . . but not be lost, both in one and one in both." Maximus is cryptic as ever.

The messages move in circles; the ineffable cannot be captured. The play's importance is not in any conclusion it arrives at, but in the question Ibsen addresses to himself. Though complex it is incomplete because it is too abstract a dramatization of the inner debate. It strains toward a doctrine (or a "philosophy") which in this form cannot be one. It takes on body in the flesh of Ibsen's future plays, in concrete situations, in "realism." No final truth is set forth. But there is some truth in every link. In Ibsen every truth is a half-truth, and every part of truth is precious. At Julian's death in battle, Ibsen speaks through the mouth of a Christian woman: "Oh brother, let us not sink to the bottom of this abyss."

In *Brand*, Ibsen was the priest, in Peer the universal tradesman-adventurer, in Julian the "apostate" seer of dramatic literature along with those other nineteenth-century apostates Darwin and Marx. In the plays which follow he takes his place among the men and women of his and our day.

6

The New Path

AFTER HARKING BACK in *Emperor and Galilean* to ancient times, Ibsen took to a new path homeward. The new path was modern realism. Compared with *The League of Youth* (1869), *The Pillars of Society*, written seven years later, is a great stride forward, though inferior compared to the plays which followed. It is in some respects a crude play, the only Ibsen play which may justifiably be dubbed "propaganda."

The Pillars of Society is constructed on a series of subplots within the main one, all of them fitting neatly into one another like little boxes. Except for the opening exposition, in which a group of gossiping women is used to impart key information—a rather threadbare device—and the hurried ending, the play is brilliantly wrought. To refine his new technical method, Ibsen worked on it for two years (1875–77), a longer period of preparation than for any other of his plays except *Emperor and Galilean*, where the difficulties were of another order. He was still serving his "apprenticeship" in realism.

The central character is Karsten Bernick, a successful ship-builder and the most influential citizen in a small Norwegian

Note: All the citations from *The Pillars of Society* in this chapter are from Michael Meyer's translation.

seaport. He jilted the woman he loved, Lona Hessel, to marry Lona's half-sister Betty, because hard pressed for funds. It was the more expedient thing to do. Fifteen years before the opening of the play's action, during his engagement to Betty, he had had a liaison with an actress of an itinerant theater troupe. Very nearly discovered with her, he escaped through her bedroom window. Being implicated in such a scrape in a provincial town would have spelled ruin for him. He allowed his fiancée's bachelor brother Johan to assume the role of the guilty party. Johan has gone off to America and is therefore not only believed to have had illicit relations with the actress but to have absconded with funds—another false rumor which Bernick allows to pass in order to cover some of his own shady dealings.

Bernick is involved in the planning of a railroad, the building of which he first opposed and then sponsors because he has learned how he may profit from it. He proceeds to cheat his business colleagues by secretly buying the land through which the railway line will run.

When Johan comes back from America and learns that he is reputed to have been guilty not only of improper sexual conduct but of theft and that these slanders are a barrier to his marriage to Dina Dorf, the abandoned daughter of the aforementioned actress, he threatens to disclose the truth about the matter. Johan consents to go back to America for a short while if in the meantime Bernick finds the means to exonerate him.

Exposure for Bernick means the collapse of his career. In despair, he allows one of his ships, on which Johan proposes to make the voyage back to America, to sail, though Bernick knows that the ship has become unseaworthy and will probably sink if the crossing is rough. Bernick then discovers that his thirteen-year-old son Olaf, impatient of the strict discipline of his home and through attachment to the adventurous Johan, has stowed away on the same ship. Fortunately the man in charge of its repair has at the last moment forbidden the sailing, so that neither Olaf nor Johan will make the voyage on the vessel.

This brings about Bernick's conversion. At a celebration as the town's most honored citizen, he confesses his several wrongdoings and promises to make amends. In short, the play ends happily not only for him—his wife forgives him and he begins to appreciate her at her true worth—but for Johan, Dina Dorf and Lona Hessel, who having been jilted by Bernick had accompanied Johan to America and almost maternally devoted herself to him.

This hasty summary of the undoubtedly melodramatic plot conveys little sense of the play's numerous strands and manifold purposes skillfully woven by Ibsen through his newly developed technical mastery.

A minor theme is implicit in the struggle between Bernick, who has brought "new machines" into the shipyard, and its foreman, Aune, chairman of the Workers' Association. When Aune is asked why he has been delegated to organize resistance against the use of these machines he says it is for the community's good. But such resistance, Bernick replies, will disintegrate the community. To which Aune counters, "I don't mean by community what Mr. Bernick does." For Bernick the workers are only "a narrow circle."

At an earlier time, in England for example, where the same difficulty and dispute had provoked the insurgence of the "machine wreckers," the fear among the working class was very much like the worry over automation today. But this incidental theme here does more than situate the historical period. Structurally, it serves as a first step in Bernick's pressure on Aune, who if he balks in this matter of the new machines will render himself the more vulnerable and liable to dismissal when he argues against sending *The Indian Girl* to sea despite its perilous condition. When, in the end, the sailing of the ship is canceled and everything turns out for the best, Aune argues that the new machines may benefit more than harm the workers. Ibsen himself was not opposed to industrial innovation.

Another subsidiary theme, initially broached in *The League of Youth*, and important in the delineation of the society in which the action occurs, is the exclusion of women from any vital role in community affairs. We know that this matter will be given fuller development not only in Ibsen's next play, *A Doll's House* (though very differently), but in several others.

Here it serves as a means to advance the plot as well as in the characterization of all the play's women, except for the afore-mentioned rumor-mongering ladies, members with Mrs. Bernick of the Society for the Redemption of Fallen Women. On this account, Dina Dorf, as the daughter of the "fallen woman" with whom Johan is supposed to have been "mixed up," has been adopted by the Bernicks and taken into their household.

Women's negligible role in important social affairs is intro-duced in an almost offhand manner. While Bernick in his private study is negotiating the railroad deal with his business associates, his wife asks him to tell her about its outcome. Bernick answers, "My dear Betty, this is not a matter for women to concern themselves with." Women's occupation, apart from household duties, is "to labor untiringly in the cause of charity."

When Lona Hessel reproves Bernick for having thrown her over to marry her half-sister, whom he admits he didn't love—in other words, he saved the House of Bernick (his business) at her expense—we not only recognize the seed of future plays (for almost every Ibsen play contains the germ of another) but a definition of Bernick's attitude and that of his coevals in regard to marriage. "The sacrifice you made for me wasn't in vain," Bernick tells Lona. His wife, Betty, is "so good and acquiescent. During the years we've lived together she has learned to mold her character to mine—She used to have a lot of over-romantic ideas about love; she couldn't accept that as the years pass it must shrink into the calm candle flame of friendship."

In this "society of bachelors," as Lona Hessel calls it, Dina Dorf has no place. She is attracted to Johan, who is no longer part of it. He has been in the land of the free. The view of America held by several of the play's characters (and probably by Ibsen) is a sunny one. Martha, Bernick's schoolteacher sister, who was once in love with Johan and hoped she might win him on his return from America, urges Dina, whom he loves, to go with him: "Go to your happiness across the sea. Oh damn that school room. I've so longed to be there! It must be beautiful there. The sky is larger and the clouds fly higher than they do here. The air that blows on the faces of the people is freer . . . " (Ibsen's brother Johan emigrated to California in search of gold.

After a few letters home, no more was ever heard from him. So too did Martin, the third of the Ibsen boys.)

This is the climax to a previous more matter-of-fact and rather charming scene in which Dina reveals her desire to escape the "provincial backwater" she has been confined to:

DINA: Is it easy as they say to become—someone—over there in America?

JOHAN: No, it's not always easy. You often have to work your fingers to the bone at first, and live pretty rough.

DINA: I wouldn't mind that . . . I can work. I'm healthy and strong and Aunt Martha has taught me a lot . . . But tell me one thing. Are people as moral over there as they are here?

JOHAN: Moral?

DINA: Yes. I mean—are they as good and virtuous as they are here?

JOHAN: Well, they haven't all got horns . . .

DINA: You don't understand. I want to go somewhere where people aren't good and virtuous.

JOHAN: Where they *aren't*. What do you want them to be then?

DINA: I want them to be natural.

JOHAN: They're that all right.

DINA: Then I think it'd be good for me if I could go and live there.

JOHAN: I'm sure it would. You must come back with us.

DINA: No, I don't want to go with you. I must go alone. Oh, I'd manage. I'd make something of myself.

The "good and virtuous" of the town are mainly typified by two characters: Hilmar Toennessen, Mrs. Bernick's cousin, and the schoolmaster, Dr. Roerlund. Hilmar is lethargic and flabby through failure to participate in the going (business) world and from lack of courage to strike out in any other way which might disturb the ease and comfort of his surroundings. Roerlund, whom Johan mockingly calls "Reverend," is a would-be intellectual and the bulwark of the town's proprieties and prejudices.

All these apparent side issues not only serve the plot but constitute rivulets in the play's main stream. In *The Pillars of Society* Ibsen makes his first unequivocal assault on society's bastions, the targets of his propaganda. Herein lies the play's strength and weakness. For though well-drawn and convincing within the limits of the play's purpose, the characters do not exceed or extend beyond these limits. They exist more as functions of the attack than as full-bodied persons with lives of their own. What is perhaps still more troubling is that the happy ending relieves them all, especially Bernick, of any of the bitter consequences which might ensue from their shortcomings and misdeeds.

Still the thrusts are sharp and accurate. They are made when Lona Hessel, who has also become a liberated spirit in America, insists that Bernick as well as his victim have suffered the evil effects of his machinations on the road to power. He defends himself: "Look at any man you choose to name; you'll find everyone has at least one skeleton hidden in his cupboard."

LORNA: And you call yourselves pillars of society?
BERNICK: Society has none better.
LORNA: If that's what your society is like, what does it matter whether it survives or is destroyed? What do people here set store by? Lies and pretenses . . .

As in his later plays, Ibsen here takes up arms against "the banner of the ideal," and speaks scornfully of "duty." The reiteration of his contempt for these shibboleths—ideals, duty—here as elsewhere is a source of grave misunderstanding of Ibsen's meaning. Ideals are not in themselves positive: "ideals" detached from action based on human and social reality lead to mendacity and destructiveness. "Duty" also becomes a distortion of honorable behavior when it is simply a catchword to conceal impersonal, unexamined, spiritually unmotivated routine. Brand battles for his ideal and duty and suffers for it. Duty as mere convention is social coercion, oppression. Duty not undertaken by free choice through the urgency of the individual self is what Ibsen considered vicious and immoral. The only true arbiter is the consent of one's conscience. ("What is most contrary to salvation," the French Catholic essayist and poet Charles Péguy said, "is not sin but habit.")

In *Peer Gynt* Ibsen dramatized his condemnation of the individualism which is only a mask for egotistical self-aggrandizement. Brand's sacrifices are not performed on official orders as so-called duties, but are self-willed and self-fulfilling actions. Indeed they are not sacrifices at all, but impulses of moral assertion on the road to the most profound happiness and, in some cases, to sanctity. It is giving up one's life to save it! The conflict inherent in the two conceptions of individual freedom will appear again in other and more familiar guises in several of the later plays of Ibsen's maturity.

Though I have indicated the play's limitation by speaking of it as "propaganda," the reservation must be qualified by adding that it is not blunt or meretricious propaganda. In Bernick's rationalization of his "mistakes" he voices his (and Ibsen's) definition of the issues. "You've no right to despise me," says the shaken pillar of society. "You can't imagine how dreadfully alone I am in this narrow, stunted society . . . What have I accomplished? It seems a lot, but really it's nothing—a patchwork of trivialities. But they wouldn't tolerate anything else here, or anything bigger. If I tried to move a step outside their conception of right and wrong, my power would vanish. Do you know what we are, we whom they call the pillars of society? We are the instruments of society. Nothing more." And in his final self-denunciation to the shocked community he promises to repair much of the harm he has done.

In the closing and cleverly though rather stagily devised scene, the town dignitaries assemble to confer a public accolade on Bernick, giving vent to all the bombast attendant on such occasions. Here he tells Lona that he has learned something else beside knowledge of the labors he will have to undertake to carry out the needed reforms: " . . . it is you women who are the pillars of society." But Lona dismisses this by saying, "Then it's poor wisdom you've learned—the spirit of truth and the spirit of freedom—they are the pillars of society."

Ibsen was not always as optimistic as he appears to be in this play. In the future he will look deeper into the hearts of such men as Bernick and at the prospects of change and social amelioration. The "new era" Bernick looks forward to will be fraught with new perils—in Ibsen's eyes as well as in ours.

Just as the conservatives were foolish and fooled in hailing the "anti-liberalism" they had found in *The League of Youth*, so the liberals who now welcomed him on the evidence of *The Pillars of Society* were soon to consider themselves deceived by

Ibsen's later doubts and reversals. Indisputably new in the era was the theatrical mode which dawned with *The Pillars of Society*; it initiated a method of playmaking which, quite apart from content, dominated Western dramaturgy for generations and has never to this day been entirely superseded. At the time he embarked on this phase of his work, Ibsen was forty-seven.

7

In Full Stride

A *Doll's House*, written in Rome and Amalfi (1879), is perhaps more often produced than any other Ibsen play. It was certainly the most socially influential of his plays. Nora's slamming of the door in farewell to her husband—a highly theatrical device since we hear no door open or shut in the course of the play—is a door slam which reverberated around the world. Largely on this account, Ibsen is commonly regarded in the theater, at any rate, as a pioneer spirit of what today goes by the name of "women's lib."

In his *History of Modern Norway*, G. Derry takes pains to note that "within five years of the publication of *A Doll's House*, women were being admitted to the private Liberal Club in the tradition bound city of Oslo!" Yet it is remarkable that in his 1888 speech at a banquet for the Norwegian League of Women's Rights, Ibsen should have said, "I am not a member of the Women's Rights League. Whatever I have written has been without any conscious thought of making propaganda."

This seems a paradox. But in view of his central conviction that there is little hope for humankind unless every individual

Note: All the citations from plays in this chapter are from Eva Le Gallienne's translations.

becomes an authentic person all of whose acts must stem from the deeper self, it is natural that Ibsen should have taken it for granted that this applied to men as well as to women. Or, to put it as Shaw does in *The Philanderer*, "If Ibsen's sauce is good for the goose, it is good for the gander as well."

If *A Doll's House* is read without preconceptions the implication is clear that men cannot be "free" (or authentic) persons unless women are equally free. It should be evident at the final curtain that while Nora is in a state of bewilderment, and she knows herself to be ignorant about everything except the necessity of her leavetaking, Torvald (Helmer), her husband, is even more bewildered. He does not quite understand what she means when she says that neither can lead an honest life unless the "miracle—the most wonderful thing of all" occurs. And if he did understand her, it would no doubt take as long for him to act on his understanding as it would take Nora to live by what she has yet to learn. Nora's abandonment of her home is not an act of defiance so much as a gesture of despair.

Few people who see the play acted grasp the full significance of Krogstad's and Mrs. Linde's presence among the personages. They appear auxiliary to the main theme rather than part of it. Krogstad is the "menace," Mrs. Linde is Nora's friend and Krogstad's redeemer. But Ibsen has placed them prominently in the picture to suggest that they will make a truer marriage than was possible for Torvald and Nora. Krogstad's struggle to sustain himself as a man who has been all but ruined by adversity and poverty, his having been forsaken by Mrs. Linde, the woman he loved, the effort to support his children while he finds himself deprived of the possibility of decent employment, will ultimately prove the ground for renewed strength. Mrs. Linde's hardship, her loveless marriage to assume help for her mother and two brothers, lends her the fortitude to enter her future relationship with Krogstad on a basis of mutual compassion and understanding. They are equal in their experience of life's trials. Krogstad, albeit "shipwrecked" and desperate, manifests a stern practicality of behavior; Mrs. Linde throughout remains staunch and, as she says, unhysterical. They know themselves in all their missteps and in their situation in society. That is why their relationship eventuates in a "happy ending." It is also to be noted that Mrs. Linde believes that if Nora were to reveal her intention to her husband, their marriage would be "saved," that is, resurrected on a firm basis of truth.

The disaster of Nora's and Torvald's marriage is a possible prelude to a future education and, only remotely possible, a reunion. Both have begun as "dolls"; at the slamming of the door, their future soundness is still only a supposition.

From the first we observe that Nora and Torvald do not know each other, though of the two Nora is certainly the more aware. What is Nora to Torvald? In the opening scene we hear Torvald, by way of endearment, call Nora "a lark," "a squirrel," "a spendthrift," "a featherbrain," "a little woman" and "a little liar." He has forgotten that she persuaded him to go on the trip to Italy which saved his life; he barely inquires how she procured the money for it. "Torvald could never bear to think of owing anything to me!" He can't possibly know that she saved most of her allowance for clothes, engaged in needlework and crocheting for others, working far into the night as a means of earning enough money to pay back the debt incurred for Torvald's sake. Speaking of those activities, she says, "Oh, sometimes I was absolutely exhausted. But it was fun all the same, working like that and earning money. It made me feel almost like a man!" Torvald owes his blissful domestic life to his thoughtlessness. In all essentials, he is more ignorant than she, for she has already faced and survived a crisis, taken difficult and dangerous action on his behalf.

Strindberg detested the play—he would! In a self-interview he took pleasure in pointing out that Torvald Helmer is an honest man—as a lawyer he never accepted a shady case—while Nora is a liar; worse still, a flirt, almost a hussy. Nora flirts, indulges in what she herself calls "pretty tricks." But this is her way, aside from an originally lighthearted nature, to penetrate the cuirass of Torvald's stuffy rectitude, his rigorous middle-class code of proper conduct. She can hardly reason with him because the heart has reasons that reason does not know. She wants above all to please him, she loves him, he is her knight. She constantly play-acts for him, and no doubt enjoys doing so. She is his baby.

Why wrangle when you get your own way by sweet cajolery? If Torvald treats Nora like a "doll," she treats him like a child. Nora's coquetry, in short, is for the most part inspired by her husband's appetite for it. If this is "insincerity" it is something even more important for the actress playing the part than for the reader to notice.

Torvald at thirty is still a boob, but certainly no "villain" as he often appears in stage performances. His preachments as to the evil effect on children of a bad mother, shocking as they may sound to contemporary audiences, are by no means untrue. He concedes that fathers too may be held responsible for similar unfortunate influences. But what is most obtuse in his moralizing is not its substance but that it is hardly the result of any felt experience; it is largely bookish. What he says is the doctrine of his day; closely examined it is hardly very different from our own.

In the crisis of his life—Nora's announced determination to leave him—after he has been literally frightened out of his wits by the prospect of dismissal from his position and said unkind and stupid things, he begs her not to believe he seriously meant them. He was so dismayed at the thought of public disgrace. Nora reacts not to the explosiveness of his vituperation, but to the realization that he has thought only of himself. In the impending calamity he neither considers its causes nor is governed by the impulse to protect her. Just before he discovers her crime, he passionately declares—with brilliant theatrical effect— "I often wish you were in some great danger, so I could risk body and soul, my whole life, everything, everything for your sake."

She to whom love is everything, above the letter of the law, public opinion, even religion, of which she knows as little as most things learned by rote, discovers that his love is a convenience, not a commitment of the self. Thus her love for him is destroyed.

For a long time it seemed to me (and to many others) that Nora's transformation from the "featherbrain" to the thoughtful woman of the final scenes, though credible as an "idea," was, as written, barely acceptable. I held it to be a technical flaw

rather than a psychological one. It was a sacrifice, I believed, to
the dramatist's need to "wind up" the story within the economy
of his tight construction. (I shall discuss this difficulty in connection with other of Ibsen's plays.) But study of the text
reveals that the premises for Nora's evolution have been laid
down from the beginning. One of the marvels of Ibsen's craft
is that he hardly wastes a word.

We find the first clue to the process of Nora's development
in her colloquy in Act One with Mrs. Linde. After she has
thanked Nora for promising to get her a job in Torvald's bank,
she says, "How good of you, Nora dear, to bother on my account. It's especially good of you—after all, you've never had
to go through any hardship," and adds, "You're just a child,
Nora." In some agitation, Nora retorts, "You needn't be so
patronizing," and she goes on to tell of her efforts to acquire the
money which enabled her husband to go to Italy for the cure of
his serious illness, which she accomplished while her father was
dying. In the recital of what she went through, followed by
what we later learn about her forging her father's signature to
the promissory note addressed to Krogstad, we come to understand the extent of her willpower and her capacity for bold
action.

After Dr. Rank's entrance, immediately following, there is
also a hint of the repression of Nora's nature even in the most
trivial matters. Torvald has forbidden her to eat macaroons:
they are bad for her teeth. But Nora likes them and like a child
continues to pop them into her mouth on the sly. She offers
one to Dr. Rank. Suddenly she exclaims, "Really I am so happy.
There's only one thing I'd like to do now." And that little
thing? "I would simply love to say 'Damn!'" And as Torvald
enters she whispers, "Sh! Sh!" and hides her bag of macaroons.

One minute touch after another provides insights into the
deeper Nora concealed in the flighty and fibbing "doll." In a
later scene with Dr. Rank, who calls her a "little rogue," she
tells him, "I always think it's tremendous fun having you here."
To which Rank reacts: "I can't quite make you out. I've often
felt you liked being with me almost as much as being with
Helmer." "Well, you see," she explains, "There are people one

loves best—and yet there are others one would almost rather be *with*—When I was still at home, it was of course Papa whom I loved best. And yet, whenever I could, I used to slip down to the servants' quarters. I loved being with them. To begin with, they never preached at me, they always talked about such exciting things." There was freedom in the servants' quarters, as there is with Dr. Rank.

When William Archer, the English theater critic and one of Ibsen's earliest translators, saw two performances of *A Doll's House* in 1883, he wrote his brother that "Nora requires an actress of even more uncommon physical and mental gifts than I imagined." This is especially necessary to render Nora's emotional coming of age convincing as well as clear. If the actress is unaware of the hazard in the scene, her "change" of character may appear too sudden and arbitrary. The director must call her attention to it.

In *reading* the play one may easily overlook the play's internal logic. After Torvald has been apprised of Nora's forgery, he bursts forth with "Do you know what you have done?" Almost as vehemently she attempts to prevent him from doing what she expects him to do. She cries out, "I won't have you suffer for it. I won't have you take the blame." He charges her with "play-acting," and after locking the door, repeats, "Answer me. Do you understand it?"

As readers we rush on without a break, to hear her reply; the play's turning point. On the *stage*, between his challenge and her answer, "I'm beginning to understand for the first time," there should be a protracted pause, or more exactly a strongly stressed silent *action* should follow, to mark her recognition of his attitude. We must *see* the terrible wrench she suffers here and the gradually mounting realization of what she must do. All she says as he continues his diatribe is, "I see." Her speeches until the moment she explains her resolve to leave are equally terse.

Most audiences now are familiar with the play's final passages. Those who have succumbed to the faddish presumptions of our day take Nora's leaving her husband and children as a matter of course or a banality; others—perhaps a minority—still consider her act foolish, cruel or dissolute. For such people she has, as Torvald says, "no religion, no moral code, no sense of duty," and possibly no common sense! Early on she tells Krogstad she doesn't know what "society" is, and to Torvald she confesses she hasn't fathomed the meaning of "religion." As for her darling children, she agrees, as she had been indirectly warned, that she is no fit mother for them. What can she teach them if she herself knows so little?

To his not wholly unreasonable protestations she very candidly replies, "It's hard to answer you. Torvald, I don't think I know—all these things bewilder me . . . I'm going to try to learn!" "Remember," he tells her, "before all else you are a mother, a wife and a mother," to which she answers, "I believe that before all else, I am a human being . . . or at least I should try to become one."

It is imperative for the understanding of the final scene to know that it is not one in which Nora as the "new woman" is mouthing portentous verities. She is groping sadly in a maze of confused feeling toward a way of life and a destiny of which she is most uncertain. And Torvald, after his first vociferous expression of indignation, arguments and pleas, is as much at sea as she is. Does he not say in a manner almost as pathetic as funny, "Just you lean on me; let me guide you and advise you; I'm not a man for nothing! There's something very endearing about a woman's helplessness."

If there is anything sure and steadfast in Nora's final posture it is that she "must take steps to educate herself" if she is ever to reach any understanding of herself and "the things around her." She "must learn to stand alone." As we have discovered in the earlier plays, and as we shall be more emphatically advised in the later ones, "to stand alone" is not Ibsen's prescription solely for women but for men as well. Perhaps, let us say, to begin with, that standing alone is a most problematic matter; that it is not in every respect possible or even desirable is something that his future plays in their alternation will demonstrate. Ibsen's forbidding "dogmatism" is more apparent than real. We always find in it a shade of forbearance, a hesitancy and a muted pulsation that made William Archer stress, paraphrasing Ibsen's constant reminder, that "the play is not a mere realistic drama, but a poem, and that its poetry should be emphasized to give it full effect." Nora's telling Torvald that she no longer loves him is not a cold but a heartbroken declaration. The ebbing of love is always profoundly painful.

What readers, audiences, actors and directors must keep in mind for a fuller comprehension of *A Doll's House* is that all its characters are bent on maintaining or achieving *worthiness*, what the Germans call *Anständigkeit*. (The same is probably true in most of Ibsen's plays.) The catch is that "worthiness" is different for each person. For Torvald Helmer as with most of the people of his class, to be worthy is to be in the "right." "Your father's conduct was not impeccable," he admonishes Nora. "But mine is, and I trust it will remain so." Helmer wouldn't borrow even to save his life. His sense of "rightness" is dictated by society. Though he is not greedy, he is extremely conscious of money and fears debt like a plague. "How nice it is to feel secure," he says, "to look forward to a good income." He is a man of his word; he feels insulted when he is called "petty." He is not petty, only petty bourgeois. In that class, the appearance of virtue is almost as important as the possession of it. Hence blindness or hypocrisy.

For Nora worthiness means to *do* right by everyone. She protected her father, she tries to shield Helmer in every way, she cares for her children, she gets a job for Mrs. Linde, she is generous with money, she won't take advantage of Dr. Rank's love for her and borrow money from him (it would be a kind of deceit in regard to her husband), and when her image of herself and her domestic life is shattered she does what she feels she must to become a true person.

Worthiness, "like individualism," has two faces: one demands responsibility to others out of deep selfhood; the other sets social propriety up as the norm of conduct—and leads willy-nilly to corruption.

To complete the picture, in this light, we find Krogstad seeking worthiness in his effort to recover his lost position, his "good name," even though out of weakness and terror he proposes to undertake the most dubious means. He is a soft man driven to hardness; a man so middle-class that he doubts anyone ever takes extreme measures to repair damage to their honor or self-esteem. "People don't do that sort of thing."

Mrs. Linde's worthiness consists in a prudent and indefatigable struggle to keep alive by dutiful occupation. This entails aid to her parents, marriage for the sake of their safety, and help to the man who needs her. "One has to have someone to work for."

Dr. Rank is the most mature and, though stricken with a fatal disease, the most integrated person in the play. He seems by that very circumstance to stand apart from the rest. He faces death with regret and dignity. There is a bitter humor in him, not unlike stoicism, and a desire, since he cannot have the woman he loves (Nora), to do some good, to leave a memory of beneficence.

In a fleeting exchange between Dr. Rank and Mrs. Linde we get another glimpse of two sides of Ibsen's nature: his submerged compassion and his moral rigor. Speaking of Krogstad, whom the doctor looks upon as a depraved person, he remarks, "I don't know if this is true in your [Mrs. Linde's] part of the country, but there are men who make it a practice of playing about in other people's business, searching for persons of doubtful character—and having discovered their secret, place them in positions of trust, where they can keep an eye on them, and make use of them at will. Honest men—men of strong moral fiber—they leave out in the cold." Mrs. Linde's response to this is, "Perhaps the weaklings need more help." Rank shrugs this off: "That point of view is fast turning society into a clinic."

Let us turn back for a moment to detail some of the short rapid strokes by which Ibsen builds character and at the same time unfolds his story, which is the secret of his technical skill.

We learn through Helmer and Nora's conversation that her father spoiled her, treated her like a doll, and was himself something of a rake. Without a mother to discipline her, she became a carefree "eater of macaroons." The world at large from which she was thus shut off hardly existed for her; hence everyone but those in her immediate circle are only "strangers." She feels responsible only to intimates whom she loves and who love her. "Why should I care about your tiresome old 'society'?" she asks. She admires bravery: for example, Mrs. Linde's taking a long train trip at midnight. When she meets Mrs. Linde after their long separation she chirps away like a bird and then stops, self-abashed: "Here I am talking about nothing but myself." Seeing that her innocence is mistaken for ingrained frivolity she protests, "You all think I'm incapable of being serious." All this leads to the revelation of the drama in her life on which the play hangs.

Helmer is not a hard man. "I am not so harsh as to condemn a man irrevocably for one mistake," he says, referring to Krogstad. What he cannot control is his middle-class revulsion at being called by his first name in the presence of his subordinates at the bank. To him all excess of temperament is embarrassing and to be discouraged even in the dancing of the tarantella. It is the tarantella Nora feverishly rehearses to postpone the terrible moment when Torvald will learn through Krogstad's letter about her forgery. It is the prelude to the play's crisis.

The tarantella scene itself is a model of inspired "theater," placed as it is just before the surge to the play's climax. But then Ibsen sets a brake on the play's forward movement. Nora and Torvald return from a party, where she has aroused everyone with the hysterically induced brio of her dancing, and stimulated sexual desire in Torvald. (An acute touch.) Still, to his credit, he desists from carrying her off to bed when she reminds him that Rank has just notified her that he has sequestered himself forever in preparation for his imminent death. The stage is set for the fatal confrontation between Torvald and Nora.

In the mid-nineteenth century, the middle class held fast to an ideal of prettiness which it mistook for beauty. To use Nora's word, it made things "cozy." Everything nice and pretty became a property, something earned through right conduct. Nora's loveliness, especially appreciated when whetted by champagne, is for Helmer "mine, wholly and utterly mine, mine alone." When he learns that she has jeopardized the prospect

of a permanently easy life he does not speak of divorce nor of
putting her out of the house but contemplates various forms of
severe punishment.

"I'm saved, I'm saved" is his first reaction to Krogstad's with-
drawal of all threats to the Helmer well-being. Turning to
Nora, he adds, "You are too, of course." Yet we cannot judge
him wholly reprehensible; any deviation from the even flow of
his life's business is "a horrible dream" to him. Rid of his fear,
he recognizes that Nora must also have suffered; that her mis-
step was an act of devotion. He acknowledges her reproaches,
and what she has said of their marriage, he admits, contains "a
grain of truth."

He wants her to remain with him; he hopes to change, to
achieve the "miracle" of which she spoke, though he only dimly
comprehends its essence. Seen in this light, the play may be
thought of as a plea for men's as much as women's liberation.
We may sentimentally hope that Nora and Torvald may some-
time in the future mend their marriage, but Ibsen certainly does
not encourage the supposition.

The play's technical virtuosity—it includes the preservation
of the classic unities of time and place—was never again to be
surpassed in Ibsen's works, except by *Hedda Gabler*. Its theatrical skill together with its superbly wrought characterizations
have made *A Doll's House* a play in which actors are eager to
test themselves and to which audiences look forward to see how
the challenge is met.

The Pillars of Society and even *A Doll's House* may be said
to end on an "upbeat." Not so *Ghosts*, the domestic tragedy,
written in 1881 in Sorrento. It offers little alleviation in its progression toward disaster, though nearly all its characters are
motivated by a desire to ameliorate their situation.

It is Ibsen's most astringent play. In the introduction to his
translation of *The Pillars of Society*, James McFarlane speaks
of these plays as "a succession of curses." But only *Ghosts* fits
the description. Society bears the brunt of the condemnation.
Though today we may be apt to say the condemnation refers
chiefly to the society of Ibsen's time because its terminology

is "dated," a closer view should convince us that the core of Ibsen's plaints are entirely relevant. The *Iliad* is valued, apart from other considerations, as a depiction of war's senseless horrors even though wars are no longer fought with yesteryear's weapons nor over the abduction of a beautiful woman.

As Ibsen cursed society, so society returned the compliment. The second paragraph of this book cites the abuse poured on the 1891 private performance of *Ghosts* in London. It was not until 1889 that Otto Brahm produced it in his Freie Bühne (Free Theater) in Berlin, a landmark in German theatrical history. It opened the way to the development of the modern realistic drama there through such men as Gerhart Hauphtmann and others. The reaction in Norway was even more violent than it was to be in England. The liberals as well as the conservative press attacked it. It was not produced there in any leading theater till 1900.

What explains these scandals? Probably the indirect but unmistakable allusion to the disease with which Oswald Alving is afflicted: syphilis. Still more appalling may have been the fact that Mrs. Alving, Oswald's mother, under special duress, is momentarily willing to countenance the possibility of her son's unknowingly marrying his half-sister. When Pastor Manders explodes with "How could you condone so abominable, so unheard of . . . ?" Mrs. Alving, with apparent calm, replies, "Unheard of you say? Why not face the truth, Manders. You know there are dozens of married couples out here in the country [a small town in the west of Norway] who are related in the same way?" But such affronts to the respectability of the period were only the red flags of insult; they were not of their essence.

For many, even to some extent today, *Ghosts* is about heredity and "the sins of the fathers." But it is with *society's* sin the play deals. Still, none of this suffices to isolate the objective of Ibsen's probing nor the scope of the play's meaning.

True, medicine can now cure hereditary syphilis, and the books Mrs. Alving had begun reading while her son Oswald was living and painting in Paris, books (Zola et al.) Pastor Mander's disapproves of though he has not read them, are no longer considered subversive or advanced. These are only the insignia of a particular epoch; we miss the play's vital point if we stop to raise objections to it on these grounds.

The play's title is frequently misconstrued. When Mrs. Alving hears Oswald making advances to Regine just as his father many years ago had done to her mother ("and had his way with her") she cries "Ghosts!" as if the event were being reenacted. But the Alving household is haunted, to quote Mrs. Alving, "not only by the things we inherit from our parents—but by the ghosts of innumerable old prejudices and beliefs—half-forgotten cruelties and betrayals—we may not even be aware of them— but they're there just the same—and we can't get rid of them. The whole world is haunted by these ghosts of the dead past . . . "

Mrs. Alving wanted to leave her idle and wanton husband after she became aware of his character. She ran off to seek refuge with the man she loved, Pastor Manders. Though he may have shared her feelings, he triumphed over his own instinct and did his duty as a pastor, insisting that she fulfill her marital obligations. Unlike Nora, and with much more provocation, she did not slam the door! The consequence was the inherited ailment of which Oswald became the victim. For despite all the "bohemianism" of the artistic circles in Paris he has led an exemplary life there.

Mrs. Alving's sacrifice to her duty as conceived by the right-thinking citizens of her day, and still so conceived in many quarters, availed her and her son nothing but misfortune. She tried to save him from knowledge of his father's nature by sending him abroad at an early age. So that her boy might always hold his father in high esteem she used his bequest to build an orphanage in his name. Because of Pastor Manders absent-mindedness at a prayer meeting just before its dedication, the orphanage burns down.

Report of the orphanage's destruction by fire opens the play's last act, and there is something vindictive in its placement there. Though Ibsen disclaimed ever injecting any personal opinions into his plays (which is of course not at all true), we know that Ibsen wished us to see the conflagration as the inevitable and desirable destruction of all institutions based on falsity and deceit. He was, however, too crafty an artist to have the orphanage fire function solely as a symbol. Ironically enough, the Pastor had objected to its being insured in fear that such a precaution be criticized in the case of a religious institution. But there is a further irony in Ibsen's use of the event. Of this more later. As for Ibsen's claims to impersonality in the expression of his own opinions in his plays, we need only recall Henry James' epigram: a writer, he said, must absolutely avoid putting himself into his work but he can't possibly keep himself out.

The bare schema I have traced of *Ghosts* and what evidence thus far has been adduced as to its theme provide only a meager sense of the extent to which Ibsen has amplified and enriched it. The logic of its compact structure makes it extremely difficult to detach any one element from the rest. There is, for example, nothing more masterly than the exposition which opens the first act. Besides its service as characterization, it lays the basis for the play's entire plot line.

The "sins of the father" applied as an abbreviation for the play's theme is literally a misnomer: it is Mrs. Alving, the mother, who committed the initial sin. To hush the scandal of her husband's affair with the housemaid and the imminent birth of their child (Regine), Mrs. Alving gave three hundred dollars to the rascally carpenter Engstrand to marry the "fallen woman." The marriage ceremony was performed by Pastor Manders, who as usual was unaware of the circumstances which led to the event. On hearing them explained to him, Manders, forever gullible, and forever in a state of shock, exclaims, "The immorality of such a marriage—and for money too!" This follows:

MANDERS: It's almost unbelievable—for a paltry three hundred dollars—consenting to marry a loose woman.

MRS. ALVING: What about me? Didn't I marry a "loose man"? Was Alving any better when he married me than the girl Johanna [the seduced maid] when she married Engstrand?

MANDERS: But good heaven—the two cases are entirely different—

MRS. ALVING: Perhaps not so utterly different, after all. There was
               a colossal difference in the price—a paltry three hun-
               dred dollars against a large fortune.

MANDERS: But there *can* be no comparison in this instance! Your
               decision was based on the advice of relations and
               friends—as well as on the promptings of your heart.

MRS. ALVING: My heart, as you call it, was involved elsewhere at
               the time—as I thought you knew.

MANDERS: Had I known any such thing, I should not have been
               a constant visitor in your husband's house.

MRS. ALVING: One thing is certain; I never consulted my own feel-
               ings in the matter.

MANDERS: Perhaps not—but you consulted your mother—your
               two aunts—all those nearest to you—as was only right.

MRS. ALVING: Yes—those three! They were the ones that settled the
               whole business for me . . . They pointed out, in the
               most forceful terms, that it would be nothing short of
               folly to refuse an offer of such magnificence!
               . . . .

MANDERS: The fact remains, that your marriage in every way
               conformed to the strictest codes of law and order.

MRS. ALVING: All this talk about law and order!—I often think all
               the suffering in the world is due to that.

She goes on to say that she will no longer be bound by "hypo-
critical conventions . . . I must work my way to freedom."

The scene establishes the fact that Mrs. Alving yielded to
the almost ritual marriage of convenience for money—a note
of alarm recurrent in the Ibsen canon—and ends with its imperative that one must countervail such conventions or "ideals"
and duties.

Ibsen does not content himself with homilies. Mrs. Alving
blames herself for creating illusions in Oswald's mind regarding
his father. She should have told him the whole truth and calls
herself a coward for not having done so. Later on Hedda Gabler
will also call herself a coward, for dissimilar but related reasons.

MANDERS: How can you call yourself a coward for doing what
               was merely your duty! Have you forgotten that a
               child should love and honor his father and mother?

MRS. ALVING: Don't lets talk in generalities! Let us ask: Should Os-
               wald love and honor Captain Alving?
MANDERS: You're his mother—how could you find it in your heart
               to shatter his ideals?
MRS. ALVING: Oh—ideals, ideals! What about the Truth?

Society, if you will, may be held to be the "villain" of the
piece, but none of its characters are. Though he is society's
spokesman, Manders is more comic a figure than anything else.
Engstrand is a wretched gnome, the grotesque bottom of the
social barrel. The play's unseen personage, Captain Alving, takes
on a new aspect in the light of Mrs. Alving's expanding consciousness. When Oswald first appears, Manders is struck by
his resemblance to his father. What this signifies is not at all
what we suppose it does.

"You should have known your father when he was a young
lieutenant," Mrs. Alving tells Oswald. "He was filled with that
joy of life [of which Oswald had spoken]. He seemed to radiate
light and warmth—he was filled with a joyous, turbulent vitality . . . And this boy—he was like a boy then—was cooped
up in the drab little provincial town, which could offer him
no real joy—only dissatisfaction. He had no real aim in life—
no work that could stimulate his mind or feed his spirit—
nothing but a dull, petty routine job. He found no one here
who understood that pure joy of life that was in him . . . "

Even Regine herself, Alving's illegitimate daughter, though
something of a slut, has inherited some of that joy of life, as
did Oswald, her half-brother.

In this sketch of Captain Alving—we find some of his traits
in at least one other Ibsen play—there is a reminder of Ibsen's
letters to his mother-in-law written in 1887: "Life there [Nor-
way] as it presents itself to me now, has something indescrib-
ably wearisome about it, it worries the soul out of me, wearies
the strength out of one's will. That is the cursed thing about
small surroundings, they make the soul small." Ibsen once considered giving up his Norwegian citizenship.

When Oswald speaks of the joy of life he could never have
found at home, the expression of which is in the light and sun-

shine of glowing happy faces of his Paris paintings, we realize
it is not frivolity he speaks of but the joy of work. "They're
really the same thing, you know." For Oswald the joy of work
is the free exercise of his truest self, an affirmation of life, the
energy of the spirit. Its symbol is the sun, that sun which ex-
hilarated Ibsen on his arrival in Italy, the sun Oswald asks to
be given as he sinks into insensibility in the play's final scene.
That sun is also Ibsen's ideal whose light is shut off by all that
Manders preaches—"artificial and dead"—of which Norwegian
society was for Ibsen the exemplar and which he came to equate
with society in general, the state everywhere.

The crippled Engstrand represents the *reductio ad absurdum*
of the society or state the artist and the revolutionary both detest.
He is determined to get ahead by hook or by crook. He horn-
swoggles and virtually blackmails Manders (still another pillar of
society) into sponsoring his project to set up a seamen's house, a
hostel for lonely sailors, in a word, a brothel. The final irony is
that for Manders' sake Engstrand speaks of it as a place dedicated
to the good of the community. It is to be named Captain Alving's
Haven. Thus the top and the bottom of the social heap conclude
a pact, indeed they are conjoined. Will the planned haven, to
be sanctified by Manders, also burn down?

In his advice to actors, Bernard Shaw once said that all roles,
including those considered unsympathetic or ludicrous, should
be played as if each of the impersonated characters was justified
in everything he or she does.

A sound tenet, it is especially helpful in producing Ibsen. It
would reduce much of the grim solemnity and the hortatory
timbre which render so many of Ibsen's performances morose
and heavily didactic.

To treat *Ghosts* with the Shavian prescription in mind we
must view all its characters as people motivated by a positive
aim: they all want to advance to a more salutary state of mind
or condition.

Mrs. Alving, following the way of her world, entered into a
marriage recommended by her family and its cohorts. Then,
following her instinct, she turned to the man she loved. He,
the pastor, led his sheep back to the path of righteousness, as

fashioned by social tradition. Having recognized her error, Mrs. Alving resolves to live her life honestly, though her past failures make the avoidance of tragedy impossible.

She has a sense of humor. She understands the absurdity of Manders' character and the mess he constantly creates with his purblind adherence to law and order. Her trials have not weakened her but on the contrary made her a confident person. She has achieved a new integrity. It has led to work, to self-cultivation, to efficiency. Her life, which has been "one long fight," gives her strength and dignity. She has battled the "ghosts" and, though defeated, she must never communicate a sense of being depressed.

Oswald must not strike us, from the very beginning, as a doomed being. He is a spirited person, not without humor, and his occasional excitability is part of his natural temperament, not a symptom of disease. His feeling for Regine is not lascivious, but an almost playful manifestation of the health which should normally be his. Regine's coy resistance makes him laugh. There is as much aesthetic as erotic enthusiasm in his exclamation "she is wonderful to look at." He wants to surround himself with beautiful people, to avoid gloom. The last words he addresses to his mother before his collapse are: "We'll live together as long as we can." Oswald has striven and has for a long time succeeded in leading a sane life. But he cannot reap its fruits because he is the heir of corruption.

Manders wants to keep everything on an even keel. His watchword is "caution." He is an innocent, "a great big baby." He should be cast by a handsome actor. For all his stuffy decorum he appreciates Regine's figure. He really knows very little about the society in which he lives. He believes, for instance, that "proper" people live according to the morality they profess. There is something charmingly helpless about him when, after the fire at the orphanage, he admits, "I don't feel competent to deal with a crisis of this sort." In fact, he cannot deal with any trouble, any real problem. He fears public opinion, especially as conveyed by the press. He is sensitive to economic values, but confronted by any unpleasantness his response is "I don't understand." Mrs. Alving thinks he does, but he doesn't, he

can't. And for all his sincere respectability he is virtually compelled to yield to Engstrand's blackmail.

Wily and slippery, Engstrand is forever calculating for his
advantage. "Everything may come in handy," even, he specu-
lates, Regine's smattering of French if she were to serve as
hostess in his seamen's refuge. Spiritually and physically, he
squints. He employs a sanctimonious vocabulary as a useful
shield and instrument in slipping in among the right-thinking
and the rich. "Temptations are manifold in this world" is not
merely an indication of his hypocrisy but a serious conviction.
He too wants to escape the "godforsaken hole," and his every
word and deed is designed to accomplish that purpose.

Regine wants "to better herself" as best she may. In the
hope of accompanying Oswald abroad she has tried to teach
herself French. She is sturdy, down-to-earth, unhesitantly "go-
ahead." She is not stupid. If she can't satisfy her ambition by
taking the high road she will take the low.

Emphasis here on the performance "problems" connected with
various of the play's roles is chiefly intended to call attention to
an aspect of the plays of the middle period which all too often
escapes notice. No matter how grave or "morbid" the subject
may be—as in *Ghosts*—they still possess a compact force, almost
a buoyancy, a kind of hope against hope. It is that of a person
battered, baffled and all but destroyed who still moves with a
certain assurance as though destined to victory. Under their
fierce control, there is in these plays a heat and a beat, allaying
the suspicion of an innate or a willful pessimism. In the later
plays there is a change of tone, a different music, darker and
more profound. But between *The Pillars of Society* (1877) and
The Wild Duck (1884), let us arbitrarily say, there is a boldness, vigor, and together with the tightlipped severity, a certain smile.

8

Yay and Nay

An Enemy of the People, Ibsen's most militant play, is a comedy. Because of its headlong drive it is not often conceived or acted in that vein. It is customary to regard it as Ibsen's irate response to the hostility aroused by *Ghosts* and the obloquy it incurred. (As usual, there were exceptions: Brandes and others.) But Ibsen had begun preparations for writing *An Enemy* before he turned to work on *Ghosts*. This should cause no surprise, since the gist of the play—as "ideology" or "message"—had ripened in Ibsen's mind long before he found the means for its dramatization. Two of the play's most salient lines are to be found in a letter in 1872, nine years before the play appeared. One is "the minority is always right," the other is "the strongest man in the world is the man who stands alone." (Strange, but in *Brand*, we find the hero saying, "I am tired of fighting alone.")

The plot was based on an incident which had been reported to Ibsen. In the 1830s, a German doctor warned the people at a spa that an outbreak of cholera had occurred there. The "sea-

Note: All the citations from *An Enemy of the People* in this chapter are from Eva Le Gallienne's translation; those from *The Wild Duck* are from the translation in the Oxford University Press edition.

[127]

son" at the resort was ruined: the townsfolk stoned the doctor's house and he had to flee. There was also a case in Norway of a chemist who had denounced the Christiana Steam Kitchens for neglect of the poor. When he attempted to read a prepared speech repeating his earlier attack the chairman tried to prevent him from speaking and the audience forced him to withdraw, very much as Dr. Stockmann does in the fourth act of the play.

The material and Ibsen's preliminary work is probably one reason why he was able to finish the play more rapidly than any of his others. Its story line is the most straightforward in all his work. The locale is a coastal town in southern Norway. Very few of Ibsen's plays are set in the capital.

Dr. Stockmann's plans for establishing town Baths had been enthusiastically received by his brother Peter, the mayor, and put into effect by him. On investigating the number of deaths by typhoid which had occurred among people who had used the new facility, Dr. Stockmann discovers that its waters are contaminated by a leak from a nearby tannery, the proprietor of which is his own father-in-law. He discloses his findings to newspaper people and to his brother, who besides being the mayor is also chairman of the board in charge of the Baths.

The liberal paper eagerly pounces on the story in order to discredit the Mayor and the party in power. The Mayor points out that to repair the damage at the Baths, which had become a health resort for out-of-town visitors, would cost an enormous sum that would have to be raised by taxing the town residents and in any case would require two years' time. To close the Baths down would ruin the community; the Mayor insists they must remain open.

When *The People's Monitor*, the liberal journal, retracts its offer to publish Dr. Stockmann's disclosures, he finds that its printer, Aslaksen, who is also head of the Homeowners' Association, will not set up the type as a pamphlet even if the doctor pays for it. Stockmann calls a meeting to state his case. Before he is allowed to speak, the Mayor as well as the editors of *The Monitor* and its printer as the chairman at the meeting prejudice the audience by emphasizing the cost to the taxpayers if Stockmann's proposal is accepted. Besides, they claim adjustments at the Baths can be made without jeopardy to anyone's health. The crowd is won over. Infuriated, Stockmann now shifts his attack on the authorities to the citizens themselves. "The compact majority is always wrong," he shouts. They vote him "an enemy of the people" and threaten him with violence.

Stones are thrown through the windows of his house; he is dismissed from his post at the Baths; most of his patients will not dare consult him now; his landlord will not allow him to remain in his residence; his schoolteacher daughter, Petra, is asked to resign; his two young sons are dismissed from school; the seaman who obtained permission to use the hall where the meeting was held is deprived of his captaincy on the boat on which he planned to take Stockmann and his family to America. But instead of turning tail, Stockmann resolves not to leave the country. He will live and practice among the poor and persist in his fight. For he has made his momentous discovery, "the strongest man in the world is the man who stands alone."

Analogies with contemporary events are obvious: they are readily discernible in controversies over ecological pollution, over arms control and yesteryear's Watergate scandal. Yet the play for all its attacks on vested interests, politicians and political parties, the press (liberal or otherwise), is not "propaganda." An early and the most prestigious of Russian Marxists, Georgi Plekhanov (1856–1918), was severely critical of the play because Stockmann demands no fundamental change in the social structure, the "system." Considered in this light, Stockmann is, as Ibsen was often thought to be, both an anarchist and an aristocrat. But to apply such criteria to Stockmann denatures the quality of the play. We must see him as Ibsen portrays him.

Ibsen called Stockmann a "muddlehead." We note a charming touch of auctorial conceit in him when he responds to the editor's praise of his article on the Baths as an "absolute masterpiece" with "Yes, isn't it?" There is much of the absent-minded professor about him: he does not even remember his housemaid's name. He is extraordinarily credulous—in fact, an innocent. He has not lived in the big world, but in isolation "up north" away from the traffic of the cities and from his native town. (The same is true of that other idealist, Gregers Werle, in *The Wild*

Duck.) Stockmann does not realize that his discovery may have any other consequence that the closing of the Baths for a limited time. Hence his childish delight at his scientific acumen and pride in contributing to public welfare. He feels flattered and shy at the prospect of having banquets and parades planned to honor him for his service to the community.

He foresees no impediment to his future progress. Of sanguine disposition and good digestion, he is lavishly hospitable and immensely pleased by his well-supplied table. He is also heedless of costs. To his dyspeptic brother, who boasts of his own dietetic abstemiousness and admonishes him for his extravagance, he defends himself by commenting that "Katrine [Mrs. Stockmann] says I earn almost as much as we spend." The stage direction on Stockmann's first entrance reads that he "is heard laughing; he shouts in a loud voice."

His ebullience gives rise to clowning. When he spies his brother hiding from him in the editorial office of *The Monitor*, he dons the mayoral hat, seizes the Mayor's stick, salutes military fashion and striding up and down booms, "Show some respect, Peter, if you please. I'm in authority now . . . You may be chief of police, but I'm the Mayor. I'm the king of the whole town." When the *Monitor*'s editors and printer attempt to bribe Stockmann into making a shady deal, he grabs his umbrella and lays about with it: "Out of the window with you. Jump, I tell you—and be quick about it."

His defiant confidence at the close of the play is the stern side of the naive confidence he displays at the beginning. We are impressed and heartened at the courage of his last stand, but we hardly lose sight of the innocence within the staunch affirmation. The little man has grown big. But as Ibsen's Stockmann he remains little and lovable. A gravely thundering or "heroic" Stockmann provokes personal and intellectual skepticism; we can embrace Stockmann who replies to the Mayor's "Are you a raving lunatic?" with "Yes, I am." He is the man who, finding a hole torn in his trousers during the fracas at the meeting, can quip, "You should never wear your best trousers when you go out to fight for truth and freedom."

Though the words and behavior of the forces pitted against

Stockmann are abhorrent, they are almost as comically drawn as are the functionaries in Gogol's *The Inspector General*. For instance, take tight-fisted Stockmann's father-in-law, Morten Kiil, who owns the tannery, the source of infection at the Baths. He is hilariously incredulous of the notion that the Bath's water pipes are full of "little animals" ("infusoria" is Stockmann's term): such things don't exist. Chuckling maliciously, he supposes Stockmann is playing "monkey tricks" on the Mayor, whom Kiil detests for having hounded him out of the Town Council. "If you can put this over on the Mayor and his cronies, so help me, I'll give a *hundred* crowns to charity." On Stockmann's tart "Very handsome of you," Kiil goes on, "Mind you I've little enough to spare. But just you put this over, and, next Christmas, I'll give *fifty* crowns to charity."

Then there is the printer, Aslaksen, of the same name as the corresponding character in *The League of Youth*. (A Stensgaard, the name of the scoundrelly "liberal" in that play, and a Roerlund, the name of the stuffy schoolmaster in *The Pillars of Society*, are also mentioned in *An Enemy*—an indication of the similarity of the various communities in these plays.) Aslaksen, chairman of the meeting which branded Stockmann "an enemy of the people," acknowledges himself as a man of "discreet moderation and of moderate discretion." "Shout," he advises, "shout with moderation." It is a virtue, he explains, from which citizens reap the highest benefits. He also delivers himself of this gem: "A politician must never be too certain of anything."

Billing, the *Monitor*'s associate editor, is a "yes-man" to every winner, and Hovstad, its editor-in-chief, is a sneaky opportunist who, when a bold step is to be taken, asks, "You think that can be done?" There's also a drunk who keeps turning up and is turned out several times at the Stockmann hearing: he hasn't the faintest idea what the rumpus is all about, but is believed to be the only one who favors Stockmann. He typifies the kind of idiocy which invariably adds a farcical note to all such gatherings.

Beside his indifference to the play's humor and to its merits as a dramatic composition, Plekhanov, in calling for a social-political program in *An Enemy of the People*, failed to perceive its wider connotations. The play's fundamental conflict is Stockmann's opposition to his brother's credo: "The individual must subordinate himself to Society as a whole or more precisely to those authorities responsible for the well-being of that Society." When Stockmann begins to see how society really functions his dissension over the sewers and the waterworks becomes a minor issue. It becomes "a question of cleaning the whole community." He has moved on to "the discovery that all our resources are polluted and that our whole civic community is built on a cesspool of lies." Reduced to the most simplistic terms his motto would be: "Don't conform!"

Stockmann stiffens his attack with additional sideswipes. Political parties are "a sausage machine . . . All the brains are ground up together and reduced to hash; and that's why the world is filled with a lot of brainless empty headed numbskulls." For a while he plans to escape from the party bosses by self-exile to America. "Not that the so-called Far West is apt to be much better. I daresay enlightened public opinion, the solid majority and all that sort of trash is just as rampant there—but at least it is on a larger scale; they may kill a man, but they don't put him to slow torture; they don't clamp a free soul into a straitjacket. And, at a pinch, there's room to get away." This was in 1882.

The press had long been one of Ibsen's particular bugbears. Stockmann's daughter, Petra, refuses to translate a short story for the *Monitor* because, she tells its editor, Hovstad, it runs contrary to everything she believes in. "It's all about a supernatural power that's supposed to watch over all the so-called good people, and how everything is for the best and how the wicked people get punished in the end." To which Hovstad replies, "You're absolutely right, of course. But an editor cannot always do what he wants. After all, politics is the most important thing in life—at least, for a newspaper it is. And if I want to win people over to a certain liberal and progressive idea, it's no good scaring them off. If they find a nice normal story like this on the back pages of the paper, they are much more ready to accept what we print on the front page—it gives them a sort of feeling of security."

The play's climactic and most controversial scene—already cited—is the one in which Stockmann (and no doubt Ibsen) expresses himself with utmost vehemence in the wongheaded "The majority is never right." Stockmann shouts, "It's the fools that form the overwhelming majority. The majority has the power, but right is on the side of people like me—of the few—of the individuals. The minority is always right." At this Hovstad heckles, "Ha! Ha! Ha! Dr. Stockmann has turned aristocrat." It would seem so when Stockmann continues, "The public is only the raw material from which a people is made." And even more heatedly he thunders on, "A community based on lies and corruption deserves to be destroyed! The poison will spread throughout the country and eventually the whole country will deserve to be destroyed; and should it ever come to that, I'd say from the bottom of my heart, let it be destroyed, and let all its people perish." We understand Hovstad's taunting "Aha! Now he's a revolutionary." To which Stockmann fires back, "Yes, by Heaven, I am."

To the long pseudo-scientific harangue in which Stockmann defends his "aristocracy," differentiating between carefully bred canines and "mongrels," we should be cautious about crying "elitism." Isn't it true that the great innovators or revolutionaries of all times in science, politics and religion have nearly always been a minority? It is they who foment the aspirations and needs of the masses, who, when hard pressed by material circumstances, finally effect the drastic changes the seers and saints have called for—sometimes, unfortunately, in travesties. As someone in *Huckleberry Finn* puts it, "H'aint we got all the fools in town on our side; and ain't that a big enough majority in any town?"

Defeat of the true leaders is temporary; victory is often attained after years of arduous struggle. Stockmann is an optimist to the end. It is the young as he envisages them through his children, particularly in his brass-tacks daughter Petra, who says, "At home we're told to hold our tongue; and at school we teach the children lies," but it is she who will win the day (perhaps only for a day) for the Stockmanns of the world.

The cool and classic Paul Valéry once wrote: "Extremists give the world values; average men make it endure; the revolutionaries provide worth, the moderates stability." Stockmann is or becomes as fanatic as Ibsen in this play appears to be. But the world must include such fanatics if our societies are not to stultify and wither into nonentity.

It has been said that after *An Enemy of the People* Ibsen began to waver in his social belligerence. But we cannot be too sure of this. To the accusation that he was soon to retreat from positions previously held, he might have declared with Walt Whitman, "Do I contradict myself? Very well. I contradict myself."

There are astonishing differences of opinion as to which Ibsen play is the "greatest." For Haldvan Koht it is *The Wild Duck.* Others have been captious on this score, particularly at the time of its publication: 1884. Michael Meyer judges *Little Eyolf* to be Ibsen's best; others rate *The Master Builder* highest. James Joyce, at nineteen, ranked *When We Dead Awaken* with the greatest of the author's work, "if indeed not the greatest"; John Gassner thought it "feeble." I myself am not inclined to classify plays of unquestionable excellence in strict order of merit. Such judgments tend to hypostatize absolutes. Works of art are "human"; they change as we (and the times) change. Apart from the pleasures we take in them, what is most important is to understand what they betoken. In addition we must always remember that there is no "last word" in the interpretation of any work of art. Each one is susceptible to an almost infinite number of interpretations—as long as we do not depart too far from the artistic material and substance of the work under consideration.

My own appreciation of *The Wild Duck* has varied at different intervals of reading. It still seems to me less well contrived and, in some minor matters, ill contrived compared with other of the modern master's works. I find the first-act exposition with the guests at the elder Werle's house somewhat stiff and awk-

ward.* His visit in the third act to the home of the maidservant
he seduced, Gina Ekdal, where she lives with her husband,
Hjalmar and his presumably illegitimate daughter, Hedwig,
strikes me as strained. I am also a little troubled by Mrs. Sörby's
coming to the Ekdal's place, though the scene itself makes
a striking point. And then, too, the pistol shot which puts
an end to Hedwig's life, following the note of exultant self-
congratulation Gregers Werle has just laughingly shouted, seems
too stagily pat.

Such demurrers, even if valid, are trivial in view of the play's
extraordinary fascination. Were it not for the suicide of its
most touching character and the shadow which hovers in the
atmosphere throughout, the play might be designated a comedy
on the verge of farce. Its mood is a shadow of troubled questioning, perhaps even of despair at the near impossibility of
dispelling its doubt at answering its own question. It has sometimes occurred to me that a Russian proverb which Alexander
Ostrovsky used as a title for one of his plays, *Truth Is Good
but Happiness Is Better*, might serve as a helpful indication of
Ibsen's theme if not exactly his thesis here. (And I have also
wondered if O'Neill's *The Iceman Cometh* does not owe something to *The Wild Duck*.)

The doubt and the questions do not rise so much in the mind
or heart of the play's characters as in that of the author himself. The play marks a turning point in Ibsen's development.
I do not refer to his increasing resort to "symbolism" but to an
element of self-rebuttal which becomes steadily more evident in
his later plays. If *The Wild Duck* does not negate the affirmations of *An Enemy of the People*, it surely dampens them with
a pained "maybe." The play's humor, which at times swells to
the positively hilarious, is an aspect of its dubiety.

Gregers Werle has come to believe that it is his mission to
tell people "rock bottom" truth about themselves and that by
doing so he will liberate or at least lighten the burden of those
who dwell in error. His intellectual antagonist, the benevolent
cynic Relling, a doctor who has gone to seed, challenges Gregers
with "take away the life-lie from the average man and straight

* I now believe I am wrong about this! H.C.

away you take away his happiness." The life-lie is the illusion which every person must cling to in order to attain a modicum of self-assurance.

Hjalmar Ekdal, Gregers' boyhood friend, is an "average man." Gregers is convinced that Hjalmar, once a genial, handsome and possibly superior youth, has been reduced to a shabby, futile existence by Gregers' father, Haakon Werle. The elder Werle married Hjalmar off to his former maid, Gina. Werle senior had chosen Hjalmar to compensate for his guilt in also having helped ruin his erstwhile business partner, Hjalmar's father, Old Ekdal. Hjalmar did not know or even suspect that Gina had ever been Werle's mistress. On being enlightened on the subject by Gregers, Hjalmar is plagued by doubt as to whether Hedwig, his fifteen-year-old daughter, who adores him and of whom he is most fond, is really his child. When Hjalmar asks Gina directly, "Is Hedwig mine . . . or . . . " she answers with gruff honesty: "I don't know."

This shatters the peace Hjalmar made with his life. He treats Hedwig unfeelingly and prepares to leave his home, which indirectly precipitates Hedwig's suicide. Gregers had hoped— was virtually certain—that by telling Hjalmar the truth about his marriage—that the elder Werle had seduced Gina and then set Hjalmar up in business as a photographer—he would free Hjalmar from the falsity of his position and thus render him the mate in a true marriage, a marriage without the taint of any deceit. But the truth here wreaks havoc.

We are by no means consoled at the play's dismal and finally ironic conclusion by the rationalization that it only applies to the average man. It cannot escape our notice that it is not Hjalmar alone who is "average" but that humankind generally is composed of the same stuff.

What about the "soothsayer" Gregers himself? He hates his father for his infidelity to the delicately fibered mother he resembles and loved. His own sensibility is cruelly shocked by Werle's dishonest treatment of his former associate, Old Ekdal, once an army officer who was sent to prison for an illegal business transaction with which Werle was in collusion. Gregers left home on that account and took a job in one of his father's mines in the remote forest region in the north. That his father behaved with women as men unloved by their wives often do does not excuse him in his son's eyes. The businessman's defense for not sharing in a common blame with his partner, that it is pragmatically justified if he can get away with it, strikes Gregers as unutterably base. Gregers is an impure and threadbare Brand.

In his isolation in the North Country, Gregers went about badgering people about "the claims of the ideal." Depressed that he himself was living a drab, ineffectual existence, he had once contemplated suicide. (So, it seems, had Ibsen.) Abjuring this, he began to seek a way of life to make up for his own evasion of responsibility. The quest for a righteous path becomes what Stanislavsky-oriented theater people call the "spine" or main action of Gregers behavior.

That he believed informing Hjalmar of the role Werle senior played in his marriage to Gina was part of his mission does not show a passion for justice or devoted friendship, but as he himself confesses, "a sick conscience" and a not wholly unconscious wish to avenge himself on his father. Gregers has hardly done more to face his own motivation than to renounce the privileges offered him by his father's status as a successful industrialist.

Still we cannot content ourselves with so bare an explanation of Gregers' nature. Since his mother's death and his departure from home, this unmistakable neurotic has in every practical way become a clumsy oaf. He can't light the fire in the stove of his room without making a mess. In other respects as well we recognize him as an unhappy eccentric, an object of derision. What has made him so? He suffers from what Relling calls a national disease, variously translated as "an acute case of inflamed scruples" or a "surfeit of self-righteousness."

Max von Sydow, who played Gregers in Ingmar Bergman's admirable production of the play, exposed the man's ungainliness, his self-neglect in dress, and above all, his gullibility, the innocence but foolishness characteristic of many "serious" people.

The Ekdal household is the refuge of the wounded, submerged, as it were, at sea-bottom. The image occurs to Gregers when he hears of the wild duck which Old Ekdal keeps in the loft attached to the apartment. The bird, Old Ekdal explains, had been shot by Werle senior but it had only been winged. "Then she dived right down to the bottom . . . as deep as they can get . . . hold on with their beaks to the weeds and stuff and all the other mess you find there. They never come up again." The duck was given to one of Werle's servants, who passed it on to the Ekdals. Now it thrives and grows fat: " . . . it's forgotten what real life is like; it has become the prize of the menagerie rabbits, hens and other fowl" in which Old Ekdal practices make-believe hunting in memory of better times. The duck has become Hedwig's special pet.

That is the analogy with the Ekdals, Gregers perceives. His father maimed the duck, now roosted in its basket in the depths of the sea, just as Old Ekdal, Hjalmar and Hedwig have been isolated and cut off from a normal life and the real world.

When Gregers learns that Hedwig is slowly going blind, like his own father, the vicious circle is complete: he embarks on his mission—to redeem Hjalmar's life. But perhaps, as has been suggested, his action is chiefly a desire to avenge his father's duplicity. The result is the disaster which leads to Hedwig's death—without making Hjalmar a wiser or a stronger man. Gregers has caused as much of a tragic mess in this as in trying to light the fire in the stove in his room he created a comic one.

The sincere zealot is often betrayed by sentimentality. Gregers totally misreads Hjalmar's nature. The "spine" of Hjalmar's character, again to use the Stanislavsky term, is his wish to take the easiest path, the least-troubled one, the softest way of living. He constantly lies to himself and to others, not out of malice but from self-ignorance. Ibsen has made Hjalmar the funniest example or archetype of self-delusion and self-indulgence in modern dramatic literature. Like the duck, he has accommodated himself and grown fat by bedding himself down in the comfort of illusion and unreality. Most of his job as a photographer is done by hard-working Gina and Hedwig. Though he knows Hedwig to be threatened by blindness, he allows her to take over duties which strain her eyes: he much prefers to go "hunting" in the loft.

He is able to recite other people's poems and play the flute a little with a tearful expression. He has neither talent nor ambition. His moments of grief are brief; all genuine feeling in him is related to his own well-being. He boasts of virtues he conspicuously lacks. And, "lucky" fellow, everyone aids and abets him in his torpor. He flops about like a big, smiling, vain and selfish child. He forgets to bring Hedwig the presents he promised her, some little token from the elegant party he attended at old Werle's house; instead he shows her the menu of the dinner served there and offers to describe the various items of the feast. Orphaned on the distaff side when he was very young, and brought up by two hysterical maiden aunts, he requires constant mothering. He complains of the food bills, yet he drinks beer and stuffs himself with thickly buttered bread and sandwiches even as he swears that sorrow has killed his appetite. On the point of deserting his family he finds that collecting and packing his belongings is too much for him. "Phew!" he mutters, "all these exhausting preparations!" The lucid Relling says of him that if he had any real personality it was cleaned out of him root and branch when he was still a child.

With a sort of wry kindness, Relling has tried to sustain the morale of the derelicts around him by supplying each of them with a suitable life-lie. He has made Hjalmar accept the myth that he would someday restore the family's fortunes by inventing something. Hjalmar makes the notion his own and assures everyone that he is hard at work on it. At the shock of Hedwig's death—his only genuine attachment has been to her—he blurts out, "Good Lord, what in fact do you want me to invent? Practically everything has been invented already." As for the wretchedly alcoholic Molvik, a former student of theology, Relling has propped his last scrap of self-esteem by telling him that he is "demonic"—in the circumstances, an utterly meaningless word.

Perhaps the only sound or "whole" persons in the play, apart from Hedwig, who has been kept clear of everything but the consolation of her imagination and the desire to help Hjalmar and mother, are Mrs. Sörby and Gina. Mrs. Sörby, Werle's housekeeper, consents to marry him, fully aware of his past,

while she is frank about her own—thus establishing the basis
for a true marriage. Gina has accepted her condition in life on
behalf of her child and Hjalmar, of whom she is soberly fond.

The debate or conflict between Gregers and Relling, who
have known each other since both were living in the vicinity
of the northern mine fields, begins when they meet again in
the Ekdal flat. Gregers is about to disabuse Hjalmar and thus
upset the foundations of his friend's quiet existence by speaking
of the poisoned atmosphere in the house—he calls it a stench—
not unlike the bad smell caused by mishandling his stove. When
that accident is alluded to in an offhand and lighthearted manner, Gregers says, "No amount of living will get rid of the
stench *I* mean." Alerted by this, Relling interrupts: "Excuse
me, I suppose *you* couldn't be the one who brought the stench
in, from the mines up there."

GREGERS: It's just like you to call what I bring into the house a
stench.
RELLING: Listen, Mr. Werle, junior! I strongly suspect you are still
carrying this "claim of the ideal" about you in your back
pocket.
GREGERS: I carry it in my breast.
RELLING: Well, carry the thing where the devil you like, but I
wouldn't advise you to try to cash in on it here as long
as *I'm* about the place.
GREGERS: And if I do?
RELLING: Then you'll find yourself going head first down the stairs.

Gregers is not kicked down the stairs, as Ibsen no doubt felt
it would have been useful to do. In the confrontation after the
havoc has been wrought by Gregers' uncalled-for revelation,
which leads to Hedwig shooting herself rather than the wild
duck as he had asked her to do, he insists, "Hedwig did not die
in vain. Didn't you see how grief has brought out the noblest
in him [Hjalmar]?" To which Relling replies, "Give him nine
months and little Hedwig will be nothing more than the theme
of a pretty poetry piece."

At the last moment before the fall of the curtain this exchange
ensues:

GREGERS: If *you* are right and *I* am wrong, life will no longer be worth living.

RELLING: Oh, life wouldn't be too bad if only the blessed people who come canvassing their ideals round everybody's door would leave us poor souls in peace.

GREGERS: In that case I am glad my destiny is what it is.

RELLING: If I may ask, what is your destiny?

GREGERS: To be thirteenth at the table. [*Which he was at his father's welcome-home party for him.*]

RELLING: The devil it is! [*Another translation has it* "Relling laughs and spits."]

What this signifies—something nearly always overlooked because the audience sides with Relling against the troublemaker Gregers—is that despite his tragic error in the Ekdal instance, Gregers will persist in pressing those same "claims of the ideal." He will forever go on with his effort to transform people so that they may make their lives accord with the strictest truth. So we may presume will Ibsen, though he has begun to doubt the efficacy and perhaps even the value of the practice. In all its pitfalls and bitter disappointments, it is Ibsen's destiny too, even though we may agree with Relling that he has hardly ever seen a true marriage and that "pretty nearly everyone is sick."

In this sense, Ibsen stands by his guns: he still believes in the need for dedicated truth tellers—despite all. In most of his last plays, however, he turns his "guns" on himself: he not only confesses his misgivings but his own failings and sins.

9
Adrift: The Inner Dialogue

I
N IBSEN'S PRELIMINARY NOTES for *The Wild Duck* we read:
"Liberation consists in securing for individuals the right to
free themselves, each according to his particular need." But the
sentence does not occur in the text. If it had it might have led
to thematic confusion. For what *The Wild Duck* says, to put
it as baldly as possible, is that it may be doing a disservice to
many people to hear the whole truth about themselves.

That a change of heart must come not from external pressure
but from the roots of one's background and character is directly
expressed in Ibsen's *Rosmersholm* (1886). It was written in
Munich following his first visit to Norway after an absence of
eleven years. Ibsen could not assert anything without suggesting
the possible validity of its opposite. So it is with *Rosmersholm*.

Joahannes Rosmer is a former clergyman, whose wife Beata
committed suicide by throwing herself off a bridge into the
millrace on their estate. He now lives there in the company of
Rebecca West, who first came to the home as a companion to
Beata and as his aide. The clergyman Rosmer held conservative

Note: All the citations from *Rosmersholm* in this chapter are from the
translation in the Oxford University Press edition.

views, but in the course of time Rebecca steered him to the radical tendencies which had gradually begun to predominate among the youth. It was the period when political dispute in Norway was most intense.

The play begins with Rosmer reluctantly admitting to his ultraconservative brother-in-law, Kroll, the headmaster of a local high school, that he is now on the side of the youth, as are Kroll's own two daughters and his wife. Kroll hardly can credit this; the Rosmer family has always been committed to and representative of traditional opinion. As pastor of the community, Rosmer was looked up to as the heir and model of the long-established conservative canon.

In the first act, the nub of the discussion between Rosmer and Kroll defines their social and political views:

ROSMER: I will devote my life and all my strength . . . to create a democracy in this land.

KROLL: Don't you think we have enough democracy already? For my part I think the whole lot of us are well on the way to being dragged down into the mud where the only ones to thrive are the common people.

ROSMER: That is precisely what makes me define the true aim of democracy.

KROLL: What is that?

ROSMER: To make all my countrymen noblemen.

KROLL: All.

ROSMER: As many as possible, anyway.

KROLL: By what means?

ROSMER: By liberating their minds and purifying their wills . . .

KROLL: Rosmer, you are a dreamer. Are *you* going to liberate them?

ROSMER: No, my dear friend. I only want to try and rouse them to it. As for *doing* it, that is their own affair.

KROLL: And you think they can?

ROSMER: Yes.

KROLL: And by their own power?

ROSMER: Exactly! By their own power! There is no other.

We recognize in this the quintessence of Ibsen's social attitudes and his "politics." Kroll breaks with Rosmer, saying first, "You shall not set foot in my house," and later, "I shall fight this [anarchy] by word and deed." We feel that Kroll intends to bring Rosmer back to the fold.

The social-political dispute serves as the play's springboard. Though there are further sidelights on the matter, the play veers away from it and advances to an exploration of Ibsen's deeper preoccupations. For it cannot be repeated too often, considering the constant misconceptions on the subject, Ibsen's concerns were never primarily social or political. *Rosmersholm* is in fact the last of his plays in which social polemics appear.

We recall Ibsen's speech to students delivered seven years before writing *Rosmersholm*: " . . . no man can portray in his writing anything for which he does not to some degree find the model in himself." The prime examples, among many up to this time, are *Brand* and *Peer Gynt*. There is much of Ibsen in *both* Rosmer and Rebecca. They are two aspects of his own being. The duality coalesces into an uneasy unity. This ambiguity, added to its social-political element, has made *Rosmersholm* one of Ibsen's most puzzling and dismaying plays, and certainly the least popular. Those who on its publication could not make head or tail of it were not entirely at fault. It is a mysterious, if not a "difficult," play.

There is no mystery in the symbolic "white horses." They are the name given to a local superstition or "spook" forboding death. They are alluded to in the first scene as an intimation of what happened at the footbridge: Beata's suicide. Rosmer has never crossed it since that tragic event. This prompts Rebecca to remark, "They cling long to their dead here in Rosmersholm," which Mrs. Helseth, the maid, corrects by saying, "It's my belief it's the dead that cling to Rosmersholm." In other words, the past holds the Rosmer realm in a powerful grip—and, as we shall later have occasion to say, on Ibsen himself.

In his fight to force Rosmer back to his family tradition, Kroll begins to suspect Rebecca of having played a crucial role in Rosmer's radical conversion. He is not mistaken, as both Rosmer and Rebecca freely admit. But that is not all. There must have been some connection between Beata's suicide and Rebecca's presence in the house. It is evident to Kroll and to everyone else that Rosmer's intimacy with Rebecca was altogether chaste. Beata idolized Rebecca; Kroll himself finds her "bewitching." Beata could not have failed to notice how close Rebecca and Rosmer had become through their intellectual interests, the books they read, the discussions they engaged in, their general affinity.

It had been surmised that Beata killed herself because despair over her childlessness had affected her mood. We also learn that she was a sexually passionate woman and that, for unspecified causes, Rosmer was not entirely responsive to her. (Ibsen's women are nearly all more forthright in this regard than the men.) This too was a possible source of neurosis and insanity. Rosmer suffers the weight of the memory and the part he may have played in his wife's fatal destiny.

In his pursuit of further clues to Rebecca's influence on Rosmer and to discredit her, Kroll's investigation leads him to question her part in the tragedy. All that was confirmed was that she had arrived from a town up north and that she had lived there with a Dr. West. It turns out that Dr. West was her father through an adultery. It is also intimated that she may have had an incestuous relationship with him. In writing about the play, Freud took this possibility to be a fact and proceeded to elaborate an entire interpretation of her character on this assumption. But such psychoanalytic conjecture, though at times provocative, is in matters of literature often befuddling, and, for the most part, irrelevant.

More to the point is Kroll's surprise at Rebecca's distress at the discovery of her illegitimacy. (We recall that Ibsen himself once cried out that he was not his father's son. And that he himself had fathered an illegitimate child.) "You seem to have certain prejudices in the matter," Kroll says. She admits she has. The scene continues:

KROLL: Well, I imagine it's pretty much the same with most of what you call your emancipation. You read up on a lot of new ideas and opinion. You have a smattering of various ideas and theories, that somehow seem to upset a good many things that up to now we took for incontrovertible and inviolate. But in your case, Miss West, it never got beyond anything but an abstraction. Book knowledge. It can never get into your blood.

REBECCA: Perhaps you are right.

KROLL: . . . . And if it is like that in your case, it's easy enough to guess how it is with Johannes Rosmer. The very idea of *him* getting up and announcing his apostasy . . .

It is imperative, Kroll says, that she get Rosmer to legalize their relationship. But there is an impediment. Rosmer cannot dispel his misgivings. "Beata," Rosmer fears, "saw straight when she believed I was in love with you [Rebecca] . . . even while she was alive, my thoughts were all for you. It was you alone I longed for. It was with you I found calm, happy contentment. Our life has been a spiritual marriage perhaps from the very first day. That is why the guilt is mine . . . I had no right to it, no right for Beata's sake . . . It was for love of me, *her* kind of love, that she threw herself into the millstream. The fact is inescapable, Rebecca, I can never get away from it."

REBECCA: Oh, you must put everything out of your mind but the great and splendid task you have dedicated your life to.

ROSMER: I fear that is something that can never be done, my dear. Not by me . . .

REBECCA: Why not by you?

ROSMER: There can be no victory for any cause that springs from guilt.

REBECCA: Oh, all these doubts, these fears, these scruples—they are just part of the family tradition. The people here talk about the dead coming back in the form of charging white horses. I think this is the same sort of thing . . .

Rebecca wanted Rosmer to be "a free man in all things" and to go "from house to house like a messenger of deliverance, winning the minds and the wills of men. Creating all about you a nobility in ever wider circles. Noble men." "Happy noble men," Rosmer echoes. "For it is happiness that brings nobility of mind, Rebecca." Rebecca asks, "Don't you think . . . perhaps suffering too? Great suffering."

ROSMER: Yes, so long as you come through, get over it, rise above it.

REBECCA: That's what *you* must do.

Rebecca, we see, urges Rosmer to more than an avowal of love, though she greets his proposal of marriage with a barely suppressed cry of joy. Yet despite her self-justification, her conviction that Rosmer must go on to fulfill his mission, unfettered by prejudice or moral qualms, she herself has begun to suffer agonizing guilt.

To liberate Rosmer from the gloom of his sickly marriage and an environment in which his wife could not abide the color and fragrance of flowers, a place where children never cried and adults never laughed, so that he might live "in the clear light of the sun," she had to remove the barrier that stood in the way of his release. She had told Beata, she confesses, first, that half-paralyzed by the home atmosphere, Rosmer was abandoning his religion (which was not true at the time) and that she herself implored Beata to permit her to leave Rosmersholm because if she did not "certain things might happen." Worse still, she intimated Rosmer might also leave. Frustrated in her avid sexual appetite, Beata had got it into her head that as a childless wife, she had no right to remain: she had persuaded herself it was her duty to make room for another. Rebecca had said nothing to dissuade her of this; she perhaps encouraged the thought. It was "the choice between two lives."

Had Rebecca acted in cold blood? "I was different then from what I am now talking about it," she says. "And besides," she adds most revealingly, "it seems a person can want things both ways. I wanted to get rid of Beata, one way or another . . . Every little step I risked, every faltering advance, I seemed to hear something call out within me 'No further. Not a step further!' And yet, I could not stop . . . And then the horrible happened."

Rebecca is now determined to leave Rosmersholm forever. This inexorably willful woman who believed she could make something of herself and through Rosmer make a life that would lead to freedom for themselves and others would seemingly stop at nothing to carry out her plan. But with Beata out of the way she lost the strength to take the next step. Her personal passion for Rosmer no longer swayed her. The Rosmer philosophy of life crippled her will. She had become subject to that old ("Ibsenite") disturbance: "the inflamed scruples," the high morality of self-abnegation. "The Rosmer philosophy of life ennobles but it kills happiness." And Rosmer, in turn, has lost the power, the certainty of inner force to inspire courage and greatness in people. Her sense of guilt prevents her from accepting the marriage he proposes; he can no longer become a leader. Morality too can be contagious.

Three men had educated Rosmer. First there was Kroll, who had helped instill in him belief in the age-old verities, which are no longer firmly his, though remnants of it, as we see, are present and active. Then there is the brilliantly depicted Ulric Brendel, once Rosmer's teacher, a philosophic-radical, now a wastrel, who in his last appearance declares himself bankrupt of all ideas. Just as Ejnar in *Brand* is the aesthete without intellect and later the evangelist with more bitterness than conviction, so Brendel is the quasi-revolutionary without moral stamina: both human wrecks. Rosmer had also counted on support for his democratic "crusade" from Peter Mortensgaard, the editor of the left-wing newspaper *The Beacon*.

Brendel, though himself an empty shell, describes Mortensgaard with devastating prescience: "Peter Mortensgaard is lord and master of the future . . . [He] possesses the secret of omnipotence . . . [He] never wants to do more than he *can* [because he] is quite capable of living his life without ideals. And it is precisely that . . . that is the great secret of political success . . . " Brendel also insinuates that if "Rebecca wishes to help Rosmer fulfill his mission she had better disfigure herself!" We are reminded once again that while Ibsen exercised an icy self-control there was the fire of virile passion in him.

In *Rosmersholm* Ibsen closes his account with preoccupations about and criticism of political establishments, journalistic unreliability and corruption, programmatic radicalism. Rosmer can no longer sustain faith in his cause. He cannot even believe unreservedly in Rebecca's love. He would be convinced of it if she had the courage to go with him "the way Beata went." She is now in the grip of the fundamental and ineradicable Rosmer morality. She has sinned; it is right, she now asserts, that she must atone. There is no longer a judge over them; they must judge themselves. In this we find Ibsen's fixed idea that no cause can be considered entirely sincere unless tested by its exponent's willingness to die for it. It is a further reverberation of Brand's absolutism. Having lost faith in their worthiness to enact the envisioned mission of liberation, Rosmer and Rebecca will go to the millstream, to a union in death.

Before they leave to yield to "the white horses of Rosmersholm," Rebecca asks Rosmer, "Is it you who goes with me, or I with you?"

ROSMER: That is something we shall never fathom.
REBECCA: Yet I should so much like to know.
ROSMER: We go together, Rebecca. I go with you and you with me.
REBECCA: Yes, now we are one.

Indeed they are. The two together are Ibsen himself, Ibsen adrift. *Rosmersholm* is the dramatization of his inner dialogue. He forgoes his battle for social good: he has neither the aptitude nor the unwavering conviction needed to effect it. He no longer possesses the arrogance to regard himself as fit to guide his countrymen to nobility: he doubts his spiritual courage or moral qualifications.

Dense with meaning and poetic allusion, *Rosmersholm* closes one phase of Ibsen's life work. Pessimistic in a mundane sense, there are in it elements of romantic purity and exaltation. In his next two plays Ibsen will turn to the revision, extension and deepening of the theme inherent in *A Doll's House*. *Rosmersholm*, however, is the bridge to a later stage in which Ibsen progresses from baleful self-accusation to renunciation and a special sort of apotheosis.

10
Toward New Heights

he Lady from the Sea (1889) and *Hedda Gabler* (1890)
considered together mark crossroads on Ibsen's way to the
wonders of his last four plays. As I have noted in the final paragraph of the preceding chapter, *The Lady from the Sea* and
Hedda Gabler revert to the manner and matter of *A Doll's
House* and of several other plays of his maturity. But it would
be more correct to say that they throw a sharper light on them.
Hedda Gabler is certainly a masterpiece in its own right.

In a letter to his publisher regarding *The Lady from the Sea*,
Ibsen wrote that "it marks a new direction I have taken." It is
generally assumed that the statement refers to the increased
use of symbolic motifs. For me the statement means something
different: that henceforth there would be hardly any social
polemics in his plays. There is no more symbolism in *The Lady
from the Sea* than in *Rosmersholm* or *The Wild Duck*. What
symbolism there is, is overt.

The burning of the orphanage in *Ghosts* may be thought of
as a symbol, but is wholly intelligible on its own level of reality.
The same applies to Oswald's inherited disease: both inescapably

Note: All the citations from the plays in this chapter are from the Oxford University Press edition.

signify that whatever issues from a corrupt source is doomed to some form of destruction. Symbolism chiefly occurs in the near-allegorical plays: *Brand* and *Peer Gynt*. Ibsen's symbolism has very little in common with the symbolism in Maeterlinck or in Strindberg's *A Dream Play* and *The Ghost Sonata*. To insist on the symbolism in most of Ibsen's later plays would justify our saying that all art is symbolic, and if it is not it is probably not art at all.

Many critics have indulged in fun and games in the extrapolation of recondite meanings in the Norwegian master's plays. Their richness lends itself to the practice.

We may find stimulation in it, but, generally speaking, it is idle to unearth "secret" interpretations where an artist creates dramatic or verbal metaphors so precise and penetrating that their significance is immediately and unmistakenly evident. There is mystery in every true work of art, and with Ibsen, as I shall have occasion to particularize, it is the better part of aesthetic wisdom to demystify him. Why add layers of adventitious speculation to what already possesses its own intrinsic complexity?

"It's extraordinary what profundities and symbols they ascribe to me," Ibsen said. " . . . Can't people just read what I write? I only write about people. I don't write symbolically. I draw real, living people. Any considerable person will naturally be to some degree representative of the generality, of the thoughts and ideas of the age, so that the portrayal of such a person's inner life may seem symbolic. And I create such people. And with good reason. I have often walked with Hedda Gabler . . . And have undergone somewhat of the same experience myself."

The sea in *The Lady from the Sea* is where its central figure, Ellida Wangel, the daughter of a lighthouse keeper, was born and raised. She associates it, as most of us do, with endless horizons, limitless space, unknown distances, constant movement, change and adventure.

In her youth, after a brief infatuation with a seaman (he was a second mate) whom she promised to marry and who was later believed lost at sea, she married Dr. Wangel, a widower with two daughters. Though they still cherish their mother's mem-

ory, they are at the play's opening, sufficiently grown up not
to require routine maternal supervision. Ellida had a child by
Wangel but it soon died. Following this she "had trouble with
her nerves" and probably on this account occasionally drank
too much. The good and considerate doctor is busy with his
patients in a small summer resort in a fjord town. (A fjord is
to the sea as a lake or an inlet is to the ocean.) Ellida says of the
waters in the fjord that they are never fresh, they have no
zest or sparkle. Though she wholly respects and is genuinely
fond of her husband, the thought of the *man* of the sea to whom
she considered herself betrothed haunts her.

The man who has been presumed dead returns as the Stranger.
He claims her as if their early vow of engagement, mystically
sealed by an exchange of rings thrown into the sea, were a marriage. Though frightened, she is drawn to him as if by an
undertow. She feels she must yield to his claim despite or because of its strangeness. Wangel's rational arguments against the
folly of her impulses are of little avail. His strenuous effort to
prevent her immediately leaving him as the sailor says she must
(he is due on the morrow of his arrival to resume his duties
on board) only makes the temptation to follow him all the
more urgent. Impressed by the powerful hold the man exerts
on her, Wangel consents to let her go. If that is her will he
cannot stand in her way.

The release and a growing sense that she may find a real place
by her husband's side breaks the Stranger's spell. Realizing that
she may act of her own free will, Ellida chooses to stay with
Wangel. *She has freedom and responsibility too.* "That puts a
different aspect on things."

The play presents a central tenet of Ibsen's belief: without
responsibility there can be no valid meaning in freedom. In the
course of the play's exposition we have been informed, almost
casually, as an explanation for the Stranger's long absence, that
he had killed his captain. Ibsen tells us nothing further about
this but we are left to infer, if we have noticed it, that murder
too may be the consequence of *complete* "freedom."

We are not entirely certain (nor is she) that Ellida will ever
find peace as a "domesticated" wife, but she will have freely

decided on her destiny as much as she, or anyone else, can. There will always remain a yearning for something else: the unknown, a different home, a different career, even at times, a different country. Still one must choose what is compatible with the most consistent reality of one's nature and situation. Ellida is a woman, not a mermaid; men and women can "acc-acc-acclimatize themselves," as Ballested, the tourist guide and Sunday artist of the play, has some difficulty in saying.

The little idiosyncrasy of articulation which Ibsen gives Ballested—it is repeated several times—and which to begin with appears to be no more than a cute bit of characterization is typical of much of Ibsen's "symbolism." What Ibsen suggests here, I repeat, is that to achieve a measure of stability in life we must "acclimatize" or adjust ourselves to necessity, necessity of the real despite its ebb and flow, its shifting direction. Nothing is entirely clear and sure. The accommodation or "acclimatization" to reality is much more difficult to achieve than Ballested's trouble in pronouncing the word. As the French critic Jacques Rivière told the half-demented poet Artaud, "The only cure for madness is the innocence of facts."

A further word in regard to symbolism in Ibsen's plays should be added in view of their stage presentation. The Stranger in *The Lady from the Sea* is a real person, not a figment of Ellida's imagination intended to "stand for" something else. It is clearly pointed out to her (and to us) that her troubled spirit has made her see him in a light which in no way corresponds to her normal observation.

In this play, the "miracle" which Nora hoped for takes place. Wangel perceives that if he insists on maintaining the *bonds* of matrimony, Ellida is deprived of a choice, she cannot be free, she cannot be a true companion, mate or wife. She is certainly a special case because of the particular circumstances of her situation, but what she learns obtains for everyone.

Bolette, the elder of Wangel's two daughters, endowed with some of Wangel's stability and common sense, also speaks disconsolately of the house by the fjord as a "fishpond . . . so cut off from things." When asked what she most longs for, she answers "to get away . . . and after that to learn." When her erstwhile tutor, Arnholm, seventeen years her senior, an "old man" to her, offers her through marriage the opportunity to go away, to travel and thus to learn, she recoils from the proposal. When he then adds that even if she rejects him as a husband, he will hold to his offer, she agrees to marry him. She too will learn to "acclimatize" herself: free and responsible.

Hilde, Wangel's younger daughter, bereft of a mother, yearns for a new attachment. She would find it in Ellida, but since she is distracted and pays little attention to her, Hilde behaves as if she dislikes Ellida. When Ellida's departure seems imminent, Hilde becomes conscious of her true feelings for her—she adores and needs Ellida. Ellida, being needed, realizes in turn that she can indeed become Hilde's mother.

Hilde fits the play's overall pattern and significance because her feeling for Ellida is due to their resemblance. Hilde is impetuous and slightly mischievous. She too longs for the mysterious, the awesome, even the possibly wicked or, to use her own expression, the *exciting*. She is a preliminary sketch for the Hilde we shall meet in *The Master Builder*.

The only shadow cast on this sunniest and most "optimistic" of Ibsen's plays is the young aspiring artist, Lyngstrand, who can never attain anything of his ambition not only because of a possible lack of talent but because he is ill and will die before he has had a chance to test himself. Bolette, good girl that she is, encourages him with the "life-lie" that he may succeed.

Ibsen, incidentally, pokes gentle fun at Lyngstrand's view of women's dependency on men for their inspiration and instruction. The momentary detail points to a richness of texture so extraordinary that to do Ibsen's major plays justice one would be obliged to cite virtually every long speech and stage direction. They all count both in narrative and thematic import. Here are a few more disparate examples.

The first-act setting calls for a large roofed verandah; outside it in the garden is an arbor. Ellida finds the atmosphere "stiflingly hot" under the verandah roof. She prefers to sit in the garden arbor, where there is *air*. The verandah is domestic, the garden has the freshness and freedom of the world at large.

Arnholm remembers that Ellida's father had called her "The

Heathen," meaning an untamed, untrammeled creature. Bolette calls Hilde "a cruel little beast" to which she retorts "I want to be—so there!"

When Ellida is asked to sit down, she objects, "I don't want to sit, I don't want to—" Her restlessness is the physical manifestation of her mind's disquiet wandering, a useful hint to the actress who plays the role. Ellida, like other of Ibsen's "favorite" women—though he never chose one to live with—is drawn to the "demonic." For all his medals and decorations, there was much of the "demonic" in Ibsen himself, though he scoffs at the word when applied to the inebriate Molvik in *The Wild Duck*.

One is puzzled at critics' and audiences' having been puzzled by *Hedda Gabler*. The lack of understanding which even some of Ibsen's admirers shared when the play was first produced may have been due to its tight weave, its racingly rapid exposition. The speeches are altogether explicit but in the main unusually terse—they convey story elements, social and personal background, individual psychology, all in one. Only a close reading of the play can unravel its full import. An actress recently looked to a psychoanalyst for an explication of Hedda's complex character. She would have been much better advised if she had been told to consult the text.

Except for one flaw—to be identified later—the play's construction is perfect. In this matter, *Hedda Gabler* reveals Ibsen at the peak of his power. To novices in dramatic craftsmanship in the realm of modern realism I would recommend the play as a model.

One of the most admired facets of Ibsen's technique is his ability to make the exposition of conditions preceding the immediate action of his plays dramatic in themselves. "We find," says William Archer in his invaluable manual *Play Making*, "that in only two out of the fifteen plays (after *The Vikings*) does the whole action come within the frame of the picture. These two are *The League of Youth* and *An Enemy of the People*. In neither of these are there any antecedents to be stated; neither turns upon any disclosure of bygone events or emotions. We are, indeed, afforded glimpses into the past of Stensgaard or Stockmann, but the glimpses are incidental and inessential . . . *Hedda Gabler* is perhaps that [play] in which a sound proportion between the past and the present is most successfully preserved. The interest of the present action is thoroughly vivid; but it is all rooted in facts and relations of the past, which are elicited under circumstances of high dramatic tension."

Perhaps some sense of this technique may be conveyed by a paraphrased sketch of the opening portion of the play. In the first scene, before Hedda's entrance, we quickly and "naturally" learn (A) that Hedda, a young bride, has just returned from her honeymoon with Jörgen (George) Tesman. (B) He has "inherited" the maid Berte from the home he had lived in with his two old maiden aunts—he had been an orphan from an early age—and that he has been cared for by Berte since he was a little boy. (C) Berte is worried that she may not suit her new mistress, Hedda, who as a general's daughter is "very particular" and "used to having everything 'just so.'" (D) Hedda is described as cutting a fine figure "riding along the road with her father in a long habit with a feather in her hat." (E) There is a peculiarity in Hedda's having made a match with Tesman. (F) He has been made a "doctor" abroad and there is a prospect of his becoming a professor (a highly honored position in Europe at the time). (G) Hedda, not Tesman, had ordered the covers to be removed from the chairs in the very handsome living room, in which the stage direction has it, there hangs the portrait of a good-looking elderly man: Hedda's father.

Tesman enters. Miss Tesman, Tesman's aunt, mentions a Mr. Brack who met Hedda at the steamer on which she and Tesman had arrived and took *her* right to the door. Hedda had a great many bags with her, and Tesman's suitcase was crammed full of notes, which during his honeymoon he had picked up from old archives. Miss Tesman explains that she has bought a new hat so that Hedda would not be ashamed of her, if they should be seen walking together. Tesman says that his aunt (Miss Tesman) has been both father and mother to him. She congratulates him in delighted surprise: "To think that you'd be the

one to walk off with Hedda Gabler! The lovely Hedda Gabler!
So many admirers she always had around her!" Many friends,
Tesman preens himself, would like to be in his shoes. The
honeymoon lasted almost six months. It was also an academic
trip, Tesman explains. He had to look through all those records
and he had to plow through so many books. Miss Tesman asks
if he has any "prospects." Tesman thinks she means of his becoming a professor!

The journey must have cost a pretty penny. Miss Tesman
wonders how his fellowship could have covered all his expenses.
Yes, but Hedda had to have that trip. And the fine house they
were now to occupy, which Tesman says Hedda also insisted
on having, would only add to the expense. But Brack got the
house for them on very favorable terms. Hedda wrote to arrange them. Besides, Miss Tesman has given security for the
furniture and all the carpets: she has put a mortage on her and
her sister's annuity. Tesman is shocked by this. Miss Tesman
assures him that it was only a formality: Mr. Brack said so too,
and he's a judge.

Tesman has had a rough time on life's road. But, thank God,
he's made good. He has outdistanced his most dangerous adver-
sary, Ejlert Lövborg, who, Miss Tesman says, "fell lower than
them all . . . the poor depraved creature." However, she's heard
that Lövborg has published a new book. She doesn't think it
will be much compared to the book Tesman is preparing to
write. What is it about? "It will be an account of the domestic
crafts of medieval Brabant." He still has to sort out extensive
collections of material. "Yes," Miss Tesman confirms, "collecting things and sorting them out, you've always been good
at that." But best of all, he's won the wife of his heart . . . "And
here she is, isn't she? Eh?"

And Hedda enters. She is twenty-nine. (Too often played
by an older actress.) "Her face and figure," Ibsen tells us,
"are aristocratic and elegant." The information provided in the
first two scenes, which lays the foundation for much that is
to follow, is supplemented by more about two already mentioned
personages: Brack and Lövborg. We also observe Hedda's snob-
bish disinclination to be on familiar terms with Tesman's aunts.

Miss Tesman has brought Tesman a pair of his old bedroom slippers. Tesman, who feels a positive affection for them, invites Hedda to admire them. Yes, she says, he mentioned them often on their honeymoon.

Much too long to summarize, the scene contains a little episode in which Hedda unexpectedly exclaims that the new maid, Berte, will never do: she has left her old hat on the sofa. It is the new hat Miss Tesman bought to please Hedda. In a later scene Hedda confesses that her jibe sprang from a sudden and recurrent malevolent impulse over which she has no control. One may also remark a stage direction which has Hedda pace about the room, clench her hands as though in desperation—a nervous trait very much like, though much sharper than, Ellida's restlessness in *The Lady from the Sea*.

A later scene in the first act, following a conversation in which Brack and Tesman have been discussing Lövborg and his well-received but not particularly remunerative book, ends with Tesman saying, "But I can't imagine what he [Lövborg] is going to do with himself now? What on earth can he possibly find to live on now? Eh?" Hedda, overhearing this, laughs scornfully. "Tesman's forever worrying about what people are going to find to live on." This follows:

BRACK: Perhaps I could tell you about that . . . You must remember that he's got relations with quite a lot of influence.
TESMAN: Oh well, his relatives . . . I'm afraid they've disowned him entirely.
BRACK: They used to regard him as the hope of the family.
TESMAN: Yes, they used to, yes! But they've washed their hands of him long ago.
HEDDA: Who knows? Up at the Elvsteds' they've been reforming him.

Mrs. Elvsted has appeared in a previous scene. She is Hedda's former and younger schoolmate. Married now to a grossly selfish husband, she has attached herself to Lövborg, helped him with another new book and through her purity and devotion brought about his rehabilitation.

Brack, Tesman and Hedda continue:
BRACK: And there's this new book he has written . . .

TESMAN: Oh well, I hope to goodness they will help him to get something. I've just written him— Oh, Hedda, I've asked him to come around this evening.

This is followed by a brilliant passage combining exposition and action.

BRACK: But, my dear Tesman, you're coming to my bachelor party this evening. You promised last night at the quay.

HEDDA: Had you forgotten, Tesman?

TESMAN: Yes, by all that's holy.

BRACK: In any case, you may rely on him to find an excuse.

TESMAN: Why should you think that? Eh?

BRACK: My dear Tesman . . . And you too, madam. I can no longer allow you to remain in ignorance of something that . . . that . . .

TESMAN: Something to do with Ejlert Lövborg?

BRACK: Both to him and yourself . . . You ought to prepare yourself for the discovery that your appointment may not come as soon as you hope and expect.

TESMAN: Has something happened to delay it? Eh?

BRACK: The appointment to the professorship might conceivably be contested by another candidate . . .

TESMAN: But who on earth! Surely not . . .

BRACK: Quite correct. Ejlert Lövborg.

TESMAN: Oh but my dear sir . . . but that would be quite incredibly inconsiderate of him. Yes, because . . . just think I'm a married man! We got married on our expectations, Hedda and I. Borrowed vast sums. We're in debt to Aunt Julie [Miss Tesman]. Because, good God, the post was as good as promised to me.

BRACK: Come, come, come . . . you'll probably get it too. But only after a competition.

HEDDA: Just think, Tesman, it'll be quite a sporting event . . .

After Brack's leavetaking, this ensues:

TESMAN: Ah, Hedda, one should never build castles in the air.

HEDDA: And do you?

TESMAN: Yes, it can't be denied . . . it was idiotically romantic of me to go and get married, and buy a house, on expectations alone.

HEDDA: You may be right about that.

TESMAN: Well, at least we have got our lovely house, Hedda! . . .
Our dream house I might almost call it. Eh?

HEDDA: The agreement was that we were to live a social life. En-
tertain . . .

TESMAN: Yes, oh Heavens. I was so looking forward to it. Just think,
to see you as hostess, presiding over a select group of
friends! Well, well, well, for the time being we'll just have
to be the two of us, Hedda. Just see Aunt Julie once in a
while . . .

HEDDA: And I suppose I won't get my footman just awhile.

TESMAN: Oh, no . . . a man servant, you must see that's quite out of
the question.

HEDDA: And the saddle horse I was to have had.

TESMAN: The saddle horse!

HEDDA: I suppose I daren't think of that, now.

TESMAN: No, God preserve me . . . that goes without saying!

HEDDA: Oh well, I've got one thing at least I can pass the time with.

TESMAN: Oh, thank the good Lord for that! And what might that
be, Hedda? Eh?

HEDDA: My pistols, Jörgen.

TESMAN: Pistols!

HEDDA: General Gabler's pistols.

On Tesman's exclamation of alarm at these dangerous and,
for the play, crucial weapons, the curtain falls on the first act.

It is late twilight as the second act begins. (It has been pointed
out by several critics that time changes and the resultant modu-
lations in the degree and quality of illumination help set the
dramatic mood of the various scenes.) Hedda stands at the open
glass door loading a pistol. Brack approaches the house through
the garden below. Hedda raises the pistol and takes aim. "I'm
going to shoot you, sir." Brack shouts back, "No, no, don't
stand there aiming right at me!" She answers, "That's what
comes of sneaking around the back!" and fires.

"Are you mad . . . Stop fooling around, I tell you," Brack
says as he enters. He's dressed for the evening party at his place.
"What the devil . . . do you still play at that game? What are
you shooting at?" "Oh," Hedda replies, "I just stand here and
shoot into the blue." He takes the pistol, looks at it and puts
it back in its case, and notices another one there.

In the two first-act scenes and in the opening moments of the second mention is made of preceding events and portents of the future. The introduction of the pistols, for example, tells us something of Hedda's connection with her father (her mother is never mentioned), the isolation and boredom she will suffer in her new home. The shooting into the trees is violence without objective. It is also a preparation for the later use of the pistols: one which she offers Lövborg for his planned suicide, the other with which she kills herself, and the fact that Brack, having seen the pistols, is in' a position to use his knowledge of them as a means to blackmail her into an affair with him.

The play contains one of the very rare scenes in Ibsen of an overtly sexual nature. Though physical passion, if not always love, plays a crucial role in his major dramas, there are few oustanding love scenes except for those in *Peer Gynt* (Peer and Solveig) and their parody in Peer's contacts with Ingrid, the Troll King's daughter and Anitra. In *Rosmersholm*, Rebecca confesses desire for Rosmer and he his love for her, but these feelings are more verbal than dramatically specific. In the last plays the *idea* of love becomes central.

Following Brack's entrance in the second act, there is a passage of flirtation between Brack and Hedda, teasingly provocative on her part, subtly menacing on his. This is still relatively mild compared to Lövborg's approach to Hedda when he comes to visit Tesman on Tesman's invitation. Though Lövborg's "advances" to Hedda are made while they pretend to be looking into an album of photos taken during the Tesman's honeymoon, the suppressed tone of the scene—Tesman is nearby—makes it all the more torrid.

Lövborg in the past had been a special guest at General Gabler's gatherings. He had been in love with Hedda. At the Tesmans' now he cannot take his eyes off her. He murmurs, "Hedda Gabler!" and with increasing ardor repeats her name. "Hedda Gabler! . . . Hedda Gabler married. And married to Jörgen Tesman!" A moment later, though she has tried to restrain and forbid him to address her by her maiden name, he presses on with: "Oh Hedda, darling Hedda, how could you throw yourself away like that?"

In Ingmar Bergman's production of the play, Lövborg thrust his hand under her skirt, and she slapped his face with the next line, "Now, none of that." This directorial byplay struck me as entirely wrong for the mode and manners of the period, hence for the play's inherent style, but it was clear that through it Bergman intended both to emphasize the heat of Lövborg's feelings and also to show the impetuosity of his nature and something of his "bohemianism."

They had been "good companions," Hedda and he. Why then had nothing further developed? In their intimate talks he had imparted the secrets of the sort of life he led. It was their common *lust for life*, he believes, which lent fire to their companionship. But there had been no question of marriage: he had spent days and nights of drinking, passion and frenzy. A strictly raised general's daughter wasn't supposed to know anything about such things or even to be associated with anyone who was suspected of them.

When he attempted to pass from speech to action—to make love to her—she stopped him. "Oh why didn't you shoot me down, as you threatened?" he now asks her. Her answer: "I'm too much afraid of a scandal." "Yes, Hedda," he says, "at bottom you're a coward!" "A dreadful coward," she admits.

This gives us an insight into the crux of her behavior, though not of her nature. She is a passionate being in a society where marrying a "wild poet" was unthinkable and an affair with a known debauchee scandalous. The general's daughter, Hedda, fears scandal above all. Now as a married woman she resists the very thought of adultery; she will countenance no "triangle." In other respects independent, she will allow no man to dominate her. Mrs. Elvsted, the poor stupid woman, as Hedda calls her, has the candid courage that Hedda, the lady of high society—and a general's daughter in those days was part of the aristocracy—cannot muster. Mrs. Elvsted abandons her husband; Hedda Gabler is "stuck" with hers. She is now imbedded, trapped in bourgeois mores.

"Experts" have suggested that Hedda is a victim of sexual frigidity. The "diagnosis" is totally without dramatic relevance. It would make the play a case history of very little interest except perhaps to the medical profession. The repeated reference to Hedda's social position explain much of her behavior. Brought up as a "lady," she was required at all times to conduct herself correctly. Even more important is the fact that because among her father's guests many were "fast gentlemen"—always present in the "upper circles"—none of Hedda's admirers ever proposed marriage to her. Brack, who was among them and is still a womanizing bachelor, was then pursuing someone else. The turbulently profligate Lövborg was no proper marital partner for anyone. He was moreover of a lower class and while considered amiable and possibly brilliant, he had not earned a doctorate and had no prospects of a professorship. He would not have offered to marry Hedda, even if he had wished to.

We may recall another general's daughter: Masha in Chekhov's *Three Sisters*. She married a high-school teacher because she imagined him to be the cleverest man in town only to find that he was only the kindest. Generals in those days may have been favored by honor and distinction, but were not, on that account, wealthy. Hedda Gabler, aristocrat by birth and upbringing, married the *bourgeois* Tesman, the only respectable man who asked her to.

Hedda is one of those festeringly passionate women we have encountered in several of Ibsen's earlier plays. The first were the rather abstractly conceived Furia in *Catiline* and Hjördis in *The Vikings* and later and most decidedly Rebecca in *Rosmersholm*. Rebecca too was a seemingly "cold" woman of sovereign will, with a strong hold on the man she had come to love. She had "conspired" to free Rosmer from the narrow doctrines of a stagnant environment. An illegitimate child, suspected of having incestuous relations with her father, in a word, an "outlaw," she is in every way exceptional. But she too failed in all her designs, through having been overcome by Rosmer's ineradicably moral nature.

Repressed, Hedda's passion and power can only manifest themselves destructively. A moral coward under the pressure of social inhibition, she becomes a corrupting and malefic force. She destroys the man she has not dared to love, and destroys herself to avoid the consequences of her cowardice. Hedda lacks the courage to slam the door on an unloved husband. If Nora may be said to have flapped her wings to escape the marital and social cage, Hedda is a Nora with clipped wings. She cannot assert herself in any positive way; she has only the desperate boldness to do away with herself.

The play takes place at a much earlier time—perhaps thirty years—than the date of its composition. It was a period, Ibsen once remarked, when women were not allowed to play any role apart from marriage and motherhood. The "protection" they enjoyed separated them from the realities of life. Hedda shuns everything painful and ugly; she cannot tolerate the sight of sickness or death. She is already pregnant when the play opens, but mention of it is abhorrent to her, not only because she does not love her milquetoast husband but because she cannot bear the responsibility of bearing and rearing a child. Besides, it would make her unsightly. Small wonder then that she admits that all she is good for is boring herself to death. A general atmosphere of boredom, of ennui, is often stressed in the depiction of middle-class life in the mid-nineteenth century, especially in countries such as Norway and Russia.

Lövborg recognized the passion in her: the "lust for life." She wanted to count in an important way. She might have found some satisfaction if Tesman were able to enter the political arena, but Brack dismisses that possibility. She cannot create, only ruin. She burns the manuscript of the book which Lövborg and Thea (Mrs. Elvsted) had worked on together: their "child." The insipid Thea has proved her capacity to arouse in Lövborg the will to discipline himself and to realize his talent. She, the magnificent Hedda, can only "inspire" him to suicide. This would be an act of bravery on his part: she sees beauty in it.

The neurotic temperament, the frustrated, the physically or morally unsatisfied often see beauty in destruction, in corruption, in self-vilification. (Much of modern and especially contemporary art exemplifies this tendency.) Balked in all her impulses, but forever the romantic, Hedda envisions Lövborg dying with "vine leaves in his hair," a mythological image of heroism. She fails even in this: Lövborg dies sordidly. Everything she touches, she says, seems condemned to have something mean and farcical about it.

Graceful, witty, proud and intelligent, the fire in her has turned icy. In playing the part, an actress must make us sense the flame within her as much as the forces which compel her to quench it. She should be acted as a dashing personality straitened to a frightening quiet. Even at school Thea was afraid of her. When they met on the steps Hedda always used to pull her hair, and once she said she was going to burn it off. Under unexpected stimulus or provocation such a being as Hedda will explode with shattering force. The burning of Lövborg's manuscript which precipitates the play's catastrophe should be played as if she were in the throes of a fierce orgasm.

Certain critics have seen in Hedda's character a reflection of Ibsen's presumed aversion to sexual contact caused by the past misfortunes already mentioned. No doubt he came to regard physical love as inferior to the spiritual. Yet we shall find in several of his last plays a man's tragic regret at having failed to yield to the urge of his passion for a beloved woman. In each case it was not a lack of sexual drive which turned the man away from consummation but quite other causes. What cannot be questioned is the presence in Ibsen of a powerful sexual drive.

That Hedda desired Lövborg is explicitly stated in his scene with her. Her rejection of him is plainly set forth, as noted, as a result of her fear of transgressing social taboos. Though the circumstances were different in Mrs. Alvings's relation to Manders in *Ghosts*, we see similar patterns repeating themselves in various modes in a number of the Ibsen plays. Beyond Hedda as an individual, Ibsen once more, and for the last time, rings a change on a central theme: the imperative of acting from a free conscience. Hedda voices her regard for Lövborg: " . . . he had the courage," she says, "to live in his own fashion." Failure to enact the dictates of one's innermost nature spells disaster. And a society which represses the innate potentialities of its members and thus the possibility of progress fosters hypocrisy, corruption, disruption and, finally, violence. *Hedda Gabler* is not only a psychological study of a certain type of woman, but (indirectly) a social parable. That the play, apart from all else, is markedly a "criticism of life" is indelibly impressed on our minds by Brack's outcry, on the discovery of Hedda's suicide—"But good God Almighty, people don't do such things!" It is the last word spoken.

The play's one flaw is, surprisingly enough, technical. Mrs. Elvsted's quick recovery from her grief on hearing of Lövborg's sudden death and Tesman's equally immediate notion of redoing Lövborg's "lost" book with the notes which Mrs. Elvsted carries around with her and their setting about then and there to do so are too pat for credibility.

The defect is due to the very tightness of the play's structure —the absolute unity of time and place in a "true-to-life" realistic vein. It is the artistic price Ibsen had to pay for his technical gain. The same fault may be charged against *A Doll's House* and *Rosmersholm*, but it is not as flagrant there as in this otherwise marvelously well-made play. The poetic form of *Brand* and *Peer Gynt* is not as susceptible to this weakness, nor quite to the same degree are the last plays. These move toward a greater openness of feeling, expression and structure.

Between 1850 and 1900 especially, modern drama, which for the most part was based on the norms of scientific or rationalist materialism, was prone to incline toward sheer functional efficiency, a kind of literary engineering. The method was, and always is, in danger of choking off inspiration.

11
Fears and Flights

I T MAY NOT BE inappropriate at this juncture to cite a historian who writes that "in the 1880s there was a preoccupation with sociological problems, in the 1890s a reaction against them, just as still earlier Norwegian writers were nationalistically concerned with historical subjects." It cannot be said with any assurance that this was either the cause or the effect of the change in Ibsen's dramatic course, but there is surely a correspondence.

The Master Builder (1892) was the first play Ibsen wrote following his return to Norway in 1891 after his twenty-seven-year absence abroad. What distinguishes the turn in his development at this point is not the further evolution of his "symbolism" but that, as in *Rosmersholm*, he not only eschews social polemics but opens an ever deeper vein of self-dissection, a further probing of his own failure as man and artist.

Something of this was always present, but whatever self-doubt may have previously troubled him, affirmations of his basic convictions were generally dominant. The feeling and tone alter unequivocally in *The Master Builder* and the three plays

Note: All the citations from the plays in this chapter are from the translations in the Oxford University Press edition.

which follow it. They are most markedly personal; Ibsen himself has become the subject.

There is always danger in ascribing a one-to-one equivalence between the man and the work. Still, with *The Master Builder* an investigation into biographical matter is inevitable. Ibsen himself said of Solness, the play's pivotal character, that he was "a man somewhat akin to me."

There is, first of all, the question of Ibsen's relation to three young women: Emilie Bardach, a Viennese girl of eighteen, whom Ibsen met when he was sixty; Helen Raff, a painter he met at about the same time; and Hildur Andersen, a concert pianist whom he first encountered in Christiana when she was a child of ten and was to meet again in 1897, nineteen years later. All three women absorbed his passionate attention. But it is the special intensity of his feeling for Emilie Bardach which has attracted most notice among biographers. It was to her he sent his photograph with the inscription "The May Sun of a September Life." She is presumed to have been the most vivid of the three (or possibly four) models for the character of Hilde who so potently inspires the architect (master builder) Solness.

For my part, I am disinclined to credit this, though there can be no doubt that Ibsen's relation to Emilie Bardach and the others contributed various details to the portrait. The Hilde Wangel of *The Master Builder* is the Hilde of *The Lady from the Sea* whose sister called her "a little beast" because she found excitement not only in danger but in misfortune. For the moment we will leave conjecture on this issue for a closer look at Ibsen's attitude toward his marriage and his life with Suzannah, his wife. There has been, as we have seen, considerable speculation on these aspects of Ibsen's personality and their bearing on this plays.

The tendency—probably justified—is to pass over these questions lightly because there is no actual proof that Ibsen's ardor ever led to a physically consummated affair with Emilie Bardach. Still, one wonders. In her diary she notes the obstacles which might (or did) keep them apart: "the difference of age! his wife! his son!" At a later date she wrote, "He means to possess me. This is his absolute will. He intends to overcome all obstacles." In a letter to her he wrote, "Was it a Stupidity or was it Madness that we should have come together? Or was it both Stupidity and Madness? Or was it neither? I believe the last is the only supposition that would stand the test. It was a simple necessity of nature. It was equally our fate."

Emilie comments in her diary about a previous letter, "He wants me to read between the lines. But do not the lines themselves say enough?" We may ask the same question and answer in one way or another. In any case we know that when Emilie persisted in keeping up the correspondence in a manner more curt than delicate, Ibsen wrote that it had to stop.

Despite the information afforded by his biographers, Ibsen's relationship with his wife has never been conclusively defined. We have read his tribute to her idealism, her devotion to him, her honesty in all things and her steady will. Still his marriage is often referred to as "loveless."

We may take the following generalization as a possible hint of the situation. "Unhappy love," he said, "is when two people who love each other get married and find that they don't suit each other and cannot live happily together." It is altogether possible that given his complex and contradictory character, his total immersion in his work, no woman could have proved entirely compatible with him. He had very little feeling for the establishment of a family hearth, a settled home. Most of his life he moved about from one residence to another; most of them were like hotel-room stopovers. One may also doubt that a man who believed, to quote a speech from *Love's Comedy*, that "love comes truly to life when it escapes from longing and desire" would make a satisfactory husband.

That Ibsen's relationship with his wife was occasionally strained we know as a matter of fact through his letter to her of May 1895. A rumor had reached her that he was "keeping company" with Hildur Andersen, and might be contemplating divorce. When his wife informed him of this he was incensed. "I can solemnly declare to you," he wrote, "that I have never thought or intended anything of the sort and that I shall never think or intend it. Whatever I may have blurted out when your moods and temperamental fits drove me to momentary desperation has no bearing on anything else and is not worth considering."

Still, it is interesting to note that Emilie Bardach in 1927 told one of Ibsen's biographers that "he had spoken to her of the possibility of a divorce and of a subsequent union with her in the course of which they were to travel widely and see the world." Michael Meyer adds, "The last entry in her diary would seem to bear her out." Was Ibsen merely fantasizing or flirting with her?

A young Dane who admired Ibsen described the condition of the Ibsen family as follows: "To find that one does not really love the woman one has married—must be a desperate situation for a man, and that is Ibsen's. He is a domineering character, egocentric and unbending, with a passionate masculinity and a curious admixture of personal cowardice, compulsively idealistic yet totally indifferent to expressing these ideals in his daily life, restlessly questing, confused, yet striving for clarity. *She* is unwomanly, tactless, *but* a stable, hard character, a mixture of intelligence and stupidity, not deficient in feeling but lacking humility. And . . . yet she loves him, if only through their poor son, whose fate is the saddest that could befall any child, to see divided what should be reconciled in him . . . "

Ibsen was most anxious to help his son, Sigurd, in every possible way, especially in his reading, his education, his career. Sigurd was at one time appointed attaché to the Swedish legation in Washington. It was hoped for a while that he might achieve the rank of prime minister in Sweden, but he was distrusted for his cosmopolitanism or lack of patriotic feeling. He resigned from the diplomatic service to write a book: *The Quintessence of Man*. He also wrote a play in 1913 which was translated into English, French and German. He had two children by his wife, Bjørnson's daughter Bergliot. He died in 1930; Suzannah Ibsen in 1914.

Still more pertinent to our immediate inquiry—Ibsen's life as it bears on *The Master Builder* and even more decisively on his later plays—is another entry in the diary of the young Dane just cited: "Does Ibsen love his wife? I don't know but she loves him, but is not happy in her love. Ibsen is so absorbed with his work that the proverb 'humanity first, art second' has practically been reversed."

That Ibsen at sixty should have attracted many young women is not surprising. Though still a controversial figure, he had become a culture hero. One of these young women said, "All the women are in love with him." And he, in turn, had, as Michael Meyer says, "a pathetic longing for young girls." But then most artists are flirts!

One reason for entering into these biographical matters is not so much to draw a parallel between the adduced facts and *The Master Builder* as well as the plays which followed it but also to suggest caution in the matter. For example, how does one reconcile a notation made by several critics that Aline, Solness' wife, was modeled on Ibsen's mother and that she also inspired the wholly dissimilar figure of Aase in *Peer Gynt*?

Then too there is surely a discrepancy between the frequent reference to *The Master Builder* as a play about sexual impulses, and the emphasis, indeed the core of the play, as something totally different. There is something absurd and aesthetically indecent about correlating the talk about the church spires and high towers in the play with a phallic symbol. This is supposed to indicate how clever Ibsen was in anticipating Freud! It is characteristic of our contemporary mania for reducing the greater to the lesser, the exceptional to the commonplace. It is an insignia of mean-mindedness. A chapel tower is surely a natural association with lofty aspiration and grandeur. There was a high belfry directly opposite Ibsen's birthplace in Skien.

The Master Builder might be called "Sorrows of the Artist," the price paid to create anything of great import. (By extension, the term "master builder" may be applied to a great scientist, statesman or industrialist.) It is not Hilde who provokes Solness to dissatisfaction with the achievement of his career, though she sharpens it and urges him to extend himself. The dissatisfaction is already present in him when she arrives on the scene. Hilde is the play's catalyst, she is not its center.

Solness suffers all the psychological turmoil and ache of the acclaimed artist. A most touching story is told of Maurice Ravel, who, in his prime, was advised by his doctor that he had an incurable disease of which he would soon die. Working at his piano one day he was heard to cry out, "My God, what I might have accomplished!"

Solness is plagued by a sense of guilt about what he had done as an artist *and not done*, what he is and what he had wished to be. He does not possess, Hilde tells him, "a vigorous conscience." On the contrary he is tormented by that same "fragile (or sickly) conscience" which tormented Ibsen as far back as 1880 when he wrote *Rosmersholm*.

The dialogue in *The Master Builder* is extremely terse and designedly repetitious. It makes everything Ibsen wants us to grasp unmistakable. It takes either an obtuse reader or one who insists on a wholly private interpretation to miss his meaning.

Solness uses everyone and everything for the purpose of his work. He has crushed his former boss, Brovik, and made him his assistant. Solness also employs and exploits Brovik's son, Ragnar, himself a talented young architect. Solness is a more or less self-taught artist, while Ragnar has the indispensable skills in which Solness is less proficient. To make sure Ragnar will keep working for him rather than establishing himself independently, Solness uses the fascination he exercises over his bookkeeper, Kaja, who is Ragnar's fiancée, by pretending that he desires her. When, through Hilde's urging, Solness finally releases Ragnar, he dismisses Kaja, who has grown ever more infatuated with him. A Chinese proverb tells us, "The genius creates hospitals!"

Solness is aware of the wickedness of his tactics, but he protests, "I am what I am and can't help myself." Knowing himself to be a master with no one else in his class, he unreasonably believes that no one has a right to compete with him. Yet he fears the younger generation. They have other aims, different aesthetic objectives. People well acquainted with any branch of the art world know how common this fear is. We cannot be certain that Ibsen was especially troubled by Knut Hamsun's attack on him at a public lecture Ibsen attended, sitting in the front row. Ibsen listened intently, apparently unperturbed. Did the "madman" Strindberg, also Ibsen's junior, who both admired and reviled him, loom large in his consciousness? We are sure he heard their clamor in the wings. Artists' progeny are always a threat to their "fathers."

In *The Master Builder*, Hilde is the younger generation incarnate, worshipful and challenging. Ibsen introduces Hilde to us in a typical *coup de théâtre*. "One of these days youth is going to come here beating at the door," Solness says. "Well, good Lord, what of it?" his doctor friend asks. "What of it?" is the rejoinder. "Just that that will mean the end of master builder Solness." There is a knock at the door. "What's that! Did you say something?"

DOCTOR: Somebody's knocking.
SOLNESS: Come in!

And Hilde enters. "She wears working clothes (at the moment her only clothes) with her skirt hitched up, a sailor's collar opened at the neck, and a sailor hat on her head. She has a rucksack on her back, a plaid blanket on a strap and a long alpenstock." This is the kind of dress which Solness' wife later reminds Hilde will make people stare at her—very much as for a time ordinary folk stared at our beatniks and hippies.

Solness is the dream figure of Hilde's childhood. In her home town ten years before, when she was twelve or thirteen, she witnessed him climbing up the scaffolding of a church he had designed to place a wreath on its tower. She had been so vociferously elated that Solness, who was later invited to a dinner in his honor at the club and to her parents' home, noticed her loveliness, called her a "little devil" and said she looked like a princess. (This was an endearment Ibsen addressed to several girls he wrote to at the time he was planning *Hedda Gabler* and *The Master Builder*.) Seeing Solness high above her, Hilde says, she thought she heard a singing like "harps in the air." There is no "symbolism" in this, only a natural expression for the time, the place, the person. It is just as much a vernacular mode of speech connoting enthusiasm as is that of the kids today who feel "sent" or "turned on" by the heroes of stage, screen, TV, or the popular bands. Solness had also kissed Hilde with the kind of miniature gallantry such men often practice to have fun with or flatter young girls and themselves.

Hilde, lively and spunky, is certainly a tease. No doubt a sexual pulse enters into her feeling for Solness, but there is much more to it than that. She is an idealist; she wishes him to be greater than he has ever been. She wants to see all the things he has *recently* built; especially if there are wonderful church towers among them.

SOLNESS: No, I don't build church towers any more. No churches either.

HILDE: What do you build now, then?

SOLNESS: Homes for people—Strange that you should ask that. That's what I want to do more than anything.

HILDE: Then why don't you?

SOLNESS: Because people don't want that.

"How good it is you came to me now," Solness says. He'd been alone and begun to be afraid, terribly afraid of youth. "Youth brings retribution. It is the vanguard of change. Marching under a new banner." To her question "Can you *use* me, master builder?" his answer is "Yes, I can indeed! For you too seem to be marching under a new banner."

Fear of the young has haunted him before Hilde's appearance. It is specifically dramatized in one of the play's first scenes. When Brovik tells Solness that a client has observed something "new" in his son Ragnar's drawings for a house that Solness has been commissioned to build and that he showed hardly any interest in, he blurts out, "Aha! New! Not the sort of old-fashioned rubbish *I* generally build! . . . Halvard Solness—he's to start backing down now. Making way for the younger men. Much younger men maybe? Just get out of the way. Out of the way! . . . I'll never give way to anybody! Never of my own free will."

Solness has other and just as tormenting fears and guilts. He has been immensely successful but, he suspects, his success was won at other people's expense. The burning down of his house was a steppingstone to his first triumph, the beginning of his renown. It was that disaster too which was indirectly the cause of his twin infants' death. It deprived his wife Aline of the chance to cultivate her chief talent: the care and building of children's lives, a loss that laid waste to her life.

She blames this on him, he imagines, but in this he is projecting his own sense of guilt; he sees in it the source of her alienation. She is aware of his power over women, over his bookkeeper Kaja, and perhaps over Hilde, if she is to replace Kaja. Aline has other and almost more painful memories than the death of her children. She misses the dolls of her parental home, which burned in the fire, dolls more intimately real to her than the children, who died only a few weeks after their birth. After all, they were closer to her for longer than her children. She is now depressed and depressing, sustained only by her everlasting sense of *duty*. "A tomb," Hilde calls her, not without genuine sympathy. And here he is "chained to a dead woman," he "who cannot live a joyless life"!

These guilts and fears are the price he has paid for his "good luck," his artistic eminence. "I've had to renounce . . . forever any hope of having a home of my own. I mean a home with children or even with a father and mother." His "happiness for which he is everywhere congratulated or envied wasn't to be got any cheaper."

He knows, as every "great man" does, that his station was not achieved without the aid of others. He had to have all kinds of "helpers and servants," those who come of themselves, but more frequently those he summons by his inner will. He calls them "trolls or devils," good or bad, and he is not certain which are the more powerful. If his first home, the one he had lived in during the first years of his marriage, the one which had burned down, had been Brovik's house, that man would not have accomplished what he, Solness, did. Thanks to the fire, he divided up most of the grounds into building sites. There he could build as he chose. "From then on I never looked back."

These specters of regret, doubt, fear make him suspect his wife of having asked a doctor to put him under observation. She probably believes him to be on the verge of insanity. The suspicion is the voice of his own apprehensions. They certainly have made him ill. Is Hilde, who bids him overcome his self-

doubt, a good or a bad "troll"? Is she a "bird of prey"? Certain
of Ibsen's sedulous exegetes have seized on this phrase—it also
occurs in *The Lady from the Sea*—which he first used apropos
of his encounters with such young women as Emilie Bardach,
and associated with the character of the earlier Hilde. To them
the Hilde here is a malevolent creature, an agent of destruction,
tritely speaking, "unsympathetic." She tries to persuade him,
goads him if you will, to build "castles in the air." She always
employs the colorful and exalted vocabulary of the idealistic
young person. She wants him to attempt the "impossible" once
more, to abandon his building of homes for people to live in—
worthy though that achievement may have been—and erect
great monuments, houses of worship that reach to heaven. This
himself he has wished to do. He once aspired to the heroic
Viking spirit in life, so that he might regain a robust conscience.

In a frenzy of hyperbolic speech, he tells Hilde, "You know
I began by building churches . . . I thought [they were] the
finest things I could devote my life to . . . I think He should
have been pleased with me."

HILDE: He? What He?
SOLNESS: He for whom they were built, of course. To whose honor
           and glory they were dedicated . . . I soon found out that
           He wasn't pleased with me. He wanted me to become a
           great master in my own sphere, so I could go on building
           ever more glorious churches for Him. At first, I didn't
           realize what He was up to, and then suddenly I saw it
           clearly. It was when I built the church tower up at Lysan-
           ger [where Hilde had first beheld him in his glory]. I was
           up in strange surroundings. I had plenty of time to think
           and meditate. And suddenly I understood why He had
           taken my little children from me. He didn't want me to
           become attached to anything. I was to be allowed no love
           or happiness. I was to be nothing but a Master Builder,
           and I was to devote my life solely to building for Him.
           But I soon put a stop to that!
HILDE: What did you do then?
SOLNESS: And as I stood up there, high over everything, I said to
           Him: listen to me, Almighty one! From now on, I will be
           a free Master Builder, free in my sphere, just as You are

HILDE:	in yours. I will never more build churches for You, only homes for human beings.
HILDE:	That was the song I heard in the air!
SOLNESS:	Yes, but He won in the end.
HILDE:	How do you mean?
SOLNESS:	This building homes for human beings isn't worth a rap!
HILDE:	Is that how you feel?
SOLNESS:	Yes. Because now I see it. People have no use for these houses of theirs. Not to be happy in—no. And if I had such a house, I would have no use for it either. What does it amount to now that I look back on it? What have I ever built? Nothing! It all amounts to nothing!
HILDE:	Then will you never build anything more, Master Builder?
SOLNESS:	On the contrary—now I'm just going to begin.

To begin what, one may well ask? Transposing Solness for the moment to Ibsen, the answer is majestic, sublime edifices (like *Brand* and *Peer Gynt*) rather than the middle-class homes for people (like *The Pillars of Society, A Doll's House, Ghosts, An Enemy of the People*). He can do it, he imagines, if there is some good companion—Hilde herself—who would climb hand in hand with him. "The princess shall have her castle."

She has told him, before this, that she must go away. "I won't let you," he says. "What can I do here now?" "Just be here, Hilde"—"You knew it wouldn't stop at that." "So much the better," he recklessly cries. But she retreats from the thought of wounding his wife.

I find no sex symbolism in all this. Ibsen's harking back to the heights of such plays as *Brand, Peer Gynt* and possibly *The Pretenders* and, in his eyes, *Emperor and Galilean* springs from a keen intuition, even though in doing this he seems to downgrade the middle-class realistic plays on which his fame has largely rested. There are critics now who believe that those earlier ones (certainly *Brand* and *Peer Gynt*) and the last plays, beginning with *The Master Builder*, are his profoundest and most beautiful achievements. And these, we once again note, are works of auto-criticism.

Ragnar and other colleagues of his age are sure Solness will not dare ascend the heights as he has formerly done. "It is his

wish to do so," says Hilde, and, to repeat, that desire was present before her arrival: she only served to activate it. As he
climbs higher and higher in response to her challenge to place
a wreath on the tower of the newly built church, she begins
to hear the song in the air once more.

She hardly sees him when he falls to his death. Ragnar, with
ghastly thrill and perhaps unconscious satisfaction, says, "So
after all, he couldn't do it." To which Hilde, ever the romantic,
replies, "But he climbed to the very top and I heard harps in
the air!" What she hears is perhaps akin to that "mighty ballad"
Jatgeir (Ibsen) in *The Pretenders* promises to create, and a
striving with *Him* whom Solness had defied. To the very end
Solness remains for Hilde "My, my Master Builder!"

Who will deny that Ibsen for very many of us was a master
builder? Nor was he quite as fearful of the younger generation
as Solness. In an 1898 speech delivered to students Ibsen said,
"I have never been afraid of youth. I knew it would come. . . .
It came, and I greet it now with pleasure." But that was six
years after the publication of *The Master Builder*. He went and
took flight to ever nobler perceptions, he planned further "crazy
tricks" when in 1900–01 he suffered two strokes before his
death in 1906.

"There is a fact . . . about the really great artists of the past,"
Henry Moore has said, "in some way their late works become
simplified and fragmentary, become imperfect and unfinished.
The artists stop caring about beauty and such things, and yet
their works get greater."

Michael Meyer quotes this, quite appropriately, I think, apropos of *When We Dead Awaken*, though it is perhaps even more
applicable to *Little Eyolf* (1894). Each "fragment" of the play
—thread of plot or conceptual allusion—is distinct, yet the impression of the whole is one of mistiness, a floating away into
quietude. A confluence of all the thoughts and feelings of
Ibsen's later years seems to merge into a soft color field in
which the outlines fade and what remains is pure atmosphere.
We are no longer wholly in the realm of drama but of mood
and mystery. We gaze into this film of shifting images and

sentiment, and what chiefly appears discernible is the lone figure of the aging author brooding in melancholy repose.

The thirty-seven-year-old Allmers, an intellectual, once an
occasional teacher and poor, now wealthy through marriage,
has for some years been working on a book called *The Responsibility of Man*. (A major Ibsen theme and a title resembling
his son Sigurd's book!) Allmers' wife, Rita, is not his "soul-
mate"; his younger half-sister, Asta, is. But Rita, a woman of
consuming passion, took possession of him by her beauty and by
the wealth which allowed him the liberty to follow his intellectual bent. At one moment, reflecting on his marriage to
Rita, he asserts that she bought him, an accusation generally
directed in Ibsen's plays by the wife against the husband. In
this case, we should remember, she also exerts a physical hold
on him.

In a troubled state of mind, Allmers leaves Rita for some
weeks to seek solitude in the mountains, to think and to write.
On his return, he is a changed man. He will write no more, he
declares, but give up the book he has been working on and
devote himself to the education of his lame nine-year-old son,
Eyolf. He is no longer responsive to his wife's sexual ardor.
She wants to possess him entirely. "I only want you," she says.
"Nothing else in the world." She even hates his book because
it has kept them apart; she also resents sharing him with their
son. And the boy drowns.

The scene in which Rita berates Allmers for his coldness on
the night of his return from his retreat and the one in which
we hear of Eyolf's fall from the jetty to his death in the water
below—both in the first act—are among the most riveting in
Ibsen's work.

From this point the action is largely internal, or, to put it
another way, subjective. Overcome by a sense of guilt, Allmers
is inconsolable. We learn that while he and Rita were making
love, they had left the infant Eyolf on a table, from which he
fell, crippling him for life. (In Ibsen, as with more than a few
other artists, we recognize a fear or superstition that sexual
engagement somehow diminishes creative activity.) The weight
of the parents' mutual responsibility in the accident and the

fact that Rita had half desired the boy to be out of the way make their estrangement complete.

The only one Allmers seems able to talk to now is Asta, his half-sister. Theirs has been a true love. Because of it she has rejected a proposal of marriage from the honorable and hard-working Borghejm, an engineer, who has just finished building a road in the vicinity. But Asta has discovered that she is not really Allmers' sister. This makes no difference; she refuses to alter the character of their relationship. Despite her deep devotion to Allmers, she finally decides to go away and marry Borghejm.

Left alone, Rita and Allmers will heal their own and each other's wounds by working together to house, feed and help the poverty-stricken children who haunt the waterfront which they had formerly shunned. He who had written about responsibility had not been responsible; she who had lived through her senses will now enter a new relationship with him through the aid they will mutually offer to the needy.

It is a dream of personal renunciation; there is no salvation for them except in work on behalf of others. Though the specific situation is concrete enough, there is a certain remoteness in the play as a whole. Rita and Allmers speak of themselves as earthbound creatures, sensualists, but in fact the action gives the impression of occurring in some special sphere of indeterminate space. No mention of the ragamuffins down by the pier is made after Allmers and Rita have reminded themselves of their cruel neglect of Eyolf, until the end of the play. Apart from that the characters all appear strangely isolated from the rest of the world. In this "blank" environment—a scene designer might bathe the settings in pearl white and blue shadow —the only indisputably symbolic figure in any of Ibsen's last plays suddenly appears. It is the Rat Wife, a specter of retribution. Even she might pass for a real person, though it would take considerable skill to convince us of her reality. She is an "exterminator," ridding homes of rodents and other pests. There are poor people in the neighborhood, but what justification is there for a Rat Wife to enter into the wealthily appointed garden room of the Allmers home?

The Rat Wife is described as "a little thin, shriveled old grey-haired woman, with sharp, piercing eyes, wearing an old fashioned flowered dress, with a black bonnet and a black coat with tassels; she carries a large red umbrella and from her arm a black bag dangles on a string." She plays on her pipe and when the rats hear it, she explains, they "come from the cellars, down from the lofts, out of all their dark holes and crannies"—and they follow her boat into the water and drown. Fascinated by the witch, whose "assistant" is a dog with a face Eyolf thinks the most horrible he has ever seen and yet one which he thinks beautiful, "the little wounded soldier," Eyolf, is led to his destruction. Can Eyolf read Death in the dog's face?

Eyolf speaks of the street boys who jeer at his lameness, telling him he will never be a soldier. Despite his dislike of them, he notices that "they're so poor, that they have to go barefoot." Allmers murmurs, "How this gnaws at my heart," not in reference to the poverty Eyolf describes but to his son's misfortune. (Could all this possibly have some connection with Ibsen's feeling for his son Sigurd?) A moment later the Rat Wife enters, announcing herself with "Begging your pardon—have your honors any troublesome thing that gnaws here in this house?"

The entrance of this creature strikes me as a forced intrusion. Eyolf, unable to swim, might have drowned or been drowned or been fatally hurt in some other way than by the Rat Wife's intervention. A disturbing element in the play, yet it places it in the half-world which sets the tone for much that follows. We are removed from the flesh of reality and move toward the ineffability of the spirit.

As idea and thought it is clear enough: on a new plane the play sums up much of what Ibsen has said through a good part of his writing. Allmers, on his return from his holiday among "the high peaks and wide spaces," has come to the conclusion that "what one can manage to put down [in a book] is insignificant." He must *do* something more. The claim of higher duties has begun to obsess his conscience. He will give the boy a more personal rather than an academic education: " . . . no more books from now on." "Here at home," he adds, "I would

never have been able to conquer myself. I would never have
[been able] to renounce anything. Not in this home." For in
this home he cannot evade Rita's sexual rapacity. He must not
divide himself. Rita can henceforth serve only to help him
remain faithful to his high ideals.

The truest love is supra-physical, sacred love, a spiritual bond.
(It is not old age or impotence that makes Ibsen voice such
thoughts through the thirty-seven-year-old Allmers' mouth.)
Asta, with whom Allmers had shared such love before little
Eyolf's birth—he had called *her* Eyolf then—must leave him
when she has learned that she is not his sister and might come
to desire him as a man. That is why she goes off to marry
Borghejm, whom she respects and admires, for he has said of
his own work that "it's a marvellous life to be a maker of roads!"

What then remains to men and women, or at least to Allmers
and Rita, when physical passion has waned, or for some other
reason has become impossible? Allmers' sexual "coldness," it is to
be understood, is a symptom of the guilt he feels about the cause
of Eyolf's being crippled. It is the thing that gnaws in the house.
Allmers and Rita must dedicate themselves to others, to social
ideals. It is the still-passionate Rita, interestingly enough, who
arrives at the decision to do this. Having lost her child and
become deprived of sexual intimacy with her husband, she will
fill her emptiness with "something resembling love." She, as
everyone does or must, yields to the "law of change"—a phrase
which from the first days of his maturity has been recurrent in
Ibsen's vocabulary. It is not only, I insist, not necessary, it
is a falsification of the play's validity to suppose its conclusion
is based on what some critics have maintained is Allmers'
impotence.

Allmers asks Rita what she hopes to do for the town's wretched
children, whom in his former intellectual, aesthetic, sensual self-
indulgences, protected by his wife's fortune in "gold and green
forests," he had avoided or resisted. "To begin with," she answers, "I shall try to make life less hard for them." If she can
assume such human responsibility, Eyolf will not have died in
vain. Together they will endeavor to make their determination

real. The spirit of little Eyolf and the other, the "big" Eyolf (Asta), will be at their side.

"Where shall we look [for them]?" Rita asks. "Upwards, up toward the mountains," Allmers replies. "Towards the stars and the great silence." Rita, stretching out her hands toward Allmers in acceptance of their new pact, says, "Thank you."

The play which intimates the renunciation of the flesh is also a play of regeneration, a flight from egocentric indulgence of body and mind to the highest reaches of human attainment. It mirrors Ibsen's attempt to resolve his lifelong conflict, to submit to the law of change in his thought and person. Yet it cannot be considered a complete change. There never would have existed any conflict within him had there been no strong impulse and will to raise himself above his mundane ambitions and appetites. But here he expresses the effort in a new way, combining his earthbound realism with poetic exultation, an effort which has not been made without signs of artistic and stylistic strain. Ibsen's last two plays in this vein are more naturally achieved, more firmly rooted. They add a new and special dimension of personal meaning, previously only adumbrated, never wholly articulated with such clarity, force and moral gravity.

12

Confessional

WRITTEN WHEN HE WAS SIXTY-EIGHT, *John Gabriel Borkman* betrays no waning of Ibsen's powers. It is compact in construction without coming to a close in the artificial hurry and mathematical precision of *Hedda Gabler* or what, at first reading, may seem an unprepared reversal in *A Doll's House*. The dialogue is an concise as ever, with a rise to poetic utterance which matches the last pages of *Brand*. There is massiveness in the characterization of the three central characters and, in their relation to the minor ones, a fine interweaving of the play's various thematic strands. Verbally and visually the final scenes attain heroic proportion in their summation of the whole.

With the decline of the classic and romantic drama it became increasingly difficult to create personages of broad dimension, "big people." John Gabriel Borkman is such a person. His wife, Gunhild, and her sister, Ella Rentheim, stand beside him with equivalent impressiveness.

Borkman as a major figure is the only man of business in the Ibsen gallery since Bernick in *The Pillars of Society* written nineteen years before. From *The Master Builder* through to

Note: All citations from plays in this chapter are from Michael Meyer's translations.

When We Dead Awaken all the protagonists are artists or intellectuals, except Borkman, who is a former banker.

He was a banker who at the summit of his success failed ignominiously. A miner's son, he climbed to immense wealth and influence. At one time he was being considered for a post as cabinet minister. But he outreached himself. His overweening ambition led him to use his depositors' funds, stocks and bonds, illegally. After he was sentenced to a five-year jail sentence, his wife refused to talk with him or to see him. Their student son, Erhart, was sent away to live with Gunhild's sister, Ella Rentheim, the only person saved in the financial disaster. It is in Ella's house, the parental Rentheim mansion, that Gunhild and John Gabriel now live. When we first see him—in the first act the sound of his footsteps is heard in the sitting room below—he is in the former parlor, where he has immured himself for eight years. Here all during his waking hours he paces about acting as his own prosecutor, counsel and judge. He is sustained by the fantastic hope of recovering his lost empire: the monies which had come under his control and the bank which their profits had established.

Like all of Ibsen's titans, the industrialist Borkman is a romantic dreamer. Seen through his wife's eyes he might be thought a swaggering tycoon very much like those we consider characteristic of the late nineteenth century. When Ella reproves Gunhild (Mrs. Borkman) for cutting off all communication with her husband, we hear the following:

MRS. BORKMAN: ... No, no, no—I shall never see him again, never!
ELLA: You are hard, Gunhild ...
MRS. BORKMAN: Didn't he tell the courts that I had started him on the path to ruin? That I had spent too much money ...
ELLA: Wasn't there some truth in that?
MRS. BORKMAN: But he wanted it that way! He wanted everything to be so absurdly luxurious.
ELLA: I know. But shouldn't you have restrained him?
MRS. BORKMAN: Was I to know it wasn't his own money he was giving me to squander? And wasn't he ten times as extravagant as I?

ELLA: Well, I suppose he had to keep up his position.
MRS. BORKMAN: Oh yes! He always said we had "to put on a show."
                  Oh, he put on a show all right! Drove a four-in-
                  hand, as though he were a king. Made people bow
                  and scrape to him, the way they would do to a king.

In the isolation of his drawing-room lair, where Frida, fifteen-
year-old daughter of his old friend and only confidant Foldal,
plays the *Danse Macabre*, we see Borkman in a different light.
Speaking of the mines where his father took him as a boy, he
says, "Down there, the iron ore sings . . . It sings!" (In Ibsen's
poem called "The Mines," published in 1871, twenty-five years
before *Borkman*, the first stanza reads: "Downwards I must
carve my way/Till I hear the iron ore sing.")

FRIDA: It sings?
BORKMAN: When it is broken loose. The hammer blows that loosen
           it are the midnight bell that sets it free. And then, in its
           own way, the iron sings—for joy.
FRIDA: Why does it do that, Mr. Borkman?
BORKMAN: It wants to be taken up into the daylight, and serve hu-
           manity.

This egotist who speaks of industry and wealth like a poet
says, "I could have created millions! Think of all the mines I
could have brought under my control, the shafts I could have
sunk. I could have harnessed cataracts, hewn quarries. My ships
would have covered the world, linking continent to continent.
All this I would have created alone." And further on, "I wanted
all the sources of power in the country to serve me. The earth,
the mountain, the forests, the sea. So that I might create a kingdom for myself, and prosperity for thousands and thousands of
others."

Doesn't this, *mutatis mutandi*, sound like Peer Gynt, like Solness, like Ibsen himself?

The drama is brought to a head by the struggle between Gunhild Borkman and Ella Rentheim for "possession" of Borkman's
son, Erhart. To avoid having to bear the brunt of his father's
disgrace, Erhart had been sent to live with his aunt, Ella. She
alone had been saved from the wreck of Borkman's bankruptcy.

She had been in love with him and thus came to cherish his son. Grown up, the youth returned to his mother's side, though he now lives apart from her in the town.

After an absence of some years, Ella returns to the Borkman household, of which she is the actual owner and the sole support. She is ill and has not much longer to live. She plans to settle there. But what she really wants is for Erhart to bear her name after her death. This Gunhild will not tolerate. For in Gunhild's mind, Erhart has a "mission": to restore the Borkman name to honor, though she has no idea how this is to be accomplished.

Ella implores Borkman in the name of her onetime love for him to vie with Gunhild on her behalf. The confrontation of Gunhild on the one hand and Ella and Borkman on the other precipitates the climactic scenes.

Still we are not yet at the heart of the drama. Borkman gave up Ella for her sister, Gunhild, because Henkel, Borkman's business associate, a man on whom Borkman depended for financial backing, was also in love with Ella. In exchange for Borkman's renunciation of Ella, Henkel was to help Borkman in his vast industrial projects. When Ella, after Borkman had married Gunhild, persisted in rejecting Henkel, Henkel set about to discredit Borkman and refused him further financial aid, bringing about his fall.

Borkman's defense of his "deal" with Henkel is that he had to conquer or be destroyed, though she was the most precious person in the world to him. "And yet you bartered me," she charges. "Traded your love to another man! Sold my love for the chairmanship of a bank! You are guilty of a double murder. The murder of your own soul and mine . . . You destroyed my capacity for love . . . You have never loved anything outside yourself." He answers truthfully, "I have loved power—the power to create happiness all around me." It is the answer of a great magnate and of many artists. It would have been Solness' answer, if his wife had reproached him for his indifference. It is also Ibsen's self-accusation and confession.

The tug-of-war over Erhart ends in a curious, ironically significant manner, which adds another facet to the play. When

Gunhild and Ella struggle to force Erhart to choose between them, Gunhild speaks of the "mission" to reclaim the family name. But, he tells her, that is her mission, not his. And though he is genuinely fond of Ella, who raised him during his formative years, he cannot remain with her. He has become infatuated with a Mrs. Wilton, an attractive woman seven years his senior, abandoned by her husband. A sort of "merry widow," she is one of Ibsen's most appealing characters. The very night of the family "showdown," Mrs. Wilton and Erhart are to ride off together to the happiness of the South. Mrs. Wilton takes Frida, Foldal's pretty pianist daughter, along with them. The girl is to study music.

When Mrs. Borkman asks Mrs. Wilton, "Do you think you are being wise in taking a young girl with you?" Mrs. Wilton answers, "Men are unpredictable. And women too. When Erhart is tired of me and I of him, it would be good for both of us that he should have someone to fall back on, poor boy." To the query "What will you do?" she replies, "Oh, I shall manage, I promise. Goodbye everybody!" Earlier Mrs. Wilton has said, "I am quite used to finding my way alone."

Mrs. Wilton delights me, and, I am sure, delighted Ibsen. In her sense of life's realities, she very much resembles the sensible Mrs. Sörby as well as Gina in *The Wild Duck*. There is a spicy correlative to Mrs. Wilton and Erhart's departure from the Rentheim-Borkman home. As the young couple drive off in the pretty lady's sleigh they very nearly run over little old Foldal and slightly injure his foot. Foldal does not know that his daughter was in the sleigh. When Borkman, amused by the incident, tells him that his daughter was in the sleigh and she was going away with Mrs. Wilton and Erhart as Frida's tutor, Foldal claps his hands and exclaims, "My little Frida in that magnificent sleigh, a sleigh with silver bells." Borkman's comment on this: "Everything there was real. Inside and out." Erhart and Mrs. Wilton have acted of their own free will. There was no lie between them; they were moving toward the joy of life. Foldal, all candor though he be, is also in his own humble way a realist. Once again Ibsen "approves."

The final scenes are among Ibsen's greatest achievements. Borkman, having pleaded with Erhart for cooperation in re-establishing himself, a plea which Erhart has rejected, dashes from the house in a last burst of desperate energy. He is determined never to enter it again. In the snow and frosty air, he mounts a winding path high in the hills overlooking the countryside. Ella follows him, as she would follow him everywhere.

They arrive at a place where in the bygone days of their love they used to rest and stare into the distance. Now half-mad, Borkman apostrophizes the prospect before him: the fjord visible only to him, with the smoke rising from the steamers. "They come and go. They create a sense of fellowship throughout the world. They bring light and warmth to the hearts of man in many thousands of homes. That is what I dreamed of creating."

He is seized by a new rush of ardor; once more he evokes his dream and declares his own true passion. "I feel them, these buried millions, I see those veins of iron ore, stretching their twisting, branching, enticing arms towards me . . . I love you, when you lie like the dead, deep down in the dark. I love your treasures that crave for life, with your bright retinue of glory and power. I love you, love you, love you."

He collapses. Gunhild has followed her sister's and husband's tracks. Borkman is dead. To Gunhild's question whether he died by his own hand, Ella replies, "No, a hand of iron gripped his heart." A miner's son, Borkman couldn't live in the fresh air. "See what the cold has done," Ella says. Gunhild adds, "Yes, the coldness of the heart." Two shadows, the sisters join hands over the man they both loved.

Whether induced by the pursuit of holiness, artistic perfection or intellectual eminence, *the coldness of the heart* kills. In this assertion and confession Ibsen pronounces his deepest conviction.

Michael Meyer's collection which includes *The Master Builder*, *John Gabriel Borkman* and *When We Dead Awaken* could be entitled "The Neglect of Love." The last of the three plays

might bear as its epigraph these lines in F. E. Garrett's verse
translation of *Brand*:

AGNES: You painted me but you did not see me
          At one blind draught you drained life's cup . . .
          . . . .
EJNAR: Then flashed the thought and struck me through
          Why, you have quite forgot to woo.

The idea might also be illustrated by one of Picasso's drawings: a beautiful naked woman stands by the artist while he
concentrates on the picture of an animal-like figure, a monkey
or a bear. The drawing might be construed in several ways but
as I looked at it I remember thinking, "He does not see her."

Brand scorns the notion that love excuses the neglect of duty;
in Ibsen's last plays—particularly in *When We Dead Awaken*—
the neglect of love is viewed as the cardinal sin.

Ibsen called *When We Dead Awaken* (his shortest play) an
"epilogue," the closing of the circle which began with *A Doll's
House*. He no doubt meant that all the plays within the series,
whatever dramatic and scenic metaphors they may have contained, were *realistic* plays—insofar as any play may be deemed
realistic!

There is nothing abstruse or mystic about the conversation
between the aging sculptor Rubek and Irene, the model who in
her youth inspired his most famous work:

RUBEK: Do you remember what you said when I asked you if you
          would leave home and come with me into the world?
IRENE: I raised three fingers in the air and promised that I would
          go with you to the end of the world; and to the end of life.
          And that I would serve you in all things.
RUBEK: As a model for my work.
IRENE: Free and naked.
RUBEK: And you did serve me, Irene—joyfully, gladly, unstintingly.
IRENE: Yes; with all the trembling blood of my youth.
RUBEK: Too true you did.
IRENE: I knelt down at your feet, and served you, Arnold. But you
          —you—you!

RUBEK: I never wronged you. Never, Irene.
IRENE: Yes, you did! You wronged my inmost being!
RUBEK: I?
IRENE: Yes, you. I stripped myself naked for you to gaze at me. And you never once touched me. [*Very like Rita's accusation of Allmers in* Little Eyolf]

. . . .

RUBEK: I was an artist, Irene.
IRENE (darkly): An artist. Yes.
RUBEK: Before all else, I was an artist. And I was sick, sick with a longing to create the great work of my life.

. . . .

And I was convinced that if I touched you, if I desired you sensually, my vision would be profaned so that I would never be able to achieve what I was striving after. I still think there is some truth in that. [*Note the ambivalence.*]
IRENE: The child of the mind first; the child of the body second.

Rubek's masterpiece which Irene had inspired, called "The Day of the Resurrection," is repeatedly referred to as their "child," just as Lövborg's book which Hedda burned was Lövborg's and Thea's "child." Rubek's and Irene's "child" was not destroyed; it has become a world-renowned museum piece. But Rubek's turning away from Irene deadened her. She became a wanton, unresponsive yet fascinating to the men she took on. Now presumed to be insane, she no longer thinks of herself as a living person.

After the creation of his greatest work, Rubek married a pretty and perky young woman, Maja, whom he had become rich enough to take for his pleasure. He is now bored to distraction with her and is ready, almost eager, to part. His work after his marriage took a different turn. Just as Solness gave up building temples and began to fashion "homes for people," so Rubek devoted himself to portraits. Solness came to think his homes for people weren't worth a rap, so Rubek sees in his busts not the "striking likenesses" his sitters praise but "something hidden within their faces which others cannot see . . . The world sees nothing. It understands nothing." For him the portraits are "the righteous and estimable faces of horses, the

opinionated muzzle of donkeys, the lop-eared and shallow brows
of dogs, the overgorged chaps of swine, and the dull and brutal-
ized fronts of oxen . . . Just nice domestic animals."

Could this have been the seventy-one-year-old Ibsen's judgment of his plays since *The Pretenders, Brand, Peer Gynt, Emperor and Galilean*? Is that another reason why he referred to
When We Dead Awaken as "an epilogue"? "If I write anything more," he said, "it will be in quite another context, perhaps too in another form." A return to verse? Is this play then
a last testament, a confession of failure? The old self had "died."
With the impetus of this intuition he felt ready to be resurrected,
to create in the vein of some future "crazy ideas." The play is,
perhaps unconsciously, prophetic, for as Rubek sets out on the
perilous path to greater heights, he and his reawakened inspiration (Irene) are buried in the avalanche from that peak of
exaltation. Ibsen had seven more years to live, but illness pre-
vented further creation. The play might have been called "Too
Late"!

It is a mistake to think of Maja as the empty-headed and
frivolous doll Rubek has come to consider her. We must consider her role in the play's scheme. She too seeks the joy of life
without which her creator found life unendurably burdensome,
and which he was often agonizingly conscious of missing. When
Maja leaves Rubek on the mountain's icy heights to try to make
a go of it in the valley with a "heathen" country squire, hunter
and deceived husband, Ulfhagen, she and he do what is right
for them to do and what Ibsen himself thought them justified in
doing. Not everyone is a Brand or a master builder or even a
Rubek. Ibsen has no contempt for the ordinary breed of men
and women as long as they act honestly and freely according
to their own healthy natures. That, as I have remarked, is the
significance of such characters as Mrs. Sörby, Gina, Mrs. Wilton
—and here Ulfhagen and Maja. As she goes off with the man
she sings:

> I am free! I am free!
> No longer imprisoned! I'm free
> I can fly like a bird, I'm free.

This is an affirmation of "all the glory in the world" which Rubek had promised her and was too "dead" to fulfill. Little remains in him now except bitter regret and the vain hope of spiritual renewal.

Time and again, Ibsen said through his most articulate characters that he'd never had a home. His first thirty-six years in Norway had been spent in painful struggle. His father and brothers and probably even his mother had not won his enduring affection. As we have seen he achieved success only during his years abroad, traveling from one place to another. On his return to Norway when generous tribute and honor had been gained, he settled in lasting solid comfort. The opening lines suggest something else. As Rubek and Maja sit outside the Spa Hotel at a resort on the Norwegian coast, just having had lunch, they are drinking champagne and each has a newspaper:

RUBEK: Well, what's the matter with you?
MAJA: Just listen to the silence.
RUBEK: Can you hear it?
MAJA: Hear what?
RUBEK: The silence.
MAJA: I certainly can.
RUBEK: Perhaps you're right, my dear. One can sometimes hear silence.
MAJA: God knows one can. When its deafening as it is here.
RUBEK: Here at the spa, you mean?
MAJA: Everywhere in Norway. Oh, down in the city it was noisy. But even there, I thought all that noise and bustle had something dead about it.
RUBEK: Aren't you happy to be home again, Maja?
MAJA: Are you?
RUBEK: I?
MAJA: Yes, you've been abroad so much, much longer than I. Are you really happy to be home again?
RUBEK: No, to be perfectly honest. Not really happy . . . Perhaps I have been abroad too long. This northern provincial life seems foreign to me.

Yet Ibsen was thoroughly Norwegian in his romanticism, his ancestral memory of Viking fortitude and heroics, his practicality, his vigor, his mysticism, his idealistic conscience. He carried Norway wherever he went, as Joyce did Ireland. The "normal" Norwegian middle class was the "world" to him as, by extension, it is to us. But with it the sea, the fjord, the mountains, the gloomy dark, the summer sun, the cold and frost, the yearning for something else in the unknown distance are also present.

In *When We Dead Awaken* we find them all in miniature. Yet there is something *big* about it, an adumbration in the background of grandeur beyond our immediate sight. Ibsen was never content.

13
Conspectus

T HE SOURCE OF Ibsen's self-contention, the constant shift in his intellectual and emotional attitudes, may be traced to his yearning for perfection, or more exactly, for an *absolute*. If there is a permanent symbol in his work it relates to his passion for ascent to the empyrean: physically the mountain, philosophically the absolute. But Ibsen had too realistic a mind not to know that absolutes are, practically speaking, impossible, and humanly speaking, dangerous. Brand and Rubek perish in their climb to the mountain's peak; Solness falls from the high point of his church.

To achieve the absolute Ibsen demanded freedom (or sincerity) of the self. This ideal too, however, he found wanting. Peer Gynt, Emperor of the Self, is a much more dismal failure than Brand. Freedom with responsibility limits the self: it is a surrender to necessity. Necessity implies the recognition of forces outside the self. Even in his most drastic criticism of social convention, *Ghosts*, Mrs. Alving in debate with Pastor Manders yields for a moment to his defense of custom by saying, perhaps ironically, "You may be right." Hence the indissoluble dilemma, the perpetual doubt. Yet when the Shade (or Figure) of Agnes tells Brand,

Remember, an angel with a flaming rod
Drove Man from Paradise
He set a gulf before the gate.
Over that gulf you cannot leap.

Brand cries out, "The way of longing remains." The longing
for the absolute still possesses him. And the Figure pronounces
the fateful words "Die! The World has no use for you."

Our name for the absolute is God. He who looks upon the
face of God, we are also reminded in *Brand*, cannot live. Irene,
speaking to Rubek in *When We Dead Awaken*, refers to God as
"the one in whom you do not believe." But Solness, another of
Ibsen's "great men," speaks to God on high, and Rosmer cannot
free himself from the age-old heritage which finally destroys
the "emancipated" or radical will of Rebecca West. We remember that when she says, "They cling long to their dead here
at Rosmersholm," the housekeeper corrects her by saying, "It's
my belief it's the dead that cling to Rosmersholm." We also
remember that when a friend took it for granted that Ibsen was
an unbeliever, he grew angry and rebuked him.

Michael Meyer in his preface to *Brand* relates the following:
"In 1906, when Ibsen was dying, Christopher Bruun, the man
who had largely inspired the character of Brand nearly half a
century before, came to visit him. The two had remained
friends, and Bruun had baptized Ibsen's grandchild. They had
always kept off the subject of religion, but now, in the presence
of death, Bruun tentatively touched on the subject of Ibsen's
relationship to God. Ibsen's answer was short and characteristic:
'You leave that to me!' he growled; and Bruun did."

Ibsen only once attempted to dramatize the core of his religious faith—in *Emperor and Galilean*. That is why, as already
noted, though it was a well-nigh unproducable play, he held it
in especial esteem. The line which states its hero's (Julian's) crises
of conscience is, to repeat, "The old beauty is no longer beautiful, and the new truth is no longer true." Historically speaking, the apothegm is misplaced. In its dramatic context, "the old
beauty" refers to paganism; "the new truth" to Christianity.
It is an anachronism to have a Christian—for at the moment of

speaking Julian is still a devout though troubled Christian—say in the fifth century A.D. that "the new truth is *no longer* true." Ibsen himself was speaking through Julian, and "the new truth" Ibsen had in mind was something· wholly contemporary. We shall see what the issue for Ibsen, rather than for Julian, actually was.

What is true in this connection is that particularly as a Norwegian Protestant, in the mid-nineteenth century, Ibsen associated Christianity with a restrictive, forbidding, "sunless" way of life. Paganism in the play is a generic term for that "joy of life" viewed as the opposite of Christian truth. "I often wonder," Julian reflects, "whether truth is the enemy of beauty." As early as *Love's Comedy*, Ibsen as Falk declared, "I'm paralyzed between two alternatives, flesh on the one hand, on the other spirit," which is a cruder way of expressing Julian's malaise. So much for Ibsen's "paganism"!

Central and permanent in this opposition of tendencies for Ibsen as for Julian is the outcry: "There must be a new revelation. Or a revelation of something new. There *must*, I say— the time has come—Yes, a revelation." Like Julian, Ibsen was racked by the inner conflict which underlies the social. The solution as expounded by the mystic prophet Maximus is "the third empire . . . the empire which shall be founded in the tree of knowledge and the tree of the cross together, because it hates and loves them both, and because it has its living springs under Adam's grove and Golgotha." Then Maximus adds, " . . . the signs conflict."

That "the third empire" was not Ibsen's name for a concept momentarily inspired for purposes of the play, but an enduring idea or rather a burning hope, is attested to by the fact that he speaks of it again in an address in 1887 more than fourteen years after its composition. "I believe that poetry, philosophy and religion will be merged in a new category, and become a new vital force, of which we who are living can have no clear conception . . . I believe the ideals of our time, while disintegrating, are tending toward what in my play *Emperor and Galilean* I designated as the third empire."

In all this, I am reminded of Walt Whitman saying toward the end of his·life, "I seem to be reaching for a new politics, a new economics. I don't know what, but for something."

It is necessary for any essential understanding of Ibsen's contribution to the cultural history of the West to define his position and importance within it, to the extent that it may be considered apart from his influence on dramatic aesthetics, and the theater of his day and our own.

There was a time in which God as absolute was everywhere worshipped. Through His church a new civilization was born. Everyone believed or acted as though they believed in Him. It was the age of Faith—at its height in the thirteenth century. The very dissensions, schisms, and heresies from the earliest years A.D. to the Reformation were not contradictions but largely efforts to define the exact nature or theological locus of the "true" Faith. Renaissance humanism enriched rather than erased it. The dissolute Popes were still believers. The mathematician Pascal in the seventeenth century still "bet" on the existence of God. The mathematician and physicist Descartes, in his attempt to establish new pillars of belief on purely rational grounds, still had to find a place for the Deity. Voltaire and the Encyclopedists in the so-called Age of Reason dared not deny Him. Only at the beginning of the nineteenth century—the age of science—could the astronomer Laplace, in explaining his cosmogony, venture to tell Napoleon that there was no place for God in it. But no doubt Laplace still considered himself a believer.

Such men as Dostoevsky in the nineteenth century grew to be the enemies of their church but remained fervid in their faith. Then Nietzsche cracked down on the Western world with "God is dead." As André Malraux was to put it in a dictum which for the moment I shall leave incomplete, " . . . the mission of the nineteenth century was to get rid of the gods . . . "

The age of science shook but did not bring down the temple. Capitalism did. Its god was Profit. This does not mean that capitalists were atheists. On the contrary, they would have felt homeless and naked without faith. They used it as a prop and justification for the acquisition of wealth. It proved that they were favored by God. They could not have preserved their confidence if they had not believed this, very often with something like ferocity. Everything they undertook—including wars —required His blessing. The faith shaped a vast array of rituals, secular as well as religious. But inner and *active* faith waned, then sickened into mere formalism, succumbing in death throes to rabid fanaticism or hypocrisy, turning "God" into a bad name!

Ibsen found the old beauty—the Christianity of the saints— "no longer beautiful" because it had become disfigured and very nearly annihilated by middle-class capitalism. The bulk of his work from *The Pillars of Society* through to *Hedda Gabler* is in the main a dramatization of the process and of its human consequences. Signs of the attack on church and state were already evident in *Brand* and *Peer Gynt*—couched in more general terms than in the later plays. "We have only exchanged an old lie for a new," declares Brand.

The "new truth" which was "no longer true" for Ibsen included the rationales of science, government, democracy and even art as understood and practiced under capitalism. In relation to these he was as he often has been called an "anarchist," though others, more perceptive, sensed the "aristocrat" in him. Remember his inscription in a friend's album: "The absolute imperative task of democracy is to make itself aristocratic."

The supreme value for Ibsen, as we decipher it from his last plays, is love. To sacrifice it for art, career or wealth constitutes the greatest sin—"coldness of heart." It is the "hand of iron" which cripples the soul. He says as much half apologetically and with perhaps a touch of irony in an 1889 letter to Emilie Bardach three years before writing *The Master Builder*: "To create is beautiful; but to live in reality can now and then be much more beautiful."

Ibsen then stands in the halfway house between the age-old and vanishing world of faith and the future, of which "we can have no clear conception." That is the halfway house of capitalism, of which we are now the descendants, though our capitalism is no longer what it was in the days of Ibsen's maturity between 1886 and 1890.

The future he hoped for is not at all our present state. Even for the most optimistic among us, ours is an age of disarray. The very idea of belief is foreign to us; we hardly believe in what we profess to believe. Most of us dare not put our beliefs to the test of personal risk. We will not face death for them according to Ibsen's prescription.

The historic development since Ibsen's death has taken a course of ever greater fragmentation. On all sides we observe outbreaks of theological, philosophical, quasi-religious, medical, technological, economic and anti-rational panaceas to restore the shattered unity.

The other seminal figure in late-nineteenth-century and early-twentieth-century drama, Strindberg, tossed on a bed of personal psychological thorns till his spirit turned to an agonized mysticism, or the near-Christian solace of *The Dream Play* (1902) and *To Damascus* Part II (1908). Much admired by O'Neill and preferred over Ibsen by certain other critics and dramatists, Stringberg's expressionism has exercised greater influence in Germany and Poland than anywhere else. Apart from for his formal venturesomeness in the above-mentioned plays and his psychological acuity, the Scandinavians generally admire Strindberg above all for the plangent vitality of his dialogue. For most theatergoers, the realism of *Miss Julie*, *The Father*, *Creditors* and *The Dance of Death* are better known and more highly regarded than *The Dream Play* and other of Strindberg's innovative plays. It can hardly be said that his thought, spirit or mood, though certainly appreciated, have everywhere entered the mainstream of our era. His technique in *The Father* and other realistic plays derives from Ibsen.

Chekhov, whose four major plays date from 1896 to 1904, has left a deeper imprint on the world stage than any other dramatist since the earlier masters. He is reported to have smilingly commented that Russian actors were not right for Ibsen— even though Ibsen aroused great enthusiasm among the Russians, particularly with *Brand* and *An Enemy of the People*. There is no record I know of in which Chekhov explains his remark. But one may guess his meaning. In Ibsen's characters there is little of the sentimental idealism, the humble sweetness, the forgivable addlemindedness that we find in Chekhov's. Ibsen's people, for all their occasional vagaries, usually follow the stiff and soberly correct behavior of a staid Protestant middle class. Chekhov broke the back of Ibsen's dramatic structure and created a special mode for his presumably passive characters. His plays, dubbed by many the "drama of inaction," called for a new technique. This is not at all the same thing as saying, as many have said, that his plays are formless. For contrary to this common notion, Chekhov's dramatic method is as controlled as Ibsen's. The main difference is that the scenes in Chekhov do not move in .linear progression from one narrative point to the next in regular order. Whenever a scene seems to be approaching a climactic point, it is interrupted or "broken" by a new strand of action seemingly irrelevant to the one which preceded it. This produced among the early playgoers and theater people—including Stanislavsky—a sense of confusion. Chekhovian structure consists of a subtle, seamless interweaving of dramatic lines of action. On close inspection, the form is as secure and coherent as in any "well-made" play.

Techniques and structures in art are not things in themselves. In the hands of a master they arise from content, that is, from the artist's point of view, his nature and what he aims to express. Though Ibsen did nòt write "thesis" or "propaganda" plays, his art proceeds from an ideology. Whether his moral or social standards are positive or negative, they are unmistakably present. Though his procedure is thoroughly objective, there is always an implicit judgment, which we find little difficulty in identifying—even when we mistake it. Ibsen condemns or chastises his miscreants, hypocrites and weaklings. Chekhov only smiles in tender forbearance as if to say we cannot expect too much of human beings, although we wish them wiser and better.

Chekhov lacks all ideology or forgoes it. Some of his most simpleminded people reveal his attitude best and often win his greatest affection. They are such humble souls, Christians without theological or ecclesiastic consciousness, as the pockmarked Telyegin ("Waffles") ˙and Marina, the old nurse in *Uncle Vanya*.

After Voinitski (Vanya) has spoken of the heat and stifling

weather, Telyegin, apparently oblivious to all the injuries which
have befallen him, says, "Whenever I ride in the countryside,
or walk in the shade of your garden, or gaze at this table I know
the meaning of bliss! The weather is enchanting, the birds are
singing, we live in peace and harmony . . . what more can we
want?" He cannot bear the sight and sound of discord. "My own
wife betrayed me with another man on the day after our marriage, just because of my unattractive appearance. But I did not
forsake my duties. I still love her and I am faithful to her. I help
her as much as I can and have given her my possessions for the
education of the children she had by the other man. I have lost
my happiness, but I have kept my pride." Still more delicious
is his response to what he believes are Vanya's cynical remarks
about marital fidelity. "I don't like it when you say such things.
Really, you must know that he who deceives his wife or husband is of course an unfaithful person and may very well betray
his own country!" Poor fool, one thinks, as one laughs; *pure
fool* is what Chekhov makes one feel.

Marina, the old and loyal nurse in the household, speaks of
the animosities and strife which beset it as no better than the
cackling of geese. When Telyegin tells her he has a "bitter feeling" because he has been called a sponge, she says quietly, "We're
all sponges on God." When the pained idealist, Dr. Astrov, asks,
"I wonder if the people who will live one or two hundred years
from now, the ones we're paving the way for now, will remember us with a kind word," Marina answers, "The people won't
remember, but God will."

Chekhov's "holy of holies," as he expressed it, consists of "the
human body, health, intelligence, talent, inspiration, love, no
matter what form the latter two take." We cannot call this an
ideology. What it comes down to is generosity and kindness of
disposition. He hoped that through such virtues in addition to
work and education men and women might someday, somehow,
make a less frighteningly stupid and disordered world.

There is a sense in which Chekhov is a more genuine realist
than Ibsen. The great Russian director Meyerhold said that
Chekhov's characters are like figures reflected in the eddies of

a stream: this would make the Chekhovian manner a kind of impressionism. But remember, the impressionists claimed they were more scientific (hence "realistic") than their predecessors, for they set out to study the effects of light on color: blue in their painting is not entirely blue, nor red entirely red, and all colors change according to the time of the day, etc. Ibsen proceeds according to a rigorous order; Chekhov flows with the loose, undulating, unplanned movement of living events—and thus may be said to be "truer" to life!

(Of course, we forget in all such discussion that "realism" is itself a stylization, since it pretends to mirror actual life, which of course it can't do, while the classic plays are *real* in the sense that they present themselves as frankly artificial, in other words, nothing but *theater* or poetry.)

In comparing Brand and Peer as personages, W. H. Auden said that while we may admire Brand, we *love* Peer. In a time of deliquescent values, in which everything is regarded as "relative" and absolutes are more or less shunned, it is natural for Ibsen to stand in the same relation to Chekhov as Brand and Peer, according to Auden, stand to each other. Ibsen would insist with Dostoevsky that "neither nation or man can exist without a sublime idea." His art, behind its objective "front," is conceptual. Chekhov's spiritual modesty and heartbreaking comedy is very close to the "floating" uncertain spirit of our day.

The complete quotation from Malraux which I left suspended at the opening of this chapter reads: "If the mission of the nineteenth century was to get rid of the gods, the mission of the twentieth is to replace them." But though there are signs of this all around, they do not agree with the direction modern drama has taken since Ibsen and Chekhov.

Substantiality of the facts and events of daily existence are also cast in doubt by Pirandello. He questions the very idea of a coherent identity or a consistent psychology, which, if they exist at all, can do so only in the mind of the artist. Reality disappears almost entirely in the (misnamed) theater of the absurd, or, if you will, reality is seen there for what many now think it: a tragic farce, an indecipherable chaos, a comedy of disgust. Beckett has most succinctly and devastatingly depicted the impasse of which the best we can say is that we are *waiting*.

Another style and dramatic vein are to be found in Brecht. But if we examine his work closely we may find that his report on the world is not so very different from that of his more anguished contemporaries. With a sort of classic coolness and a quizzical smile he asks us to judge the dismal picture and to think our way out of the maze. His earliest plays are marked by a convulsive anarchism; the didactic plays which followed point to a social solution; his last plays, outwardly serene, can hardly be categorized or serve as effective social propaganda, though they are often viewed in that light.

In whatever direction we look either for enlightenment or escape, one thing is clear: the personal and social dilemma since Ibsen stated it has grown ever more appalling. For we lack supreme guidance, a belief in something to lift us from the mess in which we are now plunged. Beckett is right when he tells us that his two tramps are better than most of us because they hear mankind's cries for help and they know they are *waiting*—for rescue, a new vision? Here too, "the longing remains."

It was Ibsen who first in modern drama realized that we stand between the certainties of the old faith and the "new truth," that is, the fraudulence of the still existent society. He felt homeless between the two, but clung to the dream and hope for a perfection he sought in the "mountains," a perfection travestied for all but a few honest souls who must dwell in the "valley." All his major plays are single acts of one *magnum opus*. His unity is to be found in his contradictions. There is nobility in his disquiet. The still-unanswered questions he posed are, on the highest level, still left to us as a permanent challenge. That is his greatness.

Appendix

Explanatory note:

I have never directed an Ibsen play. It may be of some interest, particularly to student directors and actors, to learn how if I were to direct any of the plays discussed in the foregoing text I would approach the task.

For this purpose I offer a few brief (simplified) notes on three plays as illustrations of what is more or less a personal method of procedure as described in my book *On Directing.*

For those not acquainted with the book I adopt here a few passages to define some of the terms employed in the following pages:

1. To begin active direction (after a protracted study of the script), a formulation in the simplest terms must be found to state what general action motivates the play, of what fundamental drama or conflict the script's plot and people are the instruments. What behavioral struggle or effort is being represented? It is best that the answer should be expressed as an *active* verb. . . . (Do not tell the actor "You are in love" but "You love," that is, "you pay attention to" or "You take care of, you help" etc.)

Many things are contained in O'Neill's *Desire Under the Elms*: passion, Oedipal impulses, confessions of unhappiness and hate, filial vindictiveness, retribution. But what holds all these ingredients together, makes a single specific drama of them all, is the play's "spine," or, if you will, its main action. It is the struggle for the Farm, abbreviated into the bare "To possess the Farm."

With this as both starting point and interpretive goal, I was able to make a dramatic whole from the various strands in the script. The older brothers, learning that they will never possess the Farm, give up their share of it, abandon it to their younger brother and go off to seek material satisfaction (another "Farm") in California. The young wife seduces her stepson because she has been promised the Farm if she gives birth to a boy, and her dreams of bearing a child may be more easily realized by the stepson than his father, whom she has married for the sake of goods and security. The young man is attracted to his stepmother but in taking her yields not only to his desire but to an impulse to avenge himself on his father, who dominates him. When the acquisitive drive gives way to passion and becomes transferred into love, the conflict is joined on a higher level. The play ends with the sheriff coming to arrest the guilty couple for the murder of their child; his final words—the last lines of the play—are: "It's a jim-dandy farm . . . Wished I owned it." In short, even the subsidiary characters of the play must in some way be related to its spine.

2. Each individual character has his or her own spine. The character's spine must be conceived as emerging from the play's main action. Where such a relation is not evident or nonexistent, the character performs no function in the play. There is no basis for a true characterization unless the character's prime motivation or spine is found.

3. The spine chosen for Odets' *Golden Boy* was "To win the fight of life." (It is directly applicable to the central character, Joe Bonaparte.) Joe's father enacts the play's spine by encouraging what is best in his family and friends. This may be clarified by defining his spine as "To preserve the integrity of those about

him." Joe's brother-in-law Siggie's ego is sustained by the hope of acquiring that symbol of well-being which for him is a splendid cab of his own. His spine is "To enjoy the attributes of comfort and position due his estate." The gangster Fuselli satisfies his ego by his determination to bend everything to his will. His spine is "To possess." The character called Tokyo, Joe's trainer, wants to do his job well, "To work honestly," etc.

Other "spines" I chose for my productions as set down in *On Directing*:

The spine of *Long Day's Journey into Night*: "To probe within oneself for the lost "something.' "

Tyrone's spine in that play: "To maintain his 'fatherhood'— the tradition (the crumbling grandeur)."

Mary Tyrone: "To find her bearings, her 'home,' to seek them (for they have somehow been lost.)"

In *On Directing*, after setting down the basic spine of each character, I make further remarks in explanation and justification for each spine, as my examples for three Ibsen plays will show.

I have chosen *Rosmersholm*, *The Master Builder* and *Little Eyolf* because they are less frequently produced and less familiar on our stage than many of the others.

Preliminary Production Notes

Rosmersholm

Spine of the play: To move forward to the "new."

Rebecca West

Spine: "To exert influence."
She tells Rosmer (Act Three): "I could see where your salvation lay, your only salvation. And *so I set* to work . . . "

She knows how to ingratiate herself. She is ever cordial, reassuring, almost "sweet" with Kroll. Kroll says to her, "Whom could you not bewitch if you set your mind to it . . . " She is a schemer. She's much shrewder than Rosmer. "Get Martensgaard on our side," she advises.

She tries to suppress, and she believes she has succeeded in suppressing the guilt she feels: the guilt of her past, not only the suicide which she influenced but her relationship with her foster father, Dr. West, who may actually have been her real father. She also abhors the thought of her illegitimacy. Her emancipation has not gone very deep. See Kroll's speech cited in the text.

Hedda Gabler is broken by her lack of courage: Rebecca because she has had too much "courage."

She has *passion*, which is quelled by the Rosmer morality.

Christianity "exalts and purifies, but it kills happiness" (*Emperor and Galilean*). The struggle in Rebecca is between her passion and *love*, which asks nothing for itself.

Rosmer

Spine: "To open men's eyes"; to lead them toward a true democracy, freedom, nobility, etc.

In his background are Prof. Kroll, the conservative and champion of the old way of life, and Brendel, the anarchist, who has Rosmer's tutor. (Rosmer's father showed Brendel the door. Rosmer's father was an army officer.) Two early influences—before Rebecca.

He wants the confidence of innocence. For politics? . . . Rosmer, says Kroll, is not a man to stand alone.

Rosmer says: "All our old friends were gathered at this house. They were convinced that the kind of work I had in mind was not for me. And anyway—the rehabilitation of mankind—! How hopeless it all seems! I shall give up all thought of that." In Act Four, to Rebecca: "I turned my back on the work I had to do. I *surrendered*—gave up the fight before it had actually begun."

Kroll's counterargument in his opposition to Rosmer fills out the Rosmer background: "Rosmersholm—clergymen and soldiers, high-ranking officials, worthy honorable gentlemen all!— A family that for nearly two centuries has held its place as the first in the district. You owe it to yourself, Rosmer, to all the traditions of your race to defend those things that have always been held most precious in our society."

KROLL

Spine: "To hold the 'Fort' by all means (against the *new*)." Note: To oppose the spine of the play is still to be part of it. "I shall fight [this anarchy] by word and deed." Women, he thinks, shouldn't be interested in politics.

Schools are being undermined by the senior students, who have turned radical: "The most gifted students have taken part in this conspiracy against me. The only ones who seem to have kept away from it are the dunces at the bottom of the class . . . "

REBECCA: Does this really affect you so very deeply, Professor Kroll?
KROLL: Does it affect me? To see the work of a lifetime threatened and undermined? . . . There's something worse, however . . . The spirit of revolt has entered into my own house . . . the harmony of my family life has been utterly destroyed . . .

My wife, who has always shared my opinion in all subjects . . . seems inclined to take the children's point of view in this affair. She tells me I'm to blame—that I'm too harsh with them . . .

He is determined, sturdy, courteous, intelligent and, probably, handsome.

ULRIC BRENDEL

Spine: "To risk a 'comeback' in 'existence.' " (But he has little confidence.)

A softy at bottom, he is an intellectual who plays with radical ideas when no conflict or trouble is involved in espousing them. He can't stand up to danger or even to the compromises attendant on holding to them in the face of resistance or personal adversity. There are too many contradictions within him, because he is more emotional than logical. He has a "heart," and he is a sybarite.

So he becomes an "actor," a wanderer. This embitters him at first, then makes him dissolute. He has no backbone. Self-deluded, worse still, self-disgusted; finally self-destructive. He really doesn't want to live.

This "radical" doesn't actually like the plebes, "the people."

He speaks of an "equinoctial age": the breakdown of the early nineteenth century and the dawn of the new social-democratic age. He is unable to believe firmly in either.

He intimates that a political or social leader must not couple with any woman who is not willing to sacrifice her womanliness for him.

PETER MORTENSGAARD

Spine: "To forge ahead on his own track." He is still unpopular but he is on the ascendant.

An underprivileged citizen, a minority personality.

"He never *wills* more than he can do . . . is capable of living without ideals"—which is worldly wisdom.

Falsely naive. "Political" and ironical deference *vis à vis* opponents.

He knows how to fight: a sharpy in every sense. He says, "There's no reason why a man of liberal views shouldn't be able to live his life to the full—live it exactly as he chooses: however, I repeat—*this is a time for caution.*"

When Rosmer tells him to announce his (Rosmer's) conversion to liberal views, Mortensgaard answers: "I shall include everything that respectable people need to know."

MRS. HELVSTED
Spine: "To serve and to stand fast."
The faithful and understanding servant. ("Wise," Rebecca calls her.)
Quietly observant. Without theories—as she was reared and as she acts.
Slightly superstitious, as most of those bred in the "old days" on the "soil."

The Master Builder

Spine of the play: "To achieve a fullness of being; to do one's best."
In a letter to Emilie Bardach, Ibsen speaks of "high, noble, painful joy—*to struggle for the unobtainable*"—which may be a better way to phrase the spine.

SOLNESS
Spine: "To struggle against self-doubt."
He wants to be a great man in his own eyes.

Selfish: Everything for his own needs. He hates the thought of rivals or "competition." This often becomes cruelty. Wickedly calculating, as with Kaja.

He has had quite a number of women in his life.

He always wanted to do what Hilde wants him to do—to build something that would soar to great heights.

He considers himself "sick." He speaks of healing his *wound*.

He would like to be as ruthless as a Viking—without conscience. But he is too much the Puritan or the Christian for that.

Like Faust, he yearns for youth.

HILDE

Spine: "To inspire by challenge."

Something of a hoyden, a "little devil." Independent. Courageous. Romantically imaginative. She thinks herself a "Princess." She too wants the impossible. She wants to be thrilled by life. She is eager for danger. To challenge life.

She is sexually aware.

She doesn't flinch at being called a "bird of prey." "And why not a bird of prey?" She too represents a pagan principle—a troll's morality.

She idealizes the *Master*. She can't imagine him failing. When he does fail (and falls) she finds it thrilling, because he tried to exceed himself, to accomplish the impossible.

MRS. SOLNESS

Spine: "To bear up under all her trials and sufferings."
She is the brave unlamenting victim. This gives her a special stature. "I should have been strong."

Longsuffering: she puts up with Solness, his real or supposed philandering. It is her duty not to complain of her husband. She is loyal and, in her way, loves him. Yet there is some jealousy or a touch of resentment—directed against the girls rather than her husband.

Attached to memories of the past: her parents, "the old world."

She always defends Solness. Protective of him.

Her attachment to her dolls? We often cradle the *images*—"ghosts"—even after the real is dead and gone. It is a kind of infantilism.

BROVIK

Spine: "To recover part of what he has lost (his early position) through his son." Envious, broken. If he had his full strength he would also be venomous.

RAGNAR
Spine: "To await his chance to defeat the man who suppresses him." (The younger generation-in-waiting.)

He is the young artist who submits, fears, envies and waits for the great man to fail. Such artists always know their master's weak points.

"So after all he couldn't do it"—Relief in tension.

KAJA
Spine: "To give herself."

To Ragnar when he was the chosen one. She would have married him and been devoted. But the great man, the idealized person, has instilled in her the idea that he loves her: this makes her his "slave."

By nature submissive, warm-hearted, eager to help, a soft woman.

DR. HERDAL
Spine: "To help wherever he can."

He is a "realist"; "a man of the world." Decently pleasure-seeking.

Benevolent, gently cynical or skeptical.
Observant, humorous, playful.

Little Eyolf

Spine of the play: "To exceed oneself through seeking new commitments and duties.

For most of the characters there is an element of "resurrection" in the play.

RITA

Spine: "To possess her husband, Allmers, entirely."

She changes more than anyone else in the play. In the end she reaches out to Allmers on a new level.

Her fear: "Once I let him [Allmers] go, I might never get him back again."

Examples of her possessiveness and jealousy:

ALLMERS: . . . I shall fulfill my ideal of human responsibility through my own life.

RITA: Do you really believe you will be able to stay faithful to such high ideals in this house?

ALLMERS *(taking her hand)*: With your help, Rita. *(Stretches out his other hand)* And with yours, Asta.

RITA *(withdraws her hand)*: Then you can divide yourself, after all.

She tells Allmers: "I don't want to be reasonable. I only want you. Nothing else in the world. I want you, you, you."

A passionately sexual woman. She almost wishes her child dead. Eyolf's drowning follows. Then the transformation.

She wants to find something to overcome her guilt and his.

"The change is taking place in me. It hurts me so."

ALLMERS

Spine: "To seek his true vocation"—"my ideal of human responsibility." (There are always impediments.)

He feels that Rita is strangling him.

He distrusts himself. His son's death is a matter of retribution.

His secret religious nature, though it was he who sowed doubt about God in Rita's mind.

He recognizes to his "shame" that he is earthbound—as much as Rita.

His last line: "Up toward the mountain. Toward the stars. And the great silence."

(Rita says of Allmers, "He always was secretive"—an Ibsen trait.)

Asta

Spine: "To lend support." A resolute person, calm, clear, balanced.

At first she rejects Borghejm. When she decides to go with him, because she realizes she can never be Allmers' mistress or wife, she will lend her support to Borghejm as she would have done for Allmers.

Borghejm

Spine: "To find a companion in life."

He too is a *helper* . . . A healthy idealist. The personality of a sound artist.

Characteristic lines: "It's a marvellous life to be a maker of new roads!"

Asta says to him, "You are very persistent." He answers, "You have to be to be a road builder."

He wants someone "to share the excitement and the joy of work. And that's what one must want to share . . . "

"Of course one can enjoy happiness alone for a while. But not for long. No, happiness cannot really be enjoyed except by two people."

Eyolf

Spine: "To follow the good, the beautiful, the fascinating."

He is fascinated by the Rat Wife's dog, who is horrible and beautiful. He is fascinated and touched by or sorry for the poor children by the jetty.

THE RAT WIFE
(The most "symbolic" of Ibsen's characters!)
Spine: "To rid the world of its 'gnawing things.'"

She is least convincing as a *character*, hence a weakness in the play, the most symbolically designed of Ibsen's plays—to "make a statement."

Bibliography

Ibsen: Letters and Speeches. Evert Springhorn. New York: Hill and Wang, 1964.

The following translations of Henrik Ibsen's plays were used.

Brand. Translated by Michael Meyer. New York: Dutton, 1959.

Ghosts and Three Other Plays. Translated by Michael Meyer. New York: Doubleday, 1966.

Hedda Gabler and Three Other Plays. Translated by Michael Meyer. New York: Doubleday Anchor original, 1961.

The Oxford Ibsen. Edited by James W. McFarlane:

    Early Plays. Translated by James W. McFarlane and Graham Orton. New York: Oxford University Press, 1970.

    An Enemy of the People; The Wild Duck; Rosmersholm. Translated by James W. McFarlane. Vol. 6. New York: Oxford University Press, 1961.

    The Lady from the Sea; Hedda Gabler; The Master Builder. Translated by Jens Arup and James W. McFarlane. Vol. 7. New York: Oxford University Press, 1966.

    The League of Youth; Emperor and Galilean. Translated by James W. McFarlane and Graham Orton. Vol. 4. New York: Oxford University Press, 1963.

    The Vikings at Helgeland; Love's Comedy; The Pretenders.

Vol. 2. Translated by Jens Arup. New York: Oxford University Press, 1962.

Peer Gynt. Translated by Michael Meyer. New York: Doubleday, 1963.

Six Plays. Translated by Eva Le Gallienne. New York: Modern Library, 1950.

When We Dead Awaken and Three Other Plays. Translated by Michael Meyer. New York: Doubleday, 1971.

Index

Other DACAPO titles of interest

DRAMATIC TECHNIQUE
George P. Baker
New introduction by
Harold Clurman
531 pp.
80030-6 $13.95

THE FERVENT YEARS
The Group Theatre
and the Thirties
Harold Clurman
New introduction by Stella Adler
352 pp., 32 photos
80186-8 $10.95

THE LIVELY YEARS: 1920-1973
Brooks Atkinson and Al Hirschfeld
New introduction by Walter Kerr
312 pp., 81 drawings
80234-1 $9.95

THE MAKING OF
MODERN DRAMA
Richard Gilman
New introduction by the author
304 pp.
80293-7 $10.95

A METHOD TO THEIR
MADNESS
The History of the Actors Studio
Foster Hirsch
368 pp.
80268-6 $11.95

STAGE TO SCREEN
Theatrical Origins of Early Film:
David Garrick to D. W. Griffith
A. Nicholas Vardac
358 pp., 46 illus.
80308-9 $12.95

TRAGEDY & COMEDY
Walter Kerr
New introd. by William Alfred
350 pp.
80249-X $9.95

THE WORLD OF MUSICAL
COMEDY
Fourth Edition
Stanley Green
494 pp., 321 photos
80207-4 $19.95

Available at your bookstore

OR ORDER DIRECTLY FROM

DA CAPO PRESS, INC.

233 Spring Street, New York, New York 10013